Choreographies of the Living

Choreographies of the Living

Bioaesthetics in Literature, Art, and Performance

CARRIE ROHMAN

OXFORD
UNIVERSITY PRESS

OXFORD
UNIVERSITY PRESS

Oxford University Press is a department of the University of Oxford. It furthers
the University's objective of excellence in research, scholarship, and education
by publishing worldwide. Oxford is a registered trade mark of Oxford University
Press in the UK and certain other countries.

Published in the United States of America by Oxford University Press
198 Madison Avenue, New York, NY 10016, United States of America.

Library of Congress Cataloging-in-Publication Data
Names: Rohman, Carrie, author.
Title: Choreographies of the living : bioaesthetics in literature, art,
and performance / Carrie Rohman.
Description: New York, NY : Oxford University Press, [2018] |
Includes bibliographical references and index.
Identifiers: LCCN 2017043738 | ISBN 9780190604400 (hardback) |
ISBN 9780190604417 (pbk.) | ISBN 9780190604424 (updf)
Subjects: LCSH: Science and the arts. | Biology. | Aesthetics.
Classification: LCC NX180.S3 R64 2018 | DDC 700/.46—dc23
LC record available at https://lccn.loc.gov/2017043738

1 3 5 7 9 8 6 4 2

Paperback printed by WebCom, Inc., Canada
Hardback printed by Bridgeport National Bindery, Inc., United States of America

For my husband,
ERNEST CASCINO

and our son,
GAVIN ROHMAN CASCINO

my beloved companions in this life's dance

CONTENTS

PREFACE

I have been a dancer much longer than I have been a scholar. My mother put me in dance lessons at the age of six, and she would often explain that she wanted me to "have something else." By this, I suppose she meant something besides schoolwork, or perhaps, someday, besides the labors of working or parenting. A few years later, when my father was unemployed for a stretch, we found a way to keep up my dance lessons. The director of my childhood dance school was sympathetic to our financial straits, and she appointed me as a young assistant at the small studio in Cincinnati where I took lessons. I helped the other girls with their back-bends in gymnastics and demonstrated techniques and sequences for the very beginning girls in ballet and jazz. In exchange for this, my fees were lowered, and I could continue my studies.

Although I enjoyed tap and jazz, I gravitated most toward ballet in my childhood and teenage years. I was at least partly attracted by the elegance and magisterial nature of the practice. But there was certainly the cultural pressure to be a "ballerina" at work, as well. It's not merely the tutus and sequins that re-inforce a princess-style identity for young girls in ballet, but it's also the conditioning to move in a way that is perceived as delicate and dainty. Much of ballet enacts a kind of hyperfemininity: constraint, neatness, restriction. Of course, the irony of all this is that ballet takes an extraordinary toll on the body. Its utterly punishing physicality is well known to any serious practitioner or aficionado. Appearing to float about, weightlessly, and learning to pose, balance, and turn intricately and precisely in traditional ballet requires unbelievable strength and control. It's more than a bit ironic as an allegory for being a woman.

When describing my transition from ballet to modern dance, I often refer to my "ballet crisis," assuming everyone must know what I mean. But many people don't know. For me, it happened during high school. I was a very serious dancer by that time. We had moved from Cincinnati to a rural area in Tennessee when I was in middle school. Because there were no reputable dance studios in our area, my mother began driving me over an hour, both ways, to Knoxville for my lessons. By the time I was in high school, I was not only traveling to two advanced ballet classes during the school week (evenings), but I was also rehearsing for four or five hours every Saturday with the school's small performing company. Although I was a talented enough ballet dancer, I was not the most talented. As I advanced both in my studies and with the performing company, I found that continuing to achieve at higher levels seemed to exact heavier and heavier tolls on my body and my sense of self. I had badly damaged and ingrown toenails from being on pointe for years, and sometimes the pain was excruciating. I couldn't practice the most difficult moves over and over because of the pain, and so I fell behind my more persistent peers. When I contracted mononucleosis as a high school junior, and had to spend many weeks away from classes, I gained a little weight and seemed unable to shake the feeling that I shouldn't be dancing, because I wasn't absolutely rail thin. In my final ballet concert, as a high school senior, the pain in my toenails was nearly blinding as I desperately carried out my portion of the program, furious that my body would not cooperate, but forcing it to obey. After that, I said enough. I decided that I was finished with dancing.

At the time and in the places that I received my early training (Cincinnati and Knoxville), modern dance simply wasn't on the radar of conventional studios. I had never even heard of modern dance, much less seen it. It wasn't until I went to college at the University of Dayton—and, at the urging of my roommate, auditioned for their Dance Ensemble concerts—that I was exposed to contemporary forms of dance. It was a fortuitous moment (the early 1990s), because several extremely talented choreographers from the renowned Dayton Contemporary Dance Company (DCDC) used our ensemble as a testing ground for their work. They would come to campus and set their movement on us, college students who weren't even in a dance program. We would do full concerts on campus, which included some work by these professionals and other pieces by local dancers and students. The DCDC choreographers could see how their pieces appeared on stage, and we students were helping to embody these dance works. This was a profoundly new world of dance practice that I experienced, so far removed from the conventional ballet studio.

I knew within a few months that this "modern" dance was more interesting and engaging for me than anything I had learned before. And this form became what I felt "called" to practice for the next few decades. It was only recently, however, more than twenty years later, that I began to figure out *why*. At the time, I was only able to articulate the fact that I wasn't in constant pain, and that the movement was freer, more interesting, and felt more "authentic." This is not to suggest that modern dance is "easy" or not physically demanding. I learned quickly that modern dance can be incredibly challenging for the body. But I found it had a different ethos, and the physical challenges were not as punishing or capricious. Indeed, the physical challenges in modern dance weren't humiliating or infuriating, the way they had been for me in ballet.[1]

This exposure to modern dance in college led to a lifelong avocation. I began my first experiments in choreography there at the University of Dayton. Then later, in my midtwenties—as I was making my way through a Ph.D. program in literature and critical theory—I developed a semiprofessional "second life" as a modern dance performer and choreographer. I also began to teach modern dance. After leaving Bloomington and my graduate studies, I went back to Cincinnati for a few years and worked with a contemporary dance collective there. I was immersed in dance at that time, teaching regularly, and performing and choreographing at many venues across the city. A few years later, after taking my first academic job in a less urban area, I found ways to continue performing and choreographing. Recently, in 2011 and 2012, I collaborated and performed with my colleagues Nandini Sikand and Kirk O'Riordan (composer) on our campus at Lafayette College and at the Alvin Ailey Dance Theater in New York City. And in the last three years, I set a new piece in collaboration with my colleague Lee Upton, a celebrated poet, and created a performance piece with Michael Pestel for his installation Requiem: *Ectopistes Migratorius*.[2] I also set a few solos for a local show, "Ten Tiny Dances," and had the privilege to dance for Philadelphia-based choreographer Jessica Warchal-King.[3]

Given this history, it makes sense that people who know me well often have asked why I didn't write about dance. I had a quick and firm response. I would emphatically inform them that I intentionally kept my dancing utterly separate from my academic work. I don't want to *write about dance*, I would assure them, I just want to dance. I now find my own investment in this separation really intriguing. On some level, I viewed my work as a dancer and choreographer as absolutely separate from my intellectual work. *That* activity in the studio and rehearsal room, and on stage, had nothing to do with analysis and critique and the rigors of theoretical engagements, I told myself. Or at least, I didn't want to give over my performing life to that kind of analysis. And to be sure, the processes involved in creating and executing a dance piece versus writing a scholarly essay or book cannot be simply collapsed. There are divergences in these activities, and they exist in their specificities, no doubt. But what fascinates me now is my excessive investment in keeping these realms distinct. In part, I was reinforcing some kind of mind-body, rational-affective hierarchy, without fully realizing it. And what my ongoing work in animal studies has helped me see is that the "human/animal" hierarchy was also very much at work in this distinction. I recognize *now* that I was most invested in protecting the "animal" activity—dance—from the potentially reifying constraints of intellectual analysis, from the "deadening" and overly "human" effects of the mind.

So what happened? Why am I now writing a book that has dance running through it as a major thread? My own rethinking of the connections between animality and dance is largely indebted to Elizabeth Grosz's recent work on inhuman aesthetics and to the Deleuzian insistence that art has its roots well outside the human. During the summer of 2005, I studied with Grosz at the Cornell School of Criticism and Theory. At the end of that summer, she was beginning to present the ideas that would be forthcoming in her 2008 and 2011 books about aesthetics as evolutionary excess and nonadaptive extravagance. What Grosz and Deleuze helped me see was that my own love of dance was, in fact, a love of something animal. This was a significant shift of perspective. Art was not something exclusively human and to be properly intellectualized as such. It was not primarily conceptual. Art was, rather, more affective than conceptual, and was something that connected me profoundly to the inhuman world. These ideas radicalized my own views about art and about my experience as a dancer and choreographer. They changed the way I understood my highly affective investment in dance as an especially embodied art form, and made me value it differently, through a kind of posthumanist lens. I then realized that as an animal studies scholar, or rather, as *this particular* animal studies scholar who is also a dancer and choreographer, I *must* write about dance. I must explore and investigate the ways that dance (and other artistic practices) defamiliarize the traditionally "human" and connect the living in general across species lines. And so, this quite interdisciplinary project, with dance and literature and art and performance all capering about, was begun.

ACKNOWLEDGMENTS

Writing this book has been a deeply energizing commitment for many years, and its development has been fortified by others at multiple junctures. As my preface notes, Elizabeth Grosz's 2005 seminar at Cornell University's School of Criticism and Theory was the initial spur for my thinking about art and animals, and I cannot overestimate the extraordinary impact she has had on this project. Her example of inventive and incisive inquiry, and her intellectual commitment to provocation and the new, have resonated across the life of this project. I am also grateful to Jane Bennett, whom I studied with at Cornell in 2013, and whose ideas shaped significant segments of this book. For further inspiration, encouragement, and wisdom I give special thanks to Cary Wolfe, Una Chaudhuri, and Amanda Anderson.

I have received vital institutional support for this work. From Lafayette College, multiple grants from the Academic Research Committee, and a Mellon grant, "Choreography and the Curriculum." The college also supported my research leaves, during early stages and final stages of the book. Special thanks to Paul Miller of Lafayette's Skillman Library for his impeccable work with digital images. Thanks to the Humane Society of the United States for a writing fellowship. For access to resources and for sharing their knowledge, thanks to the Merce Cunningham Trust, and its executive director Lynn Wichern, to Lori Belilove of the Isadora Duncan Dance Foundation, and Jeanne Bresciani of the Isadora Duncan International Institute, and to Laura Kuhn. I also thank the Cornell School of Criticism and Theory for the unparalleled scholarly environment they create. My undergraduate Excel scholar, Larisa Schuckle, provided valuable and enthusiastic work during early stages of this project. My son was also cared for by loving and capable staff at the Lafayette College Early Learning Center, for a good portion of this project's life.

I have been fortunate to present excerpts of this work to audiences at the University of Wisconsin-Madison, the University of Sheffield (Animals

Research Colloquium), the University of Leeds (Environmental Humanities Reading Group), Lafayette College, Wesleyan University, and State University of New York-New Paltz.

I am especially grateful to my colleague Steven Belletto, for reading nearly every word of this book in draft form, and providing invaluable feedback and moral support, sprinkled with much-needed humor. I am particularly grateful to David Herman, for his support and interest in this project, and to Kimberly Engdahl Coates for reading portions of this project. My friend and colleague Rebekah Pite has also been a crucial sounding board and irreplaceable inspiration during my labors for this book.

I want to specifically thank those I have performed with, collaborated with, and/or learned from, in the arts—including dance and performance, music, painting and other visual arts—since this project began: Nandini Sikand, especially, for her endless generosity, inspiration, and wisdom, Frank Arcuri, Karen Carcia, Sarah Carlson, Sean Delonas, Kristin Lyndal Garbarino, Rosemary Geseck, Adriano Farinella, Edward J. Kerns, Lauren Kindle, Adam MacHose, Alix Ohlin, Kirk O'Riordon, Margaret Page, Michael Pestel, Kelly Prentice, Larry Stockton, Jim Toia, Jessica Warchal-King, and Lee Upton.

Many other colleagues, friends, and students have provided feedback, ideas, editorial work, and all manner of support and camaraderie across the life of this project. Thank you to Paul Ardoin, Robert Blunt, Ron Broglio, Sascha Bru, Ben de Bruyn, Sean P. Cavanagh, Paul Cefalu, Rose and Wooly Charles, Devon Clifton, Debra Rae Cohen, John Crawford, Kim Cunningham, Kristin Czarnecki, Erica Delsandro, Michel Delville, Margo DeMello, Jane Desmond, Marianne DeKoven, Bianca Falbo, Dale Gilmore, Alessandro Giovannelli, S. E. Gontarski, Lori Gruen, Karen Haduck, Andrew Harrison, Jane Harrison, Terese Heidenwolf, Mary Jo Lodge, Ana Luhrs, Megan Masto, Laci Mattison, Susan McHugh, Robert McKay, Tresa McVicker, John Miller, Robert W. Mitchell, Pam Murray, Lauren Myers, Julia Nicodemus, Kate Noonan, Christine O'Connor, Lourdes Orozco, Seo-Hyun Park, Jennifer Parker-Starbuck, Gera Summerford, Nancy Paxton, Derek Ryan, Diane Shaw, Julie A. Smith, Vicki Tromanhauser, Tom Tyler, Carolynn Van Dyke, Kari Weil, Angelika von Wahl, and Bryn Weller.

I am grateful to Brendan O'Neill, who acquired this project initially at Oxford University Press, and to Sarah Pirovitz and Abigail Johnson, who saw it through to production.

I want to thank my mother, my beloved late father, my three brothers, and my extended family for their kindness and support. I am grateful to my son, Gavin, for keeping me honest, for teaching me to keep looking, and for his love and compassion: May you always honor the artist that you are, and may your life be filled with contentment, good friends, good health, and meaningful work. And to my husband, Ernie, who is grounding, steadfast, and truly giving—thank you for this dance, for leading and following, and finding the way forward together. And for all your care of our family—care that is so sustaining—I offer my most heartfelt thanks.

I wish to gratefully acknowledge permission to reproduce versions of my work that have been previously published, and permission to reprint the work of D. H. Lawrence:

A portion of Chapter One first appeared as Copyright © 2017 The Johns Hopkins University Press. "Nude Vibrations: Isadora Duncan's Creatural Aesthetics," in MODERNISM/MODERNITY, 2.3, (September, 2017).

Segments of Chapter Two first appeared as "The Voice of the Living: Becoming-Artistic and the Creaturely Refrain in D. H. Lawrence's 'Tortoise Shout.'" From *Experiencing Animal Minds,* by Julie Smith and Robert Mitchell, Eds. Copyright © 2012 Columbia University Press. Reprinted with permission of Columbia University Press. And as "Dancing with Deleuze: Modernism and the Imperceptible Animal." *Understanding Deleuze: Understanding Modernism,* S. E. Gontarski, Paul Ardoin, and Laci Mattison, Eds. Series: *Understanding Philosophy, Understanding Modernism.* London: Bloomsbury, 2014: pp. 169–181. Reprinted with permission of Bloomsbury Academic, an imprint of Bloomsbury Publishing, Plc.

Portions of Chapter Three were originally published as "'We Make Life': Vibration, Aesthetics, and the Inhuman," in *The Waves." Virginia Woolf and the Natural World: Selected Papers of the Twentieth Annual International Conference on Virginia Woolf,* Kristin Czarnecki and Carrie Rohman, Eds. Clemson: Clemson Digital Press, 2011: pp. 12–23. And "A Hoard of Floating Monkeys: Creativity and Inhuman Becomings in Woolf's Nurse Lugton Story." *Deleuze Studies,* 7, no. 4 (November 2013): 515–536.

A version of Chapter Four was published as "Effacing the Human: Rachel Rosenthal, Rats and Shared Creative Agency," *Performing Animality: Animals in Performance Practices.* Lourdes Orozco and Jennifer Parker-Starbuck, Eds. New York: Palgrave/Macmillan, 2015: pp. 168–186.

"Tortoise Shout" from *The Cambridge Edition of The Poems,* by D. H. Lawrence, edited by Christopher Pollnitz, Cambridge University Press, 2013, reproduced by permission of Pollinger Ltd. (www.pollingerltd.com) on behalf of the Estate of Frieda Lawrence Ravagli.

Choreographies of the Living

Introduction

In any case, there is a pure plane of immanence, univocality, composition, upon which everything is given, upon which unformed elements and materials dance that are distinguished from one another only by their speed and that enter into this or that individuated assemblage depending on their connections, their relations of movement. A fixed plan of life upon which everything stirs, slows down or accelerates. A single abstract Animal for all the assemblages that effectuate it.

—Gilles Deleuze and Félix Guattari, *A Thousand Plateaus*[1]

The Living Body is itself the ongoing provocation for inventive practice . . . for making art out of the body's capacities and actions.

—Elizabeth Grosz, *Becoming Undone*[2]

Bioaesthetics

When performance-artist and musician Laurie Anderson put on a concert for dogs in New York's Times Square on a winter night in 2016, she had previous experience to call upon. In June of 2010, Anderson and her husband Lou Reed made international headlines with their "symphony" called "Music for Dogs." The musical work, Anderson and Reed insisted, was written for an audience of dogs, and the idea for creating it had materialized when the two musicians and Yo Yo Ma were comparing their dogs' various musical preferences. The soundscape in "Music for Dogs" was partly audible to humans, but partly audible only to dogs, whose range of hearing far exceeds the human range. The score called upon traditional human instrumentation, but it also included elements such as whale song. Performed outside the Sydney Opera House in Australia, the symphony had commentators struggling to make sense of this "high" art form conceived for and performed in front of "lowly" animals. Although journalists tended to be skeptical of the authenticity of the dogs' reactions to the concert—revealing the predictable anthropocentric presumption that art is only for *Homo sapiens*—Anderson's event signals a very different set of assumptions.

1

Conceiving and writing a symphony for dogs does what much avant-garde art has done traditionally. It shocks, shatters, and provokes. In this case, however, the dog symphony shatters our deeply held illusions that music is "for" humans. It further suggests that even "high" forms of art can be appreciated by animals, who themselves have aesthetic tastes. Moreover, Anderson's animal composition not only recognizes that art is not limited to the purview of humans, but it also can be understood as staging a more radical notion of art as fundamentally of the animal. Anderson's comments about her own dog's enjoyment of music emphasize the rhythmic pleasure of sounds, a pleasure that recent theorists argue crosses species boundaries. A 2010 news story notes that Anderson and Reed's rat terrier Lollabelle was reported to be the "muse" for the piece: "Anderson claimed Lollabelle to be a music buff. 'She likes things with a lot of smoothness but with beats in them,' Anderson said. 'Things with voices and lots of complicated high-end stuff—chk-chk-chk-chk-chk—that kind of stuff.' "[3] The same news source reports that Anderson described this work and its reception as a "highlight of my life."[4] Anderson's provocations at the Sydney Opera House, and recently in New York, are very much posthumanist ones that decouple the artistic from the human.[5]

Animals, in fact, seem to be everywhere in contemporary visual art, literature, and performance. If we follow John Berger, the disappearance of animals from most sectors of daily life, and our historically unprecedented lack of engagement with "wild" animals, has likely influenced this proliferation of animal images.[6] Moreover, the climate crisis, coupled with habitat loss and other ecological factors, make animal extinction an ever-more pressing reality with which humans now grapple. But though writers, artists, and performers are now engaging more and more with ideas about animals, and even with actual living animals, their aesthetic practice continues to be interpreted within a primarily human frame of reference—with art itself being understood as an exclusively human endeavor. My critical wager in this project is that the aesthetic impulse itself is profoundly trans-species. If we understand artistic and performative impulses themselves to be part of our evolutionary inheritance—as that which we borrow, in some sense, from animals and the natural world—the ways we experience, theorize, and value literary, visual, and performance art fundamentally shift.

Increasingly, scholars in animal studies are examining the role of animality in contemporary art, including ongoing framings of taxidermic practices, uses of real or artificial animal bodies, and questions of "anthropomorphic" identifications, among other lines of inquiry. Steve Baker has undertaken the most sustained inquiry into such questions in the last twenty years. He has addressed the ways animals are represented and engaged in the work of artists such as Olly and Suzi, Damien Hirst, and Sue Coe. More recently, he continues his discussion of the complex questions of animality and animal agency in works by Eduardo Kac, Lucy Kimbell, Angela Singer, Catherine Bell, and others.[7] But in this recent work, Baker keeps returning to Olly and Suzi, a collaborative pair of artists most recognized for drawing and painting predators who are both endangered and "dangerous." Their art-making usually occurs in the animals' natural habitats, and the products often include the animals' own markings.[8] In his chapter, "An Openness to Life," Baker identifies Olly and Suzi's concerns with the "immediacy, specificity, and *intense unfamiliarity* of each new animal encounter" (*Artist/Animal* 24) suggesting how humans must become differently tuned to the precarious situation of biological life on earth in the era of endangerment and extinction. Cary Wolfe also has become increasingly focused on how contemporary art addresses animals. In *What is Posthumanism?*, Wolfe examines the recursivity of artists like Eduardo Kac, whose glow-in-the-dark creatures raise questions about the visual habits of the human, and whose video and performance pieces complicate our understanding of "contemporary forms of animal exploitation in biomedical research and factory farming as a 'holocaust.'"[9] In more recent work, Wolfe is addressing questions of extinction and "scripts of life" as they are performed and encoded in installation pieces such as Michael Pestel's 2014 "Requiem: *Ectopistes Migratorius*," an exhibit elaborating the fate of the extinct passenger pigeon that I mentioned in my preface.[10]

Other recent scholarship likewise underscores the need for an expanded frame for investigating art practices in a variety of contexts and media. Ron Broglio suggests that the "surface" world of animal phenomenology as engaged in contemporary art offers a productive site for confronting the "necessary lacuna in human knowledge" that the animal incites.[11] Moreover, Giovanni Aloi's recent book usefully surveys the contemporary world of animal art with an eye both on its statements about our current relationship with animals and, as McHugh puts it, on "alternative models through which we can look beyond ourselves for the benefit of ourselves, other life forms, and even our shared planet."[12] Although my own study has many points of overlap with these recent investigations— overlaps that will emerge in the coming chapters—my particular critical wager is that the aesthetic impulse itself is profoundly inhuman and animal. For this reason, the present inquiry focuses as much on the creative process as on creative products. What interests me is a kind of "bio-impulse" at the root of the aesthetic itself. This impulse can be situated within the increasingly profound ways that human exceptionalism is giving way to various trans-species identifications, to a certain onto-ethics in new materialist alterings of the status of human and inhuman, or in Morton's terms, to certain "queer ecologies."[13] In fact, this impulse becomes increasingly visible as frameworks for understanding premised on human exceptionalism give way to various "ecologies" that view the human as entangled with the nonhuman.

The elaboration of the field of animal studies calls for a serious recasting of received anthropocentric ecologies. The March 2009 PMLA volume included a special section on animal studies. Although critics had been addressing species questions textually and theoretically for many years prior, this volume helped usher in a more institutionally recognized version of the subfield. Rosi Braidotti's essay in that volume, "Animals, Anomalies, and Inorganic Others," situates the development of animal studies usefully in conjunction with what have been called the new materialisms in recent theory, some of that work feminist and poststructuralist. Hailing a "bioegalitarian turn," Braidotti signals the "end of the familiar, asymmetrical relation to animals, which was saturated with fantasies, emotions, and desires and framed by power relations biased in favor of human access to the bodies of animal others."[14] Extolling the virtues of "disidentifying ourselves from familiar and hence comforting values and identities" ("Anomalies" 526–527), Braidotti recommends estrangement and the "loss of familiar habits of thought and representation" when it comes to the classic human/animal divide. She goes on to explain that it is "the politics of life itself" that must become the subject of the humanities ("Anomalies" 528). Such politics have garnered the attention of many contemporary critics interested in affect, ecology, vitalism, materialism, and so on.[15]

This book should radically defamiliarize our received notions of art and the aesthetic, and reframe our understanding of life itself in its relationship to the artistic. Before discussing my conceptual frameworks, I want to indicate just how much disequilibrium the following work produces around traditional notions of art, and even some nontraditional notions of art. We need to keep in mind, therefore, how productive it can be, ala Braidotti, to disidentify with comforting values and ideas. This book in its entirety is an effort to do just that, to have us investigate a reframing of art as fundamentally nonhuman.

In his 2006 book *The Philosophy of Art*, Stephen Davies opens his discussion with a chapter titled "Evolution and Culture." He is interested in a debate between what he calls a biological basis for art and a cultural one, and he specifically addresses the question of art's origins in this debate. It becomes immediately clear on the first page of this chapter that an "evolutionary" or biological basis for art is not understood in a trans-species manner, but remains exclusively within the purview of the human, albeit the very ancient human:

> Art is universal. All over the world, mothers sing and hum their babies to sleep. Storytelling, rhyming, and dramatized enactments are present in all cultures. The same is true of music and dance, as well as of depictions of people and animals, along with designs and patterns, which are drawn in pigment and charcoal, molded from clay, and carved

or whittled from wood, bone, or stone. Humans everywhere decorate and beautify their environments, possessions, and bodies.[16]

The "universal" here is, in fact, restricted to the human. The "evolutionary" argument that Davies recounts is that art is as old as human cultures, rather than a very recent human development (in the late Enlightenment period, according to Davies' discussion of the "cultural" argument). The entire debate, therefore, is circumscribed by the assumption that art can only be a human endeavor, that only human cultures are capable of producing art. There are complicated debates about art's origins in the philosophy community,[17] but what I want to point out here is that among many, the notion that even ancient *humans* were capable of artistic practice is extremely controversial. To suggest that the aesthetic can be found/founded in animals' ways of being is an idea some would consider entirely preposterous.[18] In fact, when reading the following excerpt, in which Davies imagines someone defending this human "universality" of art, one cannot help but be struck by the way the slippage into a trans-species understanding of art might be similarly shaped:

> We share a common biology with the people of the late Pleistocene and of other cultures. As fellow humans, we have many desires, fears, emotions, and needs in common with them. Their worlds should not be completely impenetrable, therefore. After all, both anthropology and history are credible academic disciplines. There is no barrier of principle that separates their worlds from ours, so the enterprise of understanding what they do and of discovering concepts and practices they share in common with us is a legitimate and potentially successful one. (*Philosophy of Art* 18)

The work of this book takes the "evolutionary" argument about art to its actual Darwinian conclusions. After this, we can paraphrase Davies' mock defense by noting that as fellow *animals* we have many desires, fears, emotions, and needs in common with them. Their worlds, the worlds of animals, should not be completely impenetrable, therefore. In fact, in his more recent book, pointedly titled *The Artful Species*, Davies confronts the question of animal aesthetics much more directly, yet ultimately dismisses the idea that art should be understood in any meaningful way to exist beyond human boundaries. Although Davies admits that we "might share our aesthetic sense with our primate cousins and other higher animals," it would be "to a limited extent."[19] He specifically dismisses the Darwinian notion of sexual selection involving aesthetic taste (which will be a major element of my claims here) and provides what I would characterize as a circular definition of art, one that uses human art to set the standards for how art is defined. He also uses impressionistic phrases, such as, "I don't know, but I doubt it" (*Artful Species* 15), to reject understandings of birdsong as genuinely musical. Davies also claims that animals do not "sit in entranced contemplation, apparently without regard to utilitarian interests or consequences" (*Artful Species* 15). Yet we know that Jane Goodall has argued, for instance, that chimpanzees do precisely that.[20]

Davies is an interesting case study because he himself finds Kant's influential elaboration of a human aesthetic judgment too "cognitive," though Davies is ultimately a philosopher of art committed to human exceptionalism. Claiming that essential artistic capacities should be located well beyond the human profoundly revises our received wisdom about the operations of the aesthetic. Although I cannot rehearse the long history of Western aesthetic theory in great detail here, it is important to acknowledge that, beginning with Plato and Aristotle, and moving up through the recent claims of "neuroaesthetics," this history is ultimately characterized by the yoking of aesthetic experience to an exclusively human form of cognition, ethical judgment, or understanding.[21] Debates about Aristotle's concept of *katharsis*, for instance, consider whether it ought to be understood as an intellectual or emotional experience, but no one doubts that experience is part of the fully *human* life. Kant's immensely influential claims depend upon a "disinterested" perceptual judgment that he links repeatedly to what he views as exclusively human capacities. And interestingly, even John Dewey, whose ideas circulate around a somatic naturalism, nonetheless stresses how humans' more complex conscious integrations make them distinct from animals in relation to art.

Giovanni Aloi puts a finer point on the assumption that art remains within the purview of human creators. In *Art and Animals*, he discusses a classic text on artistic methodologies by Laurie Schneider Adams that includes a discussion of "'the artistic impulse,'" which is defined as "'what separates the human from the non-human'" (qtd. in *Art* xviii). Schneider Adams claims that such practices as nest building and web spinning are genetically programmed rather than expressive. Aloi then characterizes his own response to this "hollow" argument as leaving him "cold" (*Art* xviii). He goes on to state that the "well-known case for human superiority over comparative animal inadequacy . . . identifies art as the noble differentiating feature of the secular division between human and animal. It is a statement designed to stroke readers' egos, suggesting that their interest in something noble, like art, furthers their own nobility by implication" (*Art* xviii). As he further elaborates his response to Schneider Adams' position, Aloi de-emphasizes the significance of the artistic object: "What Adams fails to recognize is that the word 'art' entails a complex system of negotiations that goes well beyond the creation of an object. However if we consider *creativity* as the universal originator of all art, then we find that animals are surely capable of displaying that, at times in ways that indeed border on the understanding of the creative in humans" (*Art* xviii).

Even more, my argument will assume that human creativity is only the most recent iteration of an artistic impulse that belongs to the living in general. Aesthetics from this perspective must be understood as *bioaesthetics*.[22] Rather than looking primarily "beyond" ourselves to understand animals and aesthetics, I suggest we must also look "within" to identify a deep coincidence of the human and animal elaboration of life forces in aesthetic practices. Moreover, we ought to turn *toward* animals to revise and revivify our understanding of human aesthetic capacities. For this reason, my project focuses as much on the creative process as on creative products. The bioaesthetic force is something that humans borrow, share, or coinhabit; it manifests a human entanglement with the nonhuman. Such a viewpoint radically suggests that all human artistic propensities have some fundamental connection to animality that is based in strategies of excess, display, intensification, and elaboration or iteration. Recognizing our artistic drives as partly inhuman—re-envisioning the aesthetic domain itself as trans-species in scope—is ethically charged because we must acknowledge the shared status of art-making, one of our most hallowed and formerly "exceptional" activities.[23] To be clear, I am not simply suggesting that certain modes of aesthetic expression are closely linked to animals, but that the aesthetic itself *is* animal. To this end, the book will explore how animality, and actual animals, are at the center of the aesthetic expression of crucial modernist and contemporary artists.

The work of Gilles Deleuze and Elizabeth Grosz, in particular, has helped to make my claims about the bioaesthetic possible. Although many of us doing animal studies scholarship are deeply interested in the Deleuzian concepts of the Oedipalized animal and in questions of inhuman "becomings," other work by Deleuze (sometimes with Guattari) is even more generative for thinking about animals and the aesthetic. Deleuze insists that the territorial, the affective, and the rhythmic structures of the expressive and aesthetic are clearly locatable in animal practices. Indeed, Deleuze grounds the aesthetic itself in the animal and inhuman, rejecting the notion that art is primarily representational, and maintaining that art is linked to affects and intensities that exceed human boundaries. Thus, Deleuze and Guattari claim, "Not only does art not wait for human beings to begin, but we may ask if art ever appears among human beings, except under artificial and belated conditions" (*Plateaus* 320). Similarly, Deleuze and Guattari ask whether "art is continually haunted by the animal."[24]

Deleuze's ideas about the origins of art are scattered throughout his work, but they are most prominent in *The Logic of Sensation, A Thousand Plateaus* (with Guattari) and in their later work *What is Philosophy?* In the latter, Deleuze and Guattari's discussions of painting and abstract painting help provide a sense of the much broader claim that art is primarily affective rather than representational or conceptual. When discussing art's passage from the finite to the infinite, Deleuze quotes Van Gogh from a letter to his brother Theo, "instead of painting the ordinary wall of the mean room, I paint infinity, a plain background of the richest, intensest blue" (qtd. in *Philosophy* 181). Deleuze goes on to describe the monochromes of modern painting in which

> the area of plain, uniform color vibrates, clenches or cracks open because it is the bearer of glimpsed forces. And this, first of all, is what makes painting abstract: summoning forces, populating the area of plain, uniform color with the forces it bears, making the invisible forces visible in themselves, drawing up figures with a geometrical appearance but that are no more than forces—the forces of gravity, heaviness, rotation, the vortex, explosion, expansion, germination, and time ... Is this not the definition of the percept itself—to make perceptible the imperceptible forces that populate the world, affect us, and make us become? (*Philosophy* 181–182)

Shortly after this discussion, Deleuze conjectures, "Perhaps art begins with the animal, at least with the animal that carves out a territory and constructs a house" (*Philosophy* 183). He then suggests that the territory (which will get translated into the frame) "implies the emergence of pure sensory qualities, of sensibilia that cease to be merely functional and become expressive features" (*Philosophy* 183). This notion of the nonutilitarian, ornamental nature of animal aesthetics is of central interest to Grosz as she articulates the artistic in relation to animal excess, performance, taste, and discernment. It is worth reiterating that, in my view, Deleuze's ideas about animals and the artistic may be more useful or productive than his often-cited taxonomy of animals into Oedipalized pets, mythologized animals, and demonic or pack animals.[25]

Perhaps one of the greatest intellectual services Grosz has performed in her most recent work is to pair Deleuze in a vigorous way with Darwin. Although Deleuze has received increasing attention among critics during the last ten to fifteen years, Darwin's work is often still misrepresented and misunderstood. As Grosz puts it when she discusses Darwin's surprising compatibilities with Luce Irigaray's theories, there remains an "unrecognized radicality of Darwin's writings," and this is so even 150 years after his work tore asunder, in the late nineteenth century, a vision of humanity's preeminence in the natural world (*Undone* 155). I want to add, from the perspective of critical animal studies, that this radicality is partly rooted in the repeated and unrelenting way in which Darwin's work dismantles notions of human exceptionalism and, therefore, necessitates profound ethical investigations of the human/animal divide.

I want to further venture an analogy between Darwin and Grosz herself in the following sense. Just as Darwin revealed to us a specific (albeit scientific) mechanism for understanding the origins and development of all living species, including the human one, within a network of living organisms rather than a hierarchy of beings, Grosz provides a mechanism for understanding the origins of the artistic within the strivings of life itself. No longer a rarified product of human advancement, genius, or handiwork, artistic practice has its roots in the excesses of evolution and in the showy extravagance of sexual selection, where qualities and forces are elaborated in the name of attraction, innovation, and a becoming-other.

Grosz began to discuss these concepts publicly in 2005, both at a presentation she gave at Cornell University and in a radio interview with Julie Copeland. She suggested in the radio interview that we need to understand art as "the revelry in the excess of nature, but also a revelry in the excess of the energy in our bodies."[26] She went on to make the distinctly posthumanist claim that "we're not the first artists and we're perhaps not even the greatest artists, we humans; we take our cue from the animal world. So what appeals to us? It's the striking beauty of flowers, it's the amazing colour of birds, it's the songs of birds" ("Impulse" 2). Rather than being fundamentally about concepts or representation, Grosz maintains that art's "fundamental goal is to produce sensations," and "it's about feeling something intensely [while] there may be the by-product of a kind of understanding" ("Impulse" 3).

In what may first seem a counterintuitive locating of the artistic outside of human praxis, Grosz claims that the intersection of life itself with earthly or cosmic forces serves as the occasion for what is fundamentally an aesthetic emergence. In her 2008 book, *Chaos, Territory, Art*, Grosz describes the "productive explosion of the arts from the provocations posed by the forces of the earth . . . with the forces of living bodies, by no means exclusively human, which . . . slow down chaos enough to extract from it something not so much useful as intensifying, a performance, a refrain, an organization of color or movement that eventually, transformed, enables and induces art."[27] In the aforementioned interview, Grosz indicates the way that her ideas decenter the traditional attribution of art to a transcendent, human function:

> I think what's radical about what I'm saying is that art isn't primarily or solely conceptual, that what it represents is the most animal part of us rather than the most human part of us. Frankly, I find it really refreshing, in a way, that it's not man's nobility that produces art, it's man's animality that produces art, and that's what makes it of potential interest everywhere. ("Impulse" 3)

Just as compelling is Grosz's further claim that sexual difference lies at the heart of aesthetics. This idea is especially fascinating given Grosz's well-known work in the areas of feminist and queer theory, disciplines that have tended to resist most biological framings of sexuality and gender. Pivotal to her position is understanding nature as *dynamic* rather than static, as something that is always opening toward the new and the future in a process of becoming. She emphasizes that, because animals attract mates through various "vibratory" forces, through color and through dance, through song and cadences, the aesthetic is linked to the workings of sexual difference in evolution. In her 2008 discussion of music and sex, for instance, Grosz makes much of Darwin's claims that mammals use their voices to attract mates. For Darwin, music is "seductive" and "dangerous"; it "intensifies and excites," in Grosz's words (*Chaos* 32). Thus, there is "something about vibration," or resonance, or rhythm, "even in the most primitive of creatures, that generates pleasurable or intensifying passions, excites organs, and invests movements with greater force or energy" (*Chaos* 33). Birdsong, for instance, exists at a crossroads between sexuality and creativity.

Grosz goes on to note that "sexuality itself needs to function artistically to be adequately sexual, adequately creative, that sexuality . . . needs to harness excessiveness and invention to function at all" (*Chaos* 64–65). Referencing the work of Alphonso Lingis, Grosz discusses the forces of sexual selection and the bodily manifestations of those forces as creatures invest in enhancing "the body's sexual appeal" (*Chaos* 66): "This calling to attention, this making of one's own body into a spectacle, this highly elaborate display of attractors, involves intensification. Not only are organs on display engorged, intensified, puffed up, but the organs that perceive them—ears, eyes, nose—are also filled with intensity, resonating with colors, sounds, smells, shapes, rhythms" (*Chaos* 66). Thus taste, pleasure, performance, and staging all enter into the aestheticization of the body in sexual selection and evolution: "Art is of the animal precisely to the degree that sexuality is artistic" (*Chaos* 70). Contemporary artist Jim Toia's "spore drawings," an example of which provides the cover image of this book, are arresting examples of his collaboration with the engorgement, intensification, and "puffery" that creatures such as mushrooms (organisms considered more closely related to animals than plants) enact during reproductive processes. The excesses of mushroom bodies when sporing are the essential movements these bioaesthetic images render. In my discussions with Toia, he has described this work as "something of a dance, a collaboration or perhaps a surrender which allows nature to declare itself while offering the viewer a new awareness of what lies before them."

It is important to clarify how Grosz suggests that reproduction does not have to be viewed as the primary telos of these processes. Rather, Grosz speculates that "[perhaps] sexuality is not so much to be explained in terms of its ends or goals (which in sociobiological terms are assumed to be the [competitive] reproduction of maximum numbers of [surviving] offspring, where sexual selection is ultimately reduced to natural selection) as in terms of its forces, its effects . . . which are forms of bodily intensification. Vibrations, waves, oscillations, resonances affect living bodies, not for any higher purpose but for pleasure alone" (*Chaos* 33). We need not see sexuality as biologically "determined" or rigidly heteronormative, but rather as a fluid process of becoming that emphasizes pleasure. At the same time, Grosz aligns herself with Irigaray, who cautions that we must take seriously the existence of sexual dimorphism, even if we understand sexuality as highly fluid and historically contingent.

Grosz's claims are located within the Deleuzian framework that she outlines in her own discussion of the artistic. As mentioned earlier, Deleuze rejects the notion that art is primarily to be understood in terms of intention or representation. Rather, as Grosz explains, he suggests that "the arts produce and generate intensity, that which directly impacts the nervous system and intensifies sensation. Art is the art of affect more than representation, a system of dynamized and impacting forces rather than a system of unique images that function under the regime of signs" (*Chaos* 3). Moreover, Grosz reminds us that the idea of the affective in Deleuze involves a linkage between bodily forces and "cosmological forces," a linkage that emphasizes the human participation in the nonhuman (*Philosophy* 169).

Inhuman Humanities

The "so-called" human is under serious revision in the wake of animal studies, and I want to situate this particular investigation amid what I call the relinquishment effect of posthumanist theory. In other words, the qualities, abilities, and modes of knowledge that we once imagined as restricted to human actors are increasingly and exponentially being revealed as also present to varying degrees in nonhuman beings. And thus, we must relinquish our exclusionary claim to these processes and capacities. The range of such relinquishings is too broad to circumscribe here, but we can point to any number of scientific and philosophical developments involving mirror neurons and experiences of sympathy, complex social relations or animal "morality" in Marc Bekoff's terms, or the most fundamental dynamics of language or the "trace" in Derrida's and Cary Wolfe's work.

In *Becoming Undone*, Grosz also further complicates her thesis about life's becoming-other, particularly through sexual selection, as a dynamized and spectacular elaboration of creative intensities that humans cannot exclusively claim.[28] In the book's first chapter, Grosz makes the question of the animal more central than at any point in her prior work. Reminding us that there has been an "elusive line that has divided the animal from the human since ancient Greece . . . that denies to the animal what it grants to the human as a power or ability: whether it is reason, language, thought, consciousness, or the ability to dress, to bury, to mourn, to invent," etc. (*Undone* 12), Grosz goes on to evoke Derrida's recognition of the profound challenge Darwin set at the foot of western humanism, what is perhaps the "greatest affront" to human exceptionalism in contemporary thought (*Undone* 13). She asks, "What would a humanities, a knowledge of and for the human, look like if we placed the animal in its rightful place, not only before the human but also within and after the human?" (*Undone* 13). In fact, Grosz's question lines up with much of the theoretical and ethical work emerging in animal studies today.[29] Using the centrality of Darwin's claims, she conjures a new inhuman humanities, a humanities that "becomes possible once the human is placed in its properly inhuman context" (*Undone* 21).

Grosz's concerns in her recent book implicitly line up with a central vein of critical animal studies: the decentering of the human and the acknowledgement of animal capacities as morally relevant. Once man is properly understood in Darwin's terms, she explains, "it is no longer clear whether the qualities that man defines as uniquely his own . . . do in fact serve to distinguish man from other animals" (*Undone* 21). Moreover—and I am keen to stress this moment in Grosz's introduction—"If man is not the sole life-form that produces and judges reason, morality, art, or religion, this not only problematizes all of the humanities that have made the human the mark and measure of creativity, it also obscures the animal conditions for the emergence of so-called human qualities" (*Undone* 21).

Grosz gestures toward these monumental shifts when she claims that there are "as many forms of reason . . . as many modes of ethics or morality as there are bonds that bind together individuals and groups through relations of affection, convenience, safety, or comfort . . . as many forms of political and social organization as there are collections of large numbers, populations" (*Undone* 24). She goes on to claim that these capacities are "part of the evolutionary becoming in which all of life partakes . . . [so that] reason, language, culture, tools, and other distinctively human accomplishments must now take their place, not as the overcoming or surpassing of an animal ancestry but as its most recent elaboration" (*Undone* 24). This latter point is perhaps more profound than the elegantly crafted vehicle of this sentence allows us to recognize initially, for the ethical reverberations of the statement are somewhat comprehensive. If most of our "human" capacities and ways of being in and engaging with the world are understood as *shared* by nonhuman animals and as *originating* in nonhuman animals, even partially, then the human itself must undergo the most radical of metamorphoses via animality, in its specificity. In other words, we must purposively re-visit the misguided disavowal of animality in all our major cultural, scientific, philosophical, and ecological knowledge systems.

My searching and re-searching for this book has been motivated by the desire to elaborate the ways that "human" aesthetics are irrevocably grounded in animality and the inhuman. Because my earlier work[30] has suggested that post-Darwinian modernism represents a privileged site for the eruption of animality in artistic and cultural texts in the post-Enlightenment era, I begin in the early twentieth century. The decades after Darwin's work became widely circulated mark one of the most charged upheavals in humanism vis-à-vis animals that human history has witnessed. What is more, modernism's insistence on "making it new" resulted in a particularly resonant moment for bioaesthetics in literature and culture. That is, the coincidence of scientific and cultural acknowledgments of humans' animality with the pronounced desire to innovate and refigure forms of artistic practice, helps explain the recurrence of bioaesthetic themes in this period. Modernism is itself a kind of aesthetic "becoming-other," and thus the bioaesthetic is especially prominent in this period. I begin here by looking at Isadora Duncan, whose animal engagements that are central to the founding gestures of modern dance have been all but overlooked in recent discussions of her significance. I move on to D. H. Lawrence who, more than any other modernist writer, made animality central to his re-shaping of the conventionally human. From that point, I investigate various animal upheavals in the work of Virginia Woolf, and go on to examine more contemporary figures who reveal the inhuman roots of their artistic practices across the century and beyond it (Rachel Rosenthal, John Cage, and Merce Cunningham).

Animal Dances

Decentering human aesthetics involves locating the human "back" within the animal and the natural. Dancing in this book should, therefore, be understood first as metaphorically suggestive, describing the intricate ways in which life and species forces *move* and shape themselves in ever-surprising combinations and patterns that momentarily cohere only to become something else in the next instant (but that also return to similar forms or themes). And second, dance should be understood in its more literal sense as an often minor art form that has the (animal) body as its instrument[31] and that is routinely overlooked or elided in discussions of aesthetics and artistic practices.

Critics like Una Chaudhuri have forged important links between animal studies and performance. Chaudhuri has outlined a "theater of species" in her scholarship, and scholars of performance have begun to seriously consider the species axis in their work.[32] Chaudhuri's groundbreaking ideas on theater ecologies ask us to link animality with performativity across a number of cultural landscapes. She examines traditional and nontraditional theater as sites that move between discursive or linguistic representations and performative or affective intensities as those impinging upon the discourse of species. Her coining of the term "zooësis" draws our attention to the "myriad performance and semiotic elements involved in and around the vast field of *cultural animal practices*."[33] Chaudhuri's recent analysis of Marina Zurkow's video animation titled *Mesocosm*, for instance, unpacks a virtual representation of nature that wreaks havoc on our received notions of anthropocentrism, stage presence, the food chain, and the proper relations between species.[34] In Chaudhuri's view, *Mesocosm* reveals how the nexus of performance and animal studies can operate to unpack our experience of wilderness, the ecological imagination, and the staging of species boundaries.

I take my cue, in part, from this rich strain of work in animal studies. As this introduction has already demonstrated, however, my own critical preoccupations lead me to ask questions about modern and contemporary dance, and to query the visceral nature of dance as it foregrounds the somatic and "inhuman" in a uniquely intensified manner. In broad terms, I am compelled by the question of dance and animality on many fronts. Is dance the most "animal" aesthetic form, and does this help to explain its persistent critical marginalization? If so, then scholars ought to begin identifying and exploring the appearance of species questions related to dancing, especially in the writing and work of post-Darwinian dancers and artists. And further, how should we theorize the primacy of bodily experience and agency in dance, in relation to discourses of species? How does dance frontload the double-edged question of material agency (as in the "new materialisms") and mortal finitude that seems to figure as *the* theoretical juggernaut of animal studies at this moment? And how does the effacement of language per se in dance need to be theorized in relation to performance, animality, and posthumanism? Jane Desmond outlined a number of additional, wide-ranging scholarly frameworks for the exploration of animals and dance in a 2016 lecture at Temple University.[35] It is my hope that this study begins a sustained and long-term theoretical "pas de deux" between animal studies and dance studies.

This study asks if we can understand dance as a minoritarian art form that affords an especially creatural mode of becoming.[36] Broglio discusses artist Marcus Coates's "masks and dances" (*Surface* xxxii) as minor, noting that one of the features of minor art "espoused by Deleuze and Guattari is the move from metaphor to metamorphosis (what they will later characterize as 'becoming')" (*Surface* xxxi). A Deleuzian kind of metamorphosis characterizes the dancerly becomings in Woolf's writing, the waverings of Lawrence's "inhuman" characters, the vibratory drifting in Isadora Duncan's work, and the gestural illustrations of Rosenthal's self-portraits. By theorizing these creatural becomings, this project can encourage further dialogue across literary studies, animal studies, and performance and dance studies. It can also train discussions of the aesthetic toward animality, movement, affect, and embodiment, to counter the long historical yoking of aesthetic capacity with somewhat narrow ideas of cognitive processing.

Chapter One, "Nude Vibrations: Isadora Duncan's Creatural Aesthetic," identifies a critical embarrassment—resulting in a critical silence—surrounding Duncan's notions that one should dance like the "free animals." Duncan is hailed as the muse of modernism, and the mother of a modern dance aesthetic in the first decades of the twentieth century. Recent criticism has overemphasized her interest in the machine and neglected to examine the proliferating cosmic, natural, and animal images in Duncan's writings and choreography. This chapter reads Duncan as a paradigmatic test case for re-seeing the complexities of "naturalness" in the early twentieth century in relation to animality, performance, and an aesthetics that is specifically posthumanist. Rather than a naïve essentialist, Duncan should be viewed as a kind of vitalist who understood art as emerging from the vibrancy of matter itself and the drift or transfer of forces from earth to animal, from animal to human. By examining her animal and cosmic imagery and by discussing questions such as barefootedness and nudity as specific markers of animality in Duncan's aesthetic, I frame her dance theory as exhibiting a sophisticated posthumanist artistic position. That position situates human subjectivity in a participatory relation to the inhuman and stages aesthetics as a trans-species practice. Recognizing these elements of her artistic theories helps us re-evaluate the way Duncan has been viewed because of the natural strains in her work, but also opens new lines of inquiry regarding animality and modern dance.

Chapter Two, "Creative Incantations and Involutions in D. H. Lawrence," traces the contours of D. H. Lawrence's "blood-consciousness" through the Deleuzian refrain in his poem, "Tortoise Shout," and through the underanalyzed moments in *Women in Love* when Gudrun and Birkin partake in creatural dances. In the poem, I connect Lawrence's emphasis on living beings at extremity to ideas about evolutionary excess and intensity. The rhythm, tempo, and melody of the tortoise's shout enacts a refrain that is ultimately linked to rhythms of the poetic voice, the body, and the earth. Thus, the poem itself is an affective becoming, in which forces cross or are shared by human animal and nonhuman animal. I also suggest that poetry may provide the most resonant literary genre for expressing the overlapping aesthetic intensity of the living in general. Both "Tortoise Shout" and *Women in Love* explore the link between the artistic and the sexual in ways that dovetail with Grosz's claim that sexuality requires creativity to be itself. My discussions of Gudrun's dance of "seduction" with the cattle, and Birkin's "licentious" dancing in *Women in Love*, move us beyond received interpretations of sexuality in Lawrence. Gudrun's scene in particular reveals dance to be much more than some expressive practice, but rather a becoming–imperceptible/animal that both challenges the Oedipalized subject yet capitalizes on the rituals of sexual selection. Lawrence's Deleuzian dancing ultimately can be framed as a "lapsing out" or line of flight into the inhuman.

Chapter Three, "Woolf's Floating Monkeys and Whirling Women" frames another kind of lapsing out, one that decouples creativity and the verticality of the exceptional human artist. This chapter considers two of Virginia Woolf's most experimental texts, one being critically underexamined (her Nurse Lugton story for children), the other considered by many to be paradigmatic of Woolf's literary "genius" (The Waves). Writing as a mode of becoming-animal resides at the heart of the Nurse Lugton tale, in both of the published versions of the story and their accompanying illustrations. This tale catalogues an awareness of the way that a writer's aesthetic powers are profoundly linked to animality. Moreover, the specific becoming-other/becoming-animate of the prosaic curtain in the children's story is best understood as exhibiting a vital materialism in which matter cannot be separated from the forces of life as such. That is, the curtain in Woolf's story should be read as creative materiality itself, its folds participating in the self-varying dynamism of the virtual and actual. In the wake of such recognitions, I outline an affirmative biopoetics at the heart of Woolf's aesthetic project. Consequently, the formerly exceptional human creative genius (in this case Woolf) must be recast from her "verticality" and placed on a horizontal plateau with inhuman artistic intensities. My analysis therefore aligns Woolf's own creative powers with inhuman, biological forces. This alignment allows me, in the remainder of the chapter, to provide a counterintuitive reading of creativity in The Waves. Received wisdom about this novel links Woolf to the characters who write (Bernard and Louis) and also suggests that Rhoda is a quasi-Woolfian figure. I argue that Jinny, understood by some critics as a call-girl, may be the most creative character in the text, if we understand creativity in a posthumanist sense. Jinny, who is often dismissed as shallow or overly sexualized in Woolf criticism, is better theorized as a dancer figure who harnesses vibrational forces and engages in the becoming-artistic of life itself. It is Jinny's sensibilities, connecting affect to movement to erotic display, that most clearly register the overlap between human and nonhuman aesthetic experience in Woolf's influential text.

Chapter Four, "Strange Prosthetics: Rachel Rosenthal's Rats and Rings," also connects affective states to movement and develops critical discussions of Rosenthal's posthumanist use of Tatti the rat on stage to provide a broader examination of her trans-species artistic practice. Rosenthal's book Tatti Wattles: A Love Story, which has received scant critical attention in performance studies, feminist studies, and animal studies, reveals her aesthetic practice itself to be animated by the discourse of species. While making many references to Rosenthal's performance pieces, this discussion is also specifically invested in a reading of the Tatti illustrations that Rosenthal penned in that text. The drawings seem outrageous and fantastical, and they exhibit a pre- or extra-verbal, supplementary relationship to the written text. Although the primary subject of *Tatti Wattles* is the undeniably meaningful and personally potent companionship Rosenthal experiences with Tatti, this chapter discusses the sub-text of *Tatti Wattles*, which circulates around the way animality subtends Rosenthal's self-identification as an artist. This sub-text is presented performatively, almost entirely through the book's illustrations, both the major color illustrations and the more minor black and white drawings. These images also are marked by Rosenthal's "auto-graphy" as a mover or dancer, by an alimentary tropology highlighting the body, by the concept of mediation, and by the taming of human exceptionalism. The images also efface the human yet "en-face" rats, de-emphasizing human power and privilege. It follows that all these elements in Rosenthal's view of her artistic practice, self, and process are mediated by animality, and they challenge our received notions of art as a centrally human practice.

Chapter Five, "UnCaging Cunningham's Other Animals," excavates the natural strains in John Cage and Merce Cunningham's composing and choreographic habits vis-à-vis animality. In statements both artists made in interviews and essays about their work, Cage and Cunningham reveal their recognition that the artistic is primarily about pleasure and affect, and that it is the animal part of us that responds most fully to such provocations. For instance, Cage's discussion of the pleasure of sound in a taped interview, and his simultaneous interactions with his own cat are linked in this chapter to Cunningham's creatural style as an emerging dancer in the twentieth century. Additionally, I read the little-known Cunningham book of drawings *Other Animals* (2002) in the context of such ambitious performance pieces as *Beach Birds* (1991) and *Ocean* (1994). The latter uses whale and dolphin voices as part of its soundscape (and was inspired by comments about James Joyce). Cunningham's cultivation of "pure-dance" and his architectural, postmodernist aesthetic need to be complemented by a study of the way animality runs through his body of work. Indeed, Cunningham's propensity for drawing vibrantly colored animals links him back to Duncan, a founder of modern dance, who modeled her movement on the "free animals." Moreover, specific illustrations in *Other Animals* are remarkably reminiscent of the depictions of animal hordes in Virginia Woolf's Lugton tale. This chapter, therefore, allows us to trace the vibratory, excessive impulse of bioaesthetics from modernism to the early twenty-first century.

Such an impulse affirmatively links human and nonhuman through an innovative and improvisational force that strives to become something other and something new. Perhaps in a complementary relation to Broglio's emphasis on the "surface," this argument identifies a "deep" coincidence of the human and animal elaboration of life forces in aesthetic practices. Recognizing our artistic drives as and in the nonhuman, and thus problematizing that tired binary of human/animal, is itself creatively charged, because we must now refashion our very frameworks for understanding "human" art.

In the conclusion of my last book, I suggested that posthumanist attentions to animality might "reinvigorate" the humanities "by taking it beyond and outside of itself, by reimagining what the human really participates in and constitutes" (*Stalking* 162). Some of the "strangeness" of the texts and questions that I follow here should be understood within such a context. So, too, Braidotti has identified a "neo-materialist, embodied and embedded approach" to understanding subjectivity that she links to the "rhizomic philosophies" of Deleuze and Guattari.[37] In Braidotti's terms, the subject is "dissolved and re-grounded in an eco-philosophy of multiple belongings. This takes the form of a strong emphasis on the pre-human or even non-human elements that compose the web of forces, intensities and encounters that contribute to the making of nomadic subjectivity" (*Transpositions* 41). It is in this spirit, with an emphasis on an affirmative more-than-human re-vision of what creativity is, that I present these investigations. A conceptual opening of human creativity onto the nonhuman and animal ought to elicit many new ways of seeing and experiencing our own creative forces, and it also unfolds new ethical attentions to the richness and vitality of the nonhuman world in all its riotous becomings. As D. H. Lawrence claimed in his poem "Snake" that the animal "comes before me," so, too, we must reckon with the notion that animals' art has preceded ours.[38] Knowledge of this derivation potentially can inspire a new sense of wonder and a different kind of clarity about the aesthetic dances of all living creatures.

Nude Vibrations: Isadora Duncan's Creatural Aesthetic

It was never easy to coax Isadora Duncan into a photographer's studio.
Like a wild and wise animal, she fled from those who sought to capture
the essence of her—which was motion—by making her stand still.
—Max Eastman, forward to *Isadora Duncan: Twenty-Four
Studies* (1929)[1]

It is perhaps only the advent of animal studies in the last decade that allows us to return to the often-cited comment made here and link it in a serious intellectual manner with Isadora Duncan's own understanding of her dancing, and of the dancing body, as she was helping to shape and articulate it in modernism. While recent work on Duncan emphasizes her interest in the machine, her aesthetic commitments are more fully articulated by elucidating the pivotal animal and elemental strains in her work. Duncan recites again and again in her essays that movements ought to be "natural and beautiful like those of the free animals."[2] In conjunction with this repeated claim, she insists upon the human harnessing of earthly vibrations, the value of nudity and barefootedness, and certain border figures (woman and child) that inform her creatural aesthetic. Understanding Duncan's bioaesthetic engagements enriches our assessment of her cultural disruptions, contributions, and legacies.

One fascinating and compressed testimonial to Duncan's belief in the role of the "natural" for her artistic philosophy reveals itself in her "Notes for a Lecture":

The Dance and its place in nature; then its relation to Greek tragedy, to art, etc. The freeing of the child's body. The body controlled by mind and spirit. The effect of music on the growing child; the joining of the child's life to nature. Every child's love for music. The educational value of music (quote Plato). The unity of movement in all nature.[3]

The refrain of the natural in this memo underscores the way in which earthly and animal forces were central to Duncan's technique, philosophies, and choreographic innovations. In rethinking Duncan's theories about waves and water, and considering the fish, birds, reptiles, lions, and other animals that populate her dances and dance writings,[4] I suggest that Duncan undertook the performing of an othered bodiliness that opens the human onto the animal, the earthly, the cosmic. Moreover, Duncan understood art as emerging from the vibrancy of matter itself and the drift or transfer of forces from earth to animal, from animal to human.

Although Duncan's attentions to "nature" and "the natural" have been widely acknowledged, they have been inadequately understood. Theorizing her investment in the creatural reveals that she ultimately stages aesthetics as a transspecies practice, rather than as something that makes humans exceptional. Duncan, therefore, provides an especially compelling case study for the intersection of post-Darwinian, modernist aesthetics and the emergence of modern dance in which the "animal" body is rendered on stage.[5] Also at stake in this reading of Duncan is the practice of modern dance as a bodily metamorphosis, a kind of becoming-animal, which might be understood as uniquely creatural or inhuman among the arts.

Scholars in modernist studies have a reinvigorated interest in Duncan's theories and practice, and in her relationship to first-wave feminism. Duncan was known as the "muse" of modernism, a potentially infantilizing characterization that nonetheless highlights her broad impact on art and culture in the period.[6] Her dancing was often a direct reaction against the rigidity and high formality of ballet. Recognizing how the creatural was central to her aesthetic principles situates Duncan's work in relation to other modernists who, as I have suggested in earlier work, were disavowing, confronting, or recuperating animality in the early twentieth century after Darwin's revisions of human exceptionalism. As I have explained elsewhere, the onset of modernism "coincides with the proliferation of Darwin's story of human origins, which indicates that the human being can be understood as a highly evolved animal" (*Stalking* 22). Like D. H. Lawrence, Duncan is a modernist figure whose "privileging of the animal" enacts "a transvaluation of humanist species values that disrupts the 'human' at its core" (*Stalking* 100).

Examining the earthly and creatural in Duncan's work also can invite a fresh emphasis on her significance within modernist scholarship. Carrie Preston has recently consolidated a carefully situated and historically balanced view of Duncan's place in aesthetic, feminist, and avant-garde modernism. As Preston points out, the broad call for a "new modernist studies" has not resulted in much attention to performance, dance, or even more traditional theater practices.[7] Particularly in terms of dance, this critical neglect is not only the result of the often-noted "feminization" of dance practices, but I suggest it also may be related to the alignment with animality that the dancing body inevitably rehearses.

Preston's work is especially valuable because it rigorously contests a critical tendency to frame Duncan as a "nymph." This designation indicates the pejorative way in which Duncan is sometimes theorized because of her attention to spirituality, classical typologies, and nature.[8] Like Felicia McCarren's 2003 *Dancing Machines*, Preston's work on Duncan is varied and complex, and Preston does characterize Duncan as an artist interested in both the "natural" and the "technological." Interestingly, though, Preston's argument about Duncan is anchored by Duncan's use of the phrase "motor in the soul," a phrase that McCarren's work on motor power in modernism has made central to recent discussions of Duncan in dance history. Preston goes so far as to suggest that "Duncan's three central movement innovations" are all "associated with the motor in the soul" (*Mythic* 146).

I don't wish to dispute the noteworthiness of the appearance of the motorized in Duncan's movement vocabulary, choreography, and writing. When one turns, however, to Duncan's essays about dance, especially, and to the ways Duncan choreography is currently taught and restaged, one comes away with the clear sense that it is natural, cosmic, and animal images that truly suffuse her work. Frankly, the motor image is dwarfed by the varied, ecstatic, and incessant images that are *not* connected to technology as such in Duncan's theories. Preston herself has pointed to a certain "technophilia" in modernist criticism on film and cinema,[9] and there can be no doubt that this has had a profound, if sometimes unspoken, impact on the way modernist critics approach writers and thinkers of the period who are deemed simplistic in their attention to the "natural" or instinctual. Lawrence's work, for instance, has been regularly excoriated in the last fifty years for its perceived "primitivism," though some significant interventions have resuscitated the ecological value of his writings.[10] Preston's own discussions of "impersonality" in the critically favored version of modernist philosophy, à la T. S. Eliot, point out such biases. Nevertheless, Preston's work also seems to display a slightly compensatory emphasis on the motor in Duncan's performance vocabulary, perhaps in order to continue rescuing Duncan from the "natural" strains in her work. This fetish-like emphasis is understandable given the way that Duncan has been consistently read. However, there seems to be a critical embarrassment—resulting in a critical silence—surrounding Duncan's notions that one should dance like the "free animals."[11] Duncan's repeated focus on earthly and creatural forces compels us to revise the prominence of the motor in the soul and turn our attention to the creature in the soul.[12]

Being "Earthy": Vibration as Species Drifting

Shifting Duncan's connections to modernist culture from the machinic to-ward the animal reframes her aesthetic as valuing and harnessing the creatural. Moreover, Duncan's ideas about rhythm and the vibratory connect human cre-ativity to supple and innovative biological and cosmological forces. One can hardly overstate the frequency with which, in *The Art of the Dance*, she discusses the concept of vibration or cosmic rhythm. In the segment "The Philosopher's Stone of Dancing," Duncan addresses her primary pedagogical aim in relation to a vibratory force: "So confident am I that the soul can be awakened, can com-pletely possess the body, that when I have taken children into my schools I have aimed above all else to bring to them a consciousness of the power within them-selves, of their relationship to the universal rhythm . . . " (*Dance* 52). Duncan elaborates upon the vibratory in her section "Movement is Life," where she provocatively writes: "When asked for the pedagogic program of my school, I reply: 'Let us first teach little children to breathe, *to vibrate*, to feel, and to be-come one with the general harmony and movement of nature'" (*Dance* 77; my emphasis). Breathing and feeling, becoming "harmonious" even, are rather straightforward in terms of our conceptual apparatus, but teaching a child to vibrate? What precisely does Duncan mean here? Ann Daly points out how Duncan's references to scientific theories of her day might be understood as both sophisticated and intentional[13] (an argument that would apply just as easily to figures like F. T. Marinetti, in fact). But Elizabeth Grosz's work allows us to rec-ognize that Duncan's notion of teaching a child to vibrate may be much more than a clever reference to atomic theory, and should be understood, rather, as a specific aesthetic statement posing dance as a kind of queer ecology.[14]

Grosz helps to put a finer point on the relation between the vibratory and what she ultimately calls aesthetic emergence. In her linking of Darwinian and Deleuzian concepts of sexual selection, the refrain, aesthetic display, and spec-tacle, Grosz returns again and again to the vibratory. When speculating that sex-uality itself is best understood in terms of pleasure rather than heteronormative reproduction, Grosz asserts, "Vibrations, waves, oscillations, resonances affect living bodies, not for any higher purpose but for pleasure alone. Living beings are vibratory beings: vibration is their mode of differentiation, the way they en-hance and enjoy the forces of the earth itself" (*Chaos* 33).

Grosz goes on to discuss vibration primarily in terms of music, but she makes it clear that her conclusions about the artistic apply to a broad range of formal modes. She also notes that music, followed closely by dance, seem to be the most intensifying, "contagious" and "seductive" of the arts (*Chaos* 29). Grosz's understanding of aesthetic emergence is grounded in a Darwinian articulation of attraction and seduction that, she makes clear, does not require an emphasis on heterosexual reproduction, but rather on pleasure and the becoming-other of the animal (or plant) body. She explains that during courtship, bodily surplus, display or spectacle, and skills in excess of the practical, all figure in to the way an animal creates a vibratory performance. Thus, it is "the erotic, indeed perhaps vibratory, force in all organisms . . . that seduces, entices, mesmerizes, that sexualizes the body, metabolizes organs, and prepares and solicits it for courtship. . . . For Darwin, this seems as close to a universal postulate as anything he claims: rhythm, vibration, resonance, is enjoyable and intensifying" (*Chaos* 32). Moreover, it is the individual's vibratory play and framing of elemental forces into aesthetic articulations that we might call the fundamentally inhuman impulse behind all aesthetics.

When Grosz writes the following, we understand much more radically what Duncan might mean about teaching a child to vibrate: "What music and the arts indicate is that (sexual) taste and erotic appeal . . . indicate that those living beings that 'really live,' that intensify life—for its own sake, for the sake of intensi[t]y or sensation—bring something new to the world, create something that has no other purpose than to intensify, to experience itself" (*Chaos* 39). Vibration, then, in Duncan's writings, might be understood as the harnessing and displaying—the participatory intensifying—of cosmic forces or possibilities. These participations inevitably link the artist, the dancer, and the child, to the forces of the earth, to matter, to "natural" rhythms and animals. In this connection, Duncan's "universal gesture," as taught by Lori Belilove of the Isadora Duncan Dance Foundation (IDDF), involves an acknowledgment of the earth and sky, and the greeting of other beings, including "animal friends."[15]

We can now revisit Duncan's "Movement Is Life" to understand its sophisticated aesthetic claims. Duncan writes at another point in that essay: "Man has not invented the harmony of music. It is one of the underlying principles of life. Neither could the harmony of movement be invented: it is essential to draw one's conception of it from Nature herself, and to seek the rhythm of human movement from the rhythm of water in motion, from the blowing of the winds on the world, in all the earth's movements, in the motions of animals, fish, birds, reptiles, and even in primitive man, whose body still moved in harmony with nature" (*Dance* 78).[16] This statement evokes Deleuze's notion of art as that which drifts between the animal and the human, between the earth and the vibrancy of matter itself. In fact, Jeanne Bresciani, Artistic Director and Director of Education for the Isadora Duncan International Institute, notes that the "Duncan Vibrato" is a fundamental concept in Duncan technique.[17] Bresciani describes this vibration as the aftermath of energy that emerges from the solar plexus and runs through and beyond fingers, toes, and eyelashes, and then through the head, which tilts back (a movement I will discuss later).[18]

In the introductory materials to Duncan's essays, too, those who knew her connect her legacy with the concept of vibration. Sheldon Cheney's striking prefatory remarks imagine her life and life's work as a spreading tremor of the unimagined:

> To me there is an epic quality in her life. The picture of the girl-figure emerging out of Victorian times and customs, out there on the very edge of Western civilization, in California, *vibrating to some wave of Whitmanesque affirmation*, starting eastward with absolute self-confidence, conquering all of America and all of Europe for her idea, by a revelation, a presentation of her dance—in this picture of the march of the spirit of Isadora Duncan across the world, I find a greatness, a stirring elemental implication. (*Dance* 6; my emphasis)

It is important to keep in mind that it is just this "elemental implication"—associated with naïve, naturist affinities—that has often been used to marginalize Duncan's role in modernist culture.

Tracing Duncan's ideas about the vibratory indicates how she understood art as harnessing the "freedom" of matter and animality, and as linking the vibrancy of human and nonhuman worlds. In fact, Max Eastman describes Duncan's cultural influence by enumerating the "bare-legged girls, and the poised natural girls with strong muscles and strong free steps wherever they go—the girls that redeem America and make it worth while to have founded a new world . . . The boys, too, who have a chance to be unafraid of beauty, to be unafraid of the natural life and free aspiration of an intelligent animal walking the earth" (*Dance* 38). An additional line of inquiry might emerge over discourses of "freedom" in Duncan's writings within the context of new materialism. As Bennett notes, "vitalism is the reaction formation to a mechanistic materialism. . . . The machine model of nature, with its figure of inert matter, is no longer even scientific. It has been challenged by systems theory, complexity theory, chaos theory, fluid dynamics, as well as by the many earlier biophilosophies of flow that Michel Serres has chronicled" (*Vibrant* 91). Even today, Bennett reminds us, human control over nature often trumps "the element of freedom in matter" (*Vibrant* 91).

Such a perspective reveals the "earthy" aspects of Duncan's dancing and theorizing as complex engagements with the inhuman rather than primitive "returns" to some purified nature. In terms of her choreography, this drifting is overtly thematized in a dance like Duncan's *Water Study*, which Preston describes as such: "The dancer both moves through the water and is the water; she appears to be splashing and playing, but her body is a wave and her arms are swirling eddies. For a moment, she leaps out of the water like a fish" (*Mythic* 177). Duncan technique in general is also highly directed by animal engagements. Belilove, in her master class, describes the motion of the leg and foot in Duncan's form of skipping as akin to "reaching like a paw." In my interview with Belilove, she further expounded that the foot/paw is to be used for "seeing," as if the dancer were blind. She also noted that according to Sima Borisovana Leake, the Elizabeth Duncan School of training would regularly take dancers to watch horses train and trot, and to watch fish swimming in ponds. While teaching a "Mermaid" sequence, Belilove characterizes the arms as shooting "up like a whale spout," and she even cues the dancers with a "pshew" noise that imitates this animal sound. Moreover, Belilove chooses to use the term "wings" rather than arms when teaching Duncan technique, and she describes the quality of a particular run by evoking the intense focus of an eagle. Although Duncan's theories linking human and inhuman movement are expansive, and would not be limited to choreography that explicitly addresses water, paws or wings, the prominence of these overt images is striking. Noting how practitioners embody Duncan's choreography as a mesh between species and natural forces provides a new critical purchase on iconic photographic images that show Duncan, for instance, exultant amidst the trees and grasses (see Figure 1.1).

It is important to clarify my caveat against viewing Duncan's attentions to nature as a simple kind of primitivism. In Grosz's discussions of Aboriginal Australian painting, she reminds us that "art is not simply the expression of an animal past, a prehistorical allegiance with the evolutionary forces that make one; it is not memorialization, the celebration of a shared past, but above all the transformation of the materials from the past into resources for the future, the sensations unavailable now but to be unleashed in the future on a people ready to perceive and be affected by them" (*Chaos* 103). This explanation clarifies Duncan's role as announcing the *future* of dance, her role in shifting the perception of what dance was, is, and ought to be. These engagements with the pre-human "past" for the sake of the future also provide a strong connection with Lawrence's work, a connection that is framed through ideas about dance in his novels, as I discuss in the next chapter. That is, in *Women in Love*, Gudrun dances a kind of becoming-cow, enacting one of Lawrence's most animal examples of the desire to inhabit new concepts and new forms of being that revive the "blood-consciousness" in the human. Birkin also dances a "grotesque step-dance" of self-overcoming in the novel, and engages in a nude becoming-plant after a violent episode with his lover, Hermione.[19]

Figure 1.1 Courtesy of the Jerome Robbins Dance Division, The New York Public Library for the Performing Arts, Astor, Lenox and Tilden Foundations.

Hard Running: Nudity and the Foot

Duncan's dancing, her manifesto-like, post-performance commentaries,[20] and her own cultural and performative choices shaped the modernist metamorphosis of dance in the broader transatlantic milieu. In many ways, Duncan's style and ideas were experienced as an *unleashing* for which people were precisely unprepared. But those people were also made ready in that experience to witness and imagine the new. As her companion Gordon Craig wrote, "Only just moving— not pirouetting or doing any of these things which we expect to see, . . . she was speaking in her own language, not echoing any ballet master, and so she came to move as no one had ever seen anyone move before."[21] Ann Daly points out that, by World War I, largely because of Duncan, "dance had been transformed from entertainment into 'Culture,' at least in New York. Duncan reimagined the form and content of dance as an aesthetic object and convinced an audience of its legitimacy as a 'high' art" (*Gestures* 248). Duncan also converted the received taxonomies of dance that prized the corseted, strained, balletic body into a framework that valued seminudity, bodily weight, barefootedness, and individual female performance. In her essay, "The Dance of the Future," Duncan repeats what can only be characterized as her ur-emphasis on the natural, rhythmic movement "of waves, of winds, of the earth," "of the free animals and birds" (*Dance* 54). She goes on to discuss the ways in which "civilized man" has lost the ability to move naturally. But she makes it clear that the "return" to the naked body is not a memorialization, but is rather an improvisation of nudity for the present (and future) of the reformed human who once again moves and dances: "Man, arrived at the end of civilization, will have to return to nakedness, not to the unconscious nakedness of the savage, but to the conscious and acknowledged nakedness of the mature Man, whose body will be the harmonious expression of his spiritual being. And the movements of the Man will be natural and beautiful like those of the free animals" (*Dance* 55).

Nudity has been a central concept in animal studies since the publication of Derrida's essay "The Animal That Therefore I Am," which opens this way: "In the beginning. I would like to entrust myself to words that, were it possible, would be naked. Naked in the first place—but this is in order to announce already that I plan to speak endlessly of nudity and of the nude in philosophy."[22] Derrida goes on to recount the now familiar episode in which he is "caught naked, in silence, by the gaze of an animal, for example, the eyes of a cat" (*Animal That* 3–4). Among a number of Derrida's immediate considerations in these pages is the question of having knowledge of one's nudity, of nakedness *proper*. In other words, the animal "doesn't feel its own nudity. There is no nudity 'in nature'" (*Animal That* 5). The naked human, on the other hand, is characterized by shame. As Rebecca Tuvel puts it, the human case "is that in which the *human* is not truly naked because it only becomes aware of its nakedness in relation to a feeling of shame, according to which it immediately desires to cover itself up."[23]

In a much broader sense, Derrida's emphasis on nudity is meant to emphasize human vulnerability, finitude, mortality, and exposure. All of these are states that we share with nonhuman animals. As Cora Diamond maintains, recognizing these affinities helps us view other animals as fellow creatures, so that we respond, "to animals as our fellows in mortality, in life on this earth" (qtd. in *Posthumanism* 77). In this light, Duncan's work can be viewed as the performance or staging of human nudity *without* that event being overtaken by feelings of shame. In fact, Kimberly Engdahl Coates reminds us of the "[u]nashamed" Duncan, who danced in a transparent tunic and while pregnant.[24] And if we follow the logic of such an event as breaking open a "new" sense of the possibilities of dance, we see that modern dance, as such, might be understood as staging human animality through performance in a way that is historically specific. Thus, the "truly" naked human animal, for Duncan, figures centrally in her modernist becoming of the future of dance.

This trans-species variety of nudity is literalized much later in the century by the modern dancer and performance artist Ann Carlson. In her five-part, 1988 series "Animals," which included goats and dogs, Carlson performed a solo (or duet, if we count the animal) described here by Jack Anderson of *The New York Times*: "In the extraordinary 'Visit Woman Move Story Cat Cat Cat,' Ms. Carlson, totally nude, frisked about with feline movements, then picked up a kitten. She resembled a mother cat. Yet, given the tenderness of her actions, she could have been any loving mother."[25] Carlson continues today to engage a variety of questions related to animality and bare bodies in her ongoing work. I won't address her more recent dances in detail here; my point, rather, is to mention her dances in the context of Duncan's animal nakedness.

Duncan's commitment to barefootedness puts a finer point on the questions of animality, exposure, and the development of a modern dance aesthetic in the early twentieth century. Performing barefooted was one of Duncan's hallmark "revolutions" in Western dance, and she insisted upon its value in her writings. She opens "The Dance of the Future" by recalling a woman who once asked her why she danced with bare feet. Immediately linking the future of dance practice with evolutionary "wisdom," Duncan cites Darwin and Haeckel as her sources, claiming that "the expression and intelligence of the human foot is one of the greatest triumphs of the evolution of man" (*Dance* 54). This claim is fascinating in its willfully unconventional posturing, for, in fact, it is the *hand* that is traditionally linked to man's putative "progression" in the evolutionary narrative that places him at the forefront of bio-developmental power. Of course, Duncan protests too much in her effort to elevate the foot over the hand. But I want to suggest that her commitment to barefootedness is a philosophical position meaningfully linked to animality and to an anti-handedness that shapes some of the broader critical arcs of twentieth-century dance.

Human hands and thumbs are often used to represent a substantive evolutionary division between the human and the animal. In *Ciferae: A Bestiary in Five Fingers*, Tom Tyler contextualizes what Stanley Cavell calls "the romance of the hand and its apposable thumb"[26] by reminding us of the long-standing claim that opposable thumbs are unique to humanity, evidence of "human exceptionalism, of an expedient, handy humanism" (*Ciferae* 243). Moreover, Cary Wolfe, in his ongoing attention to Heidegger's affair with the hand (and Derrida's troubling of that affair), reminds us just how profound this mythology is. Wolfe explains that for Martin Heidegger, "the meaning of the hand, properly understood, is determined not by biological or utilitarian function," such as grasping or clutching, "but by its expression of the *geschlecht* or species being of humanity, which, in opposition to the rest of creation, rests on the human possession of speech and thought" (*Posthumanism* 204). The human hand, handedness, handiness, these are all figures for the elevated status of the human in its evolutionary "distance" from the animal. That animal is perceived as mute and tool-less, "poor in world," and without the handed capacity for world-making.[27]

It is against this backdrop of handedness that I want to place Duncan's valorization of the foot. And despite her one attempt to claim footedness as an evolutionary sign of "progress," what her broad writings call for is a linking of animality to the foot in a way that recuperates or revivifies not a progressively evolving humanity but a persistent animality in the living in general. Duncan insisted upon the "scandalous" centrality of bare feet in her dance practice, and there is a double-edged or squared emphasis here on materiality and animality because of the foot. No one is discomfited by a bare hand, but a bare foot makes it difficult to maintain the humanist disavowal of animality. In Duncan's choreography, the bare foot in its particularity is emphasized in her early work, *Tanagra Figures*, which Preston explains is based on a British Museum collection of famous terra cotta figures: "As the dancer shifts her weight between poses . . . [she moves] both hands to her shoulder as if pinning a tunic, and she bends to the ground to take a handful of dirt," and so forth (*Mythic* 157). Belilove emphasizes a presentation of the foot that is "not coy," as the active knee does not cross in upon that of the standing leg. Rather, the bare foot in this "Boticelli leg" pose, or the "Tanagra foot," is gently placed with toes angling away from the body, in a kind of humble presentation or offering of the bare foot during performance.

If the Duncan dancer is animated as are the free animals, the birds, and the waves, if the dancer is animated by a recapitulation of earthly or natural forces, then the dancer is most dancerly as a *creature* rather than a "human." In that case, the bare foot functions as the sign or mark of animality for the Duncan dancer, and perhaps thereafter for all modern dancers in perpetuity. Duncan was constantly insisting that her art was civilized, the highest and most cultured form of "the dance." She had to insist upon this in order to make her desired changes in dance practice that have already been outlined, but also to counteract the central place of animality in her aesthetic vision. Similarly, just as she decried "savage"

African dances, her appearances in bare feet put animality itself back on the table, so to speak. Taking off the ballet shoe and performing with "animal" feet signaled the onset of a modern dance practice that took the body, the body's weight, the body's vulnerability and mortality seriously, in a way that ballet practice never could. My framework thus argues for reading Duncan's radicality in dance not as a rarified product of human advancement, genius, or handiwork, but rather as a bold commitment to the porous distinctions between humans and nonhumans.

We can read Duncan's commitment to barefootedness in any number of more "literal" ways. The bare foot opens up the possibility for contact with the earth itself, while the balletic foot, condemned to "torture" in Duncan's words, and always shod, remains civilized and cut off from earthly pulsations.[28] Moreover, as any modern dancer knows, the bare foot gets dirty, refusing the disavowal of matter or the organic. One has a fuller sense of the "scandal" of dancing barefoot with all this in mind. Such a podology reverses the typical processes of abjection and instead values a dirty and "base" creatural connection to matter and the organic. Recalibrating our view of Duncan's aesthetics along these lines resonates with the provisional emergence of an "inhuman humanities" within modernist studies, to use Grosz's phrase. As I discussed in the Introduction, Grosz asks, "What would a humanities, a knowledge of and for the human, look like if we placed the animal in its rightful place, not only before the human but also within and after the human?" (*Undone* 13).

The centrality of the bare foot in Duncan's work is recapitulated in Edna St. Vincent Millay's poetic tribute to the Duncan Dancers, "Sonnet XXI." Written in 1923, the poem reveals not only how contemporaneous audiences experienced the use of the bare foot in Duncan's choreography, but also how *other artists* in the early twentieth century experienced and responded to this choreographic element. The poem further solidifies the connection between barefootedness and an earthly organicism:

> How healthily their feet upon the floor
> Strike down! These are no spirits, but a band
> Of children, surely, leaping hand in hand
> Into the air in groups of three and four,
> Wearing their silken rags as if they wore
> Leaves only and light grasses, or a strand
> Of black elusive seaweed oozing sand,
> And running hard as if along a shore.
> I know how lost forever, and at length
> How still these lovely tossing limbs shall lie,
> And the bright laughter and the panting breath;
> And yet, before such beauty and such strength,

Once more, as always when the dance is high,
I am rebuked that I believe in death.[29]

The syntax, cadence, and punctuation of the first full sentence all emphasize the phrase "strike down!" Even the unusually large space after "down!" suggests that hearing the dancers' feet hit the ground is the cardinal element of the viewer's experience. And lest we overlook this fact, it is not a visual image of dance that opens the poem, but an auditory one. Indeed, it is a vibratory one. The reader is made to witness the rhythmic cadence of the dancers' feet, and the opening image calls to mind a kind of animal stampede. The poet further emphasizes the mortal weight of the dancers' footfall by using the term "healthily" and by claiming immediately that these are "no spirits." She goes on to reconjure the image further down with the line "running hard as if along a shore." No light skipping or whispery glissades here, but *hard* running. Also noteworthy is the way in which the dancers' tunics become leaves and grasses here (perhaps Millay was evoking Whitman?), or the surprisingly organic "strand / Of black elusive seaweed oozing sand." Millay's speaker seems to celebrate the bare- and sure-footed, panting women in precise contrast to the way that Eliot's Prufrock fears the women with bare arms who come and go (Millay's poem was published three years after Eliot's). Millay refracts Prufrock's anxiety over the "sea-girls wreathed with seaweed red and brown" into reverence for the black and oozing organicism of unbounded women who are affiliated with the sea.[30] In this case, the "new women" that Duncan trained and inspired are valued for their vital life force, in a recuperation of what might be called feminist animality for the modernist subject.

Bordering the Human: Animal, Child, Woman

In the collection *Human, All Too Human*, Diana Fuss discusses three "border identities" for humanism: animal, thing, child. In her introduction, she reminds us of the age-old alliance between children and animals, beings whose liminal status troubles the "integrity of the human."[31] She notes further that the child has been variously "idealized, demonized, eroticized, patronized, and publicized," and the same can easily be said of the animal (*All Too* 5). Ursula K. LeGuin articulates similar sentiments in her introduction to the collection of her stories, *Buffalo Gals and Other Animal Presences*. There, LeGuin writes that "In literature as in 'real life,' women, children, and animals are the obscure matter upon which Civilization erects itself, phallologically."[32] Duncan dedicated much of her life to the instruction of children. As is well known, she opened her experimental schools of dance, to varying success, in Germany, in France, and in Russia.

She believed in a dance revolution that would result in "free" and "natural" movements rather than automatic mimicry, and that would begin by harnessing the movements of the untrained child.

Duncan's essay "Youth and the Dance" helps situate the role of the child and of the child-like in her theoretical taxonomy. She opens this essay by claiming the following: "The child is gloriously full of life. He leaps endlessly, filled with the intoxication of movement. He is a young animal, growing in the midst of a joyous exaltation, drawing in with the intensity of all his being the forces for his future life" (*Dance* 97). (The use of the male pronoun seems mostly conventional; Duncan trained a few boys, but mostly girls.) We can imagine that she meant these statements to describe all children in an untrained state. Duncan's description of the child resonates with a vibratory bioaesthetics. The child is more animal than human, a creature exalting in intensities and forces that are harnessed for the future or the new.

Duncan repeatedly aligns the child with the woman in her written work: "[Poets] have mostly written of little children dancing, or of maidens dancing, or of one woman dancing" (*Dance* 73).[33] She continues to evoke the voice of poets whom she imagines asking the following of "Woman": "Dance us the sweetness of life and its meanings, dance for us the movements of birds, the waters, waving trees, floating clouds . . . Give us again the sweetness and beauty of the true dance, give us again the joy of seeing the *simple unconscious* pure body of woman" (*Dance* 73; my emphasis).

As scholars in animal studies have recently pointed out, the Freudian unconscious can be read as a figure for animality.[34] Duncan's own invocation of Bacchic dances and Dionysian movement, which Franko has theorized as "a moment of new departure for the material body" (DM 20), partially frames her engagement with discourses of animality in modernism and in dance. Thus, we see the triangulation of animal, child, woman surface repeatedly in her writings. Her essay "Terpsichore" reiterates the centrality of a Deleuzian and Darwinian aesthetic in which music once again serves as a bedrock for our understanding of inhuman artistic emergence: "All movement on earth is governed by the law of gravitation, by attraction and repulsion, resistance and yielding; it is that which makes up the rhythm of the dance. To discover this rhythm, we must listen to the *pulsations* of the earth. The great composers—Bach, Beethoven, Wagner—have in their works combined with absolute perfection terrestrial and human rhythm" (*Dance* 90; my emphasis). In an invective against ballet, Duncan discusses the "undulating line" that she sees as emblematic of Attic poses on vases, claiming she has almost never seen a Greek representation of dance "in which the foot is raised to a line perpendicular to the body. Even on the vases with figures expressing Bacchic frenzy, this movement is unknown" (*Dance* 91).[35] Bacchic frenzy is then explicitly allied with animality through a specific physiological gesture:

One of the commonest figures in the Bacchic dances is that with the
head turned backward. In this movement one senses immediately the
Bacchic frenzy possessing the entire body. The motive underlying this
gesture is in all nature. The animals, in Bacchic movement, turn back
the head: in tropic countries, at night, the elephants turn their heads;
dogs baying at the moon, lions, tigers. It is the universal Dionysiac
movement. (*Dance* 91)

This Dionysian movement is featured most prominently in two of Duncan's
dances, the *Bacchanal* (set to selections from Gluck's *Don Juan*) and the *Scherzo*
section from Chopin's Symphony No. 9 in C Major, titled *Homage to Dionysius*.[36]
As Bresciani explains, the *Scherzo* section stages a hunting scene, and in addition
to the classic Dionysian movement with the head straight back, dancers also in-
corporate a movement in which the head is angled to the side and held back.
Bresciani notes that Maria Theresa Duncan called this variation "the gazelle."
    Duncan was photographed by her brother Raymond in 1903, in Greece, in
this Dionysian position (Figure 1.2). The two dances mentioned earlier often
feature the dancers jumping in this position as well.[37] A photo of Irma Duncan,
provides another striking image of this Bacchic baying (Figure 1.3). The open
mouth is crucially "animal" in this backward gesture with the head. And "backward" has many meanings in this case. As Georges Bataille suggests, the mouth
"is the beginning or, if one prefers, the prow of animals; in the most charac-
teristic cases, it is the most living part, in other words, the most terrifying for
neighboring animals."[38] According to Bataille, the mouth and certain "profound
physical impulses" have lost prominence among civilized humans, thus "the
narrow constipation of a strictly human attitude, the magisterial look of the face
with a *closed mouth*, as beautiful as a safe" (*Visions* 59, 60). Nevertheless, "on important occasions human life is still bestially concentrated in the mouth" (*Visions*
59). Bataille qualifies this baying gesture as a kind of becoming-animal in the
human who screams. "On this subject," he continues, "it is easy to observe that
the overwhelmed individual throws back his head while frenetically stretching
his neck in such a way that the mouth becomes, as much as possible, an extension of the spinal column, *in other words, in the position it normally occupies in the
constitution of animals*. As if explosive impulses were to spurt directly out of the
body through the mouth, in the form of screams" (*Visions* 59). Belilove confirms
that the mouth is open and relaxed, not pursed, in this "Ecstatic position," in
order to emphasize release and surrender (interview).
    The photograph of Irma (Figure 1.3) eerily emphasizes the kind of excessive
and affective animality Bataille catalogues, because her mouth seems blurred in
a way that magnifies this "most living part," and also evokes abandon and terror.
Moreover, the "explosion" of impulses seems to mirror another of Duncan's

Figure 1.2 Isadora Duncan, Greece, by Raymond Duncan (1903). Courtesy of Isadora Duncan Dance Foundation.

theories about dance, that it should cultivate movement that is continuous rather than abrupt or compartmentalized. In the "Terpsichore" segment on Bacchic frenzy, she notes that in the figures on Greek vases, "one senses that the movement goes on: there is in this movement an eternal element—one which follows the undulating line of the great forces of Nature, on which I have based all the movements of my dance" (*Dance* 91). The "Bacchic" movement of affect seems coterminous here with the pulsating movement of the body.

Figure 1.3 Photo of Irma Duncan (one of Isadora's adopted daughters). Courtesy of the Jerome Robbins Dance Division, The New York Public Library for the Performing Arts, Astor, Lenox and Tilden Foundations.

Linking these insights with Duncan's commentary on the female body suggests how the "border identities" of animal, child, and woman seem to overlap in their inhuman instantiation of aesthetic forces in her ideology. In "The Dancer and Nature," Duncan suggests that women will attain knowledge of beauty not through analysis and conceptual regimens, but rather through the lived body:

> Shall she find this knowledge in the gymnasium examining her muscles, in the museum regarding the sculptured forms, or by the continual contemplation of beautiful objects, and the reflection of them in the mind? These are all ways, but the chief thing is, she must *live* this beauty, and her body must be the living exponent of it. (*Dance* 67)

These comments reject a notion of artistic comprehension as primarily conceptual and instead implicitly align the aesthetic with the reverberating body. Reviving dance as an art (thus resuscitating it from its "fallen" reputation), Duncan argues, will bring about a specifically "feminine" aesthetic practice. "I believe," she claims, "here is a wonderful undiscovered inheritance for coming womanhood, the old dance which is to become the new. She shall be sculpture not in clay or marble but in her own body which she shall endeavor to bring to the highest state of plastic beauty" (*Dance* 68).

This "highest" state of plastic beauty is specifically modern dance, and this modern dance is often expressly opposed to the restricted and prescribed movement vocabularies of ballet. In fact, in the taxonomy I have developed here, ballet becomes the reified humanist framework in which the vibratory is lost, choked out, dissipated. Duncan repeatedly writes diatribes against ballet, both in her autobiography and in her essays. The following excerpt from "The Dancer and Nature" further clarifies her position:

> First draw me the form of a woman as it is in Nature. And now draw me the form of a woman in a modern corset and the satin slippers used by our modern dancers. Now do you not see that the movement that would conform to one figure would be perfectly impossible for the other? To the first all the rhythmic movements that run through Nature would be possible. . . . To the second figure these movements would be impossible on account of the rhythm being broken, and stopped at the extremities. (*Dance* 69)

Interestingly, the corset is aligned with ballet slippers: both become instruments of repression and restriction that halt the movement of the vibratory through—and, it would seem, beyond—the woman's body. Ballet is often associated with the conventional and mechanical in Duncan's discussions. She calls ballet movements "sterile" because "they are unnatural," and emphasizes how ballet practice deforms women's bodies (*Dance* 56). Duncan also evokes Nietzsche in "Movement is Life," noting the philosopher's repeated emphasis on dancing: "Nietzsche has said that he cannot believe in a god that cannot dance. He has also said, 'Let that day be considered lost on which we have not danced'" (*Dance* 77). She goes on to suggest that Nietzsche's kind of dance is not ballet: "But he did not mean the execution of pirouettes. He meant the exaltation of life in movement" (*Dance* 77).[39]

This exaltation of life in movement is associated in both Duncan and D. H. Lawrence's ideas with a particular bodily "realm"; both modernist thinkers privilege the solar plexus in their philosophies. Preston has already pointed out that Duncan cites this area above the abdomen and between the breasts as the central source of movement. The relevant passage comes from Duncan's autobiography:

> I spent long days and nights in the studio seeking that dance which might be the divine expression of the human spirit through the medium of the body's movement. For hours I would stand quite still, my two hands folded between my breasts, covering the solar plexus. . . . I was seeking, and finally discovered, the central spring of all movement, the crater of motor power, the unity from which all diversions of movements are born. (ML 75)

Preston focuses on the solar plexus as the soul's organ and "the motor propelling dance" (*Mythic* 154). She rightly points out how thinkers at the time often associated the solar plexus with torsion and certain industrial actions (*Mythic* 97–98). But a few lines beyond the mention of a motor in Duncan's autobiography, we find the following elaboration of this movement source, as Duncan juxtaposes ballet's axis, the lower spine, with the solar plexus for modern dance: "I on the contrary sought the source of the spiritual expression to flow into the channels of the body filling it with vibrating light . . . when I listened to music the rays and vibrations of the music streamed to this one fount of light within me" (ML 75). As I mentioned at the outset of this chapter, the motor image is compelling for various reasons, but we might question it as *the* central metaphor for Duncan's aesthetic vision. It is possible to read the "motor" as a contemporary technological development that Duncan uses for troping or translating a more transhistorical and "natural" vibratory force, that is here associated with rays and eruptions of light.

Pairing Duncan's and Lawrence's attentions to the solar plexus reveals how this physical center was also understood by modernist thinkers as a seat of creatural consciousness. In Lawrence's *Fantasia of the Unconscious,* he includes a chapter called "Plexuses, Planes and So On," in which he argues that the solar plexus is the source of an other-than-rational knowledge linked to animality:

> The primal consciousness in man is pre-mental, and has nothing to do with cognition. It is the same as in the animals. . . . The first seat of our primal consciousness is the solar plexus, the great nerve-centre situated in the middle-front of the abdomen. From this centre we are first dynamically conscious. For the primal consciousness is always dynamic, and never, like mental consciousness, static. Thought, let us say what we will about its magic powers, is instrumental only, the soul's finest instrument for the business of living. Thought is just a means to action and living. But life and action rise actually at the great centres of dynamic consciousness.
>
> The solar plexus, the greatest and most important centre of our dynamic consciousness, is a sympathetic centre. At this main centre of our first-mind we know as we can never mentally know. Primarily we know, each man, each living creature knows, profoundly and satisfactorily and without question, that *I am I*.[40]

Like Duncan, Lawrence associates the solar plexus with a specific kind of knowledge. But it is a knowledge more in the blood—to use Lawrence's own terminology—than in the head. It is the same as in the animals, he writes. The creatural way of being in the world that Lawrence's characters seek throughout his oeuvre might well be linked to the becoming-animal and becoming-wave that Duncan seeks in her artistic practice. Moreover, Lawrence describes the "primal" consciousness that radiates from the solar plexus as always "dynamic" and never "static." He essentially makes the claim that primal knowledge is knowledge that *moves*.

I want to move toward a conclusion of this chapter by evoking David Wills's discussion of dorsality and the dorsal turn in relation to Duncan's affinity with the sea. She notes in her autobiography, "I was born by the sea, and I have noticed that all the great events of my life have taken place by the sea. My first idea of movement, of the dance, certainly came from the rhythm of the waves" (ML 10). Although Wills is not concerned with dance per se, he does consider Nietzsche at some length and notes the philosopher's extremely contrarian nature: "no one pirouettes or dances more provocatively, and indeed no dervish ever drove himself to such irrevocable vertiginousness, to the point of collapse."[41] Duncan would contest the precise image of Nietzsche pirouetting, as the earlier quotation demonstrates. Nonetheless, Wills mentions Nietzsche as dancer while discussing Nietzsche's engagement with images of the sea. Nietzsche seems ambivalent about the sea's potency, sometimes penning a "paean to the

waves" in *The Gay Science*, and at other times leading Zarathustra up the mountain, away from the sea, where the heights and the "pure air" are thought to "inspire one to dance" (*Dorsality* 242). But Wills counters that as one climbs away
from the sea, turns one's back to it, the sea only becomes larger: "The more one
climbs, the more the sea grows at one's back, seen or unseen, until it begins to
shimmer with the overwhelming immensity of the ocean" (*Dorsality* 243). Wills
links dorsality, the turning back or the dorsal turn, to the oceanic throughout his
book. He writes, "only water itself both offers the particular supine repose of flo-
tation and works as a medium of propulsion" (*Dorsality* 20). In other words, the
oceanic allows us a backward gesture, yet nonetheless moves us forward.

Duncan's attention to waves and the sea throughout her work and her writings
can be understood as emphasizing a rhythmic cadence that is expressly linked to
cosmic forces, fluidity, the feminine, and—following Wills—a dynamic motion
that is nonetheless attentive to what comes before:

> Where are we to look for the great fountain-head of movement?
> Woman is not a thing apart and separate from all other life organic and
> inorganic. She is but a link in the chain, and her movement must be one
> with the great movement which runs through the universe; and there-
> fore the fountain-head for the art of the dance will be the study of the
> movements of Nature.
>
> With the strengthening of the breeze over the seas, the waters form in
> long undulations. Of all movement which gives us delight and satisfies
> the soul's sense of movement, that of the waves of the sea seems to me
> the finest. This great wave movement runs through all Nature . . . all
> movements in Nature seem to me to have as their ground-plan the law
> of wave movement. (*Dance* 68)

These frameworks increase our understanding of the way Duncan privileges
dancers whom she describes in "The Philosopher's Stone of Dancing" as "those
who convert the body into a luminous fluidity" (*Dance* 51). Her emphasis on
the sea and on the universal meaning of the wave seems to have manifested itself
even in her setting and costume design choices. Although many critics have noted
the signature blue curtains that Duncan used for her performances, it would be
sensible to link that preference to the centrality of the sea in her theories and
practice. Moreover, the tunics that Duncan insisted upon as unconstrained and
emancipated costumes also seem to articulate the undulations that she names in
the previous passage, as that rhythmic force or vibration that characterizes the
movements of the "organic and inorganic." Some of the photographs from the
period give us a clearer sense of this connection between tunics and curtains that
appear to move (see Figure 1.4). The tunic seems to counterbalance the role of

the human appendage in Duncan's aesthetic. That is, arms and legs (elbows and knees, specifically) tend to create hard angles or truncations in the bodily form, the kinds of breaks that she did not see on Greek vases, as described earlier in this chapter. As the image in Figure 1.4 demonstrates, the tunic works to render continuity of the body through drapery. Additionally, the undulating curtains echo the undulations of the dancers' tunics, producing a becoming-wave even in the static photographic image. This emphasis on undulation was especially pronounced in Duncan's choreography for *Water Study*, as I mention earlier, where dancers become-water and become-fish.

Near the end of *Chaos, Territory, Art,* Grosz claims that the way "human subjects become inscribed with animal-becomings, the movements, gestures, and habits of animal existence" in aesthetics occurs not just in the visual arts but "above all in dance and music" (102). Isadora Duncan's work should be understood in this context. In the 2014 Isadora Duncan Dance Company performance of *Dance of the Furies*,[42] as the dancers lie flat on their stomachs with hands reaching forward and clenched like talons, they raise their chests up from the floor, twist and whip their heads from side to side with a piercing look, right and left, in what can only be described as the most intense creatural specularity.

Figure 1.4 Courtesy of the Jerome Robbins Dance Division, The New York Public Library for the Performing Arts, Astor, Lenox and Tilden Foundations.

Belilove's dancers confirm what Bresciani asserts: "To do this work without the consciousness of the creature . . . I find very boring[,] . . . very banal, there's no aliveness. It's the creature that gives us aliveness." Duncan's refrains about the natural and the animal signal a bioaesthetic vision that eschews the symbolism of "human" conceptualization and turns rather on the "great undulating movement" of the inhuman (*Dance* 68).

If dance as a practice of visceral, embodied transformation is particularly creatural among the arts, and if modernism is a charged site of animality's "homecoming" in cultural, artistic, and psychic discourses after Darwin, then modernism's animal dances offer an important assemblage for critical examination. In this connection, understanding art as having its roots in inhuman forces provides a new critical purchase on Duncan's work, and links her contributions to those of modernist writers such as Lawrence (and Virginia Woolf, as I will show in Chapter Three). The accession of vibratory energy connecting living beings with cosmic capacities allows us to see Duncan's very creatural reformation of "high" dance and Lawrence's images of dancing (as I elaborate in the next chapter) as related lines of flight away from a traditional humanism in modernism. Thus, modern dance's emergent experimentations with the possibilities of the body need to be recast as innovations having animal forces at their core. The way Duncan revolutionized dance must be recognized as embracing the vibrating animality of the human body and of human experience: in this sense modern dance in the twentieth century represents the eruption of the animal into Western dance practice.

Creative Incantations and Involutions
in D. H. Lawrence

Because poetry participates in the rhythmic, the musical, and the incantatory, the poetic representation of animal being is particularly salient to a discussion of cosmic and aesthetic forces. Moreover, as Jorie Graham explained during the 2006 Geraldine R. Dodge Poetry Festival, poetry must be recognized as bodily experience. Graham reiterated during her festival presentations that reading and hearing poetry are not primarily cognitive, but rather somatic processes. Such a claim forces us to rethink some of our more conventional notions about literature, the body, and even the creatural. I first want to suggest in this chapter that one of D. H. Lawrence's often-anthologized animal poems, "Tortoise Shout," reveals an aesthetics of poetry that is rooted in bodily experience, in which the nonhuman voice functions within the context of the Deleuzian refrain. That voice—the shout of the tortoise—carries a rhythmic force that connects human to animal, and both to broader cosmological powers in a posthumanist becoming-artistic of the living. This kind of becoming is also danced in Lawrence's other work, specifically his fictional vignettes of characters dancing in *Women in Love*. I will return to Deleuze's characterization of Lawrence in the second part of the chapter, where I will also suggest that Lawrence (and other modernist writers) occupy a problematic and incongruous position in Deleuze (and Guattari's) theorizing due to their valorization of individual "genius," in the place of acknowledging the specific, historical assemblage of modernist animalities.

It is somewhat remarkable to note in the context of Graham's observations what Fiona Becket pointed out in her 1997 study, *D. H. Lawrence: The Thinker as Poet*. Lawrence, she reminds us, "confirms the inseparability of the aesthetic and the ontological," especially through his concept of "art-speech" as that which "will play fruitfully across the centers and plexuses of the body of the reader."[1] One segment from Lawrence's writings is particularly salient to our discussion. It comes from his work *The Symbolic Meaning* and explains this concept of art-speech:

Art-speech is also a language of pure symbols. But whereas the authorized symbol stands always for a thought or an idea, some mental *concept*, the art-symbol or art-term stands for a pure experience, emotional and passional, spiritual and perceptual, all at once. The intellectual idea remains implicit, latent and nascent. Art communicates a state of being—whereas the symbol at best only communicates a whole thought, an emotional idea. Art-speech is a use of symbols which are *pulsations on the blood and seizures upon the nerves,* and at the same time pure percepts of the mind and pure terms of spiritual aspiration. (Becket 29–30, *Thinker,* second emphasis mine)

Given these claims about art impacting the nervous system, when Grosz refines her discussion about artistic production as that which "merges with, intensifies and eternalizes or monumentalizes, sensation" (*Chaos* 4), we realize that Lawrence's body of work, his life's work, really—with all its investment in the concept of "blood consciousness"—is especially resonant for its engagement with what might be called a bioaesthetic condition. And this Lawrencian bioaesthetics is pointedly Deleuzian.

I first want to examine this "pulsational," anticonceptual notion of art in D. H. Lawrence's poem, "Tortoise Shout." This text provides an astonishingly rich and provocative example of the kind of trans-species participation that characterizes bioaesthetics. In fact, the way in which the poem situates a becoming-artistic of the creatural, specifically through the medium of sexual difference and sexual behavior, marks it as an extraordinary example of these concepts in literary discourse.

It is useful, at the outset of this chapter, to note both the factual or scientific realities of the tortoise, as well as the mythic or symbolic resonance it has tended to carry across cultures. Peter Young's book, *Tortoise,* helps to situate the tortoise in this regard. Young notes in the opening pages of his discussion:

Tortoises look and are old, almost mythical creatures. They are primeval, the oldest of the living land reptiles, their age confirmed by fossil remains. Tortoises are the surviving link between animal life in water and on land. . . . Tortoises . . . . have survived for some 225 million years. They are living fossils. Hardy, self-contained creatures, they have endured aeons of major changes, and on a world scale survived geological upheaval, volcanic activity and climatic swings.[2]

Amid a good deal of further biological information, such as the advanced age to which tortoises often live, Young makes note of one fact that Lawrence's poem takes as its focus: the coitus cry of the male. "Tortoises," he explains, "are basically mute, except for males squealing with delight, sometimes with open mouth, at the climax of mating" (*Tortoise* 22). In fact, my further investigation of this topic suggests that the mating call, or cry, is often very pronounced during the mounting phase in some tortoises, and may continue during segments of the often-protracted coitus session. Thus, it may be more accurate to say that the tortoise is basically mute, except for the male crying during mating activities.

Young's chapter, "Myths and Symbols," addresses a variety of cultural associations linked to tortoises. Like most animals, tortoises have been sub-ject to varying and sometimes contradictory symbolic use by human cultures. The recurring association of tortoises with qualities such as longevity and per-severance is quite familiar. Young reminds us, however, that an astonishingly broad array of cultures have symmetrical creation myths that see the tortoise as supporting, literally, the world itself on its back, and sometimes simultaneously as a "model of the world itself" (*Tortoise* 42). He provides an interesting theory on the historical "route" of these myths, but also makes the Jungian claim that the tortoise seems to have an archetypal presence in "the collective unconscious of the human race" (*Tortoise* 47). For the purposes of this chapter, I want to note that the centrality of the tortoise in myths of creation—its association with a truly rudimentary force of generation—provides an especially poignant pur-chase on Lawrence's use of the tortoise.

The poem, which ultimately runs to about 120 lines, begins with three short ones: "I thought he was dumb, / I said he was dumb, / Yet I've heard him cry" (lines 1–3).[3] These opening observations emphasize several important elements of the text to come. Like some of Lawrence's other poems, perhaps most fa-mously "Snake" and "Fish" as I have argued elsewhere, the ineptitude, misappre-hension, or limit of human knowledge is made immediately evident (*Stalking*).[4] These three lines signal that the human speaker was wrong about the animal's "dumbness" or muteness. What is more, Lawrence emphasizes human reason and language specifically. The narrator *thought and then said* the animal was dumb. Typically, rationality and linguistic capacities are hailed as the hallmark of human superiority and dominion over animals, yet here, Lawrence acknowledges that his rational mind and speaking abilities were just plain mistaken. What is it that tells the truth about this animal or this event? It is what the speaker hears: the auditory sense. Not thinking or speaking in symbols, not representation or high-order analysis, but the body's sensorium. And apparently this alternative knowl-edge, which in Lawrence's terms would be blood-conscious knowledge rather than nerve-conscious knowledge, renders an immediate truth. I thought he was dumb, yet I heard him cry. At the instant when the body registers the tortoise's voice, human assumptions about the animal are revealed as naïve.

Lawrence's choice of words at this juncture is not to be overlooked. He does not say that he thought the animal was silent; he says "dumb," instead. This word's historical weight is relevant: The Oxford English Dictionary lists a ref-erence to animal muteness as the word's second primary meaning: "Applied to

the lower animals (and, by extension, to inanimate nature) as naturally inca-
pable of articulate speech." Moreover, "dumb's" polyvalence calls into question
our assumptions that animals are stupid, "bestial," unintelligent. He was wrong
about animals being "dumb." Animals are not dumb, and indeed, their apparent
muteness for the human does not indicate a mental vacuity. Similarly, the choice
of "cry" in the opening stanza seems to emphasize something particular about
animal emotion. Lawrence does use the word "scream" in the very next line, a
term we would associate more with instinct or aggression, or even simple physical distress. But the choice of "cry" suggests weeping, which clearly locates this
creature in an emotional realm more akin to humans than alien from them.

Thus, in the second stanza, while Lawrence seems to suggest that the tortoise
cry is distant, or obscure to us, we already know that this primal scream is, in
fact, deeply coterminous with the human. The stanza reads: "First faint scream,
/ Out of life's unfathomable dawn, / Far off, so far, like a madness, under the
horizon's dawning rim, / Far, far off, far scream" (lines 4–8). Rather than intimate that the scream is "far" ontologically from the human—foreign, that is, to
human being—this stanza sets up the poem's broad ideological claim that the
tortoise brings us back to the fundamental, the primeval scream or vibration of
the living in general. The scream may be far off to the hapless, unattending, or
overly rationalized human passerby, caught unawares. But as the text unfolds,
we recognize how it brings the human speaker and the tortoise irrevocably into
the same ontological space. This making coextensive of the human and tortoise
takes place in large part through a discursive meditation on extremity.

I will come back to the specific image of the tortoise *in extremis* shortly. For
now, I want to focus on the poem's subsequent question: "Why were we crucified
into sex? / Why were we not left rounded off, and finished in ourselves [?]" (10–
12). Lawrence often focuses on a kind of suffering involved in the problem of
individual sovereignty versus communal experience and intersubjectivity. These
themes are well-outlined by critics of his writing and frequently play themselves
out through the problematics of sex. Indeed, Richard Ellmann noted early on
the connections between images of crucifixion and sexuality in Lawrence's
work: "The metaphor of the cross," he reminds us, "is one of his most dramatic
and successful images, for it implies the sacredness, terror, and pain which were
for him essential parts of the sexual experience."[5] What interests me here, however, is the way that Lawrence's question evokes the most fundamental biological realities about sexual difference. Grosz helps us recognize those realities
when she discusses the role of sexual selection in the elaboration and creativity
inherent in organic life forms:

> The evolution of life can be seen not only in the increasing specializa-
> tion and bifurcation or differentiation of life forms from each other, the
> elaboration and development of profoundly variable morphologies

and bodily forms, but, above all, in their becoming-artistic, in their self-transformations, which exceed the bare requirements of existence. Sexual selection, the consequence of sexual difference or morphological bifurcation—one of the earliest upheavals in the evolution of life on earth and undoubtedly the most momentous invention that life has brought forth, the very machinery for guaranteeing the endless generation of morphological and genetic variation, the very mechanism of biological difference itself—is also, by this fact, the opening up of life to the indeterminacy of taste, pleasure, and sensation. Life comes to elaborate itself through making its bodily forms and its archaic territories, pleasing (or annoying), performative, which is to say, intensified through their integration into form and their impact on bodies.

There is much "art" in the natural world, from the moment there is sexual selection, from the moment there are two sexes that attract each other's interest and taste through visual, auditory, olfactory, tactile, and gustatory sensations. (*Chaos* 6–7)

There's a kind of delicious irony embedded in this angle on sexuality, for Lawrence readers and scholars. Grosz explains that sexual difference is perhaps the prime generator of the excesses and transformations that ultimately establish the becoming-artistic of life itself. In other words, the origins of art at least partly reside in the ways that bodies overcome themselves, create something nonutilitarian, in conjunction with the forces of the earth and the cosmos in the great dance of seduction and mating (not necessarily driven only by reproduction, as I have noted already). I think that Lawrence might hate this idea if confronted by it, with its profound yoking of sexual difference and artistic capacity, given that Lawrence was often so distraught by the necessities of sex. But perhaps, in a psychoanalytic register, Lawrence's ambivalence toward sexuality reveals a subterranean recognition on his part of this very linkage that requires a moving beyond the self and a deep connection to the body and animality in order to become-artistic.

When Lawrence asks his next question in the poem, we are ushered into a world of vibration. Lawrence writes: "A far, was-it-audible scream, / Or did it sound on the plasm direct?" (lines 15–16). A scream that is potentially not audible, a sound that bypasses the ear and "sounds" directly on and throughout the body. This is vibration, the vibratory, and emphasizes the primal connection between bodies, rhythm, and cosmic energies. That Richard Ellmann in 1953 recognized this element of Lawrence's animal and plant poetics is noteworthy. Although Ellmann's overall sense of the tortoise sequence remains insistently anchored in an unquestioned human exceptionalism, he nonetheless clearly senses the importance of the vibratory for Lawrence. Ellmann's general claim begins to acknowledge Lawrence's deep sensitivity to animal ontology, though its quick return to human subjectivity as something implicitly nonanimal disappoints: "No poet has a more uncanny sense of what it is like to be, for instance, a copulating tortoise. At their best the poems about tortoises, about elephants, about plants, reveal Lawrence's attitudes toward men, but without relinquishing their hold on the actual object" ("Demon" 195–196). My own previous readings of Lawrence's poetry in *Stalking the Subject* depict a writer much more attentive to animal ontology. Indeed, I would argue that when the animal poems become mere metaphors for human action, they often fail. The "passion" with which Lawrence writes about other creatures, however, leads Ellmann to conclude that "Nature for Lawrence *is pullulating*; his landscape, his flowers, his animals have *radiant nodes of energy within them*, and he sets up an electric circuit between them and himself" ("Demon" 196–197; my emphasis).[6] This notion of the pullulating, radiant circuit of energy in Lawrence brings to mind Van Gogh's appearance in Deleuze's writings about art and the percept, which I noted in the Introduction: there Deleuze discusses how abstract painting goes about "drawing up figures with a geometrical appearance but that are no more than forces—the forces of gravity, heaviness, rotation, the vortex, explosion, expansion, germination, and time . . . Is this not the definition of the percept itself—to make perceptible the imperceptible forces that populate the world, affect us, and make us become?" (*Philosophy* 181–182).

Grosz notes that for Darwin, the use of rhythm and cadence, sometimes located in the voice, is an essential element of sexual selection. These powers not only seduce, intensify, and excite, but they also can endanger the creature who excels at them. "Nevertheless," Grosz explains, "it is the erotic, indeed perhaps vibratory, force in all organisms, even those without auditory systems, that seduces, entices, mesmerizes, that sexualizes the body, metabolizes organs, and prepares and solicits it for courtship" (*Chaos* 32). Darwin, she explains, insists that "rhythm, vibration, resonance, is enjoyable and intensifying" (*Chaos* 32).

Tellingly, Lawrence's subsequent stanza in the poem elaborates the tortoise vibration in ways that suggest an excessive polyvalence associated with this rhythm: "Worse than the cry of the new-born, / A scream, / A yell, / A shout, / A paean, / A death-agony, / A birth cry, / A submission, / All tiny, tiny, far away, reptile under the first dawn" (lines 17–26). Lawrence seems to tap into the broad and universal instantiations of the vibratory among the creatural in this riff: birth, death, celebration, pain, vulnerability all resonate with the narrator's experience of this tortoise's shout. Citing Alphonso Lingis, Grosz notes that the "first vocalizations in any articulated life are those of a cry: sobbing, gulping, breathing with a more and more intense rhythm. Pain articulates itself in many creatures, even those without vocal apparatus in roars, hisses, screams and squeals. For Lingis, expression is bound up with the rhythmic forces inhabiting and transforming bodies, the pleasure and pains the body comes to articulate" (*Chaos* 51).

Grosz reminds us of Deleuze's conceptualization of the refrain and helps to clarify its function.[7] She writes, "The refrain is a kind of rhythmic regularity that brings a minimum of livable order to a situation in which chaos beckons" (*Chaos* 52). In music, for instance, the refrain "wards off chaos by creating a rhythm, tempo, melody that taps chaos by structuring it through the constitution of a territory" (*Chaos* 53). It is in her discussion of the Deleuzian refrain and the connection between cosmic and bodily forces that Grosz points to the very life rhythms that Lawrence catalogues in his renaming or rephrasing of the resonances of the tortoise's shout: "These rhythms of the body—the rhythms of seduction, copulation, birth, death—coupled with those of the earth—seasons, tides, temperatures—are the conditions of the refrain, which encapsulates and abstracts these rhythmic or vibratory forces into a sonorous emblem, a composed rhythm" (*Chaos* 55). The impact of this rhythm is most powerfully felt by bodies of the same species, but as Grosz often points out, these refrains are transmuted and transferred from cosmos to earth, from animal to animal, from animal to human and back, as I emphasized in the previous chapter on Isadora Duncan. In the case of Lawrence's poem, then, the refrain of the tortoise resonates through the body of the human narrator, connecting both of them to the "primeval rudiments of life, and the secret" (line 61). Ellmann's description of the "electric circuit" connecting human and nonhuman in the earlier quotation seems especially insightful.

One of Grosz's comments in her discussion of rhythms and refrains is particularly salient here. She asks, "[w]hat else is both labile enough and appealing enough to slip from its material to its most immaterial effects, from the energy of the universe to the muscular oscillations that constitute pleasure and pain in living things? What else enables the body itself, the internal arrangement of its organs and their hollows, to resonate and to become instruments of sonorous expression?" (*Chaos* 55). Thus, when Lawrence writes about the "male soul's membrane / Torn with a shriek half music, half horror" (lines 31–32), we recognize the implicit reference to a Deleuzian refrain.

Moreover, in the poetic genre, rhythm itself is embedded in the communication of content. Lawrence repeats the tups, the jerks, the screams of the tortoise in coition, just as he includes variations of the refrain of the reptile's shout as they appear in other living organisms. What follows is Lawrence's renaming and rephrasing that connects the poem most specifically to the Deleuzian refrain. A very long stanza begins with the opening line, "I remember, when I was a boy,

/ I heard the scream of a frog, which was caught with his foot in / the mouth of an up-starting snake" (lines 69–72). The narrator goes on to catalogue "hearing a wild goose out of the throat / of night," "the scream of a rabbit," "the heifer in her heat, blorting and / blorting," and "a woman in / labour, something like an owl whooing, / . . . The first wail of an infant, / And my mother singing to herself/ And the first tenor singing of the passionate / throat of a young collier" (75–97) among several other vibrations. The refrain of the tortoise's shout is connected to other vocalizations that cross species lines and represent the universal rhythms of life—and especially the bringing forth of life in the birthing process—that I have already mentioned as the conditions of the refrain.

This long passage, which is situated near the center of the poem, is especially crucial for my reading of the poem in its posthumanist context. The connections that Lawrence makes here are not to be overlooked. The scream of a rabbit is collocated with the cries of the woman in labor, yes, but perhaps even more strikingly, these vibrations are coterminous not only with the maternal singing voice, but even with the young tenor's voice. These final connections to human song, to human aesthetic practice traditionally construed, make Grosz's point about the becoming-artistic of the vibratory quite clear. For Lawrence, all of these practices are fundamentally about life-rhythm, about the cosmic forces in which all creatures, human and nonhuman, participate. This segment of the poem, therefore, seems especially demonstrative of a bioaesthetic view of artistic capacities and activities.

What is more, each of these comparisons highlights living beings at extremity, which is importantly connected to Grosz's understanding of excess and intensity. After the catalogue of refrains, Lawrence returns to the tortoise: "And more than all these, / And less than all these, / This last, / Strange, faint coition yell / Of the male tortoise *at extremity*, / Tiny from under the very edge of the farthest far-off horizon of life" (lines 101–107; my emphasis). It goes without saying that the organism is intensified through sexuality. Moreover, the biological fact of the male tortoise's coition scream brilliantly underscores this intensification. As I noted at the beginning of the chapter, and as Peter Young documents, tortoises are mute *except for* the male's cries during mating activities. We might imagine a life of continual muteness only to be broken in this most acute and physically radical circumstance.

Grosz also reminds us that "Art is where intensity is most at home" (*Chaos* 76). "[P]erhaps," she continues, "we can understand matter in art as matter at its most dilated, matter as it most closely approximates mind, diastole, or proliferation rather than systole and compression and where becoming is most directly in force" (*Chaos* 76). In the poem, the proliferation of matter seems to be registered through the voice's discharging of bodily intensity in the poem. And of course, that bodily intensity is frequently sexual here. More generally, the extreme and, for the tortoise, somewhat singular cry tends to underscore the idea that it is the excesses of evolution, the pressing beyond oneself and beyond the mundane routines of the body that manifests aesthetic practice.

Grosz continues to link the sexual and the artistic in her final chapter, where she discusses aboriginal Australian art. Within that discussion, she notes that "[q]ualities and territory coexist, and thus both are the condition for sexual selection and for art making—or perhaps for the art of sexual selection and equally the sexuality of art production. It is this excess, of both harnessable forces and of unleashed qualities, that enables both art and sex to erupt, at the same evolutionary moment, as a glorification of intensity, as the production and elaboration of intensity for its own sake" (*Chaos* 102). Lawrence's poem seems to thematize this very eruption given that he emphasizes, in the poem's final considerations, the opening that sexuality both requires and results in: "Sex, which breaks up our integrity, our single inviolability, our / deep silence / Tearing a cry from us. / Sex, which breaks us into voice, sets us calling across the / deeps, calling, calling for the complement, / Singing, and calling, and singing again, being answered, / having found" (lines 113–117).

Referencing the Platonic myth that gender breaks some originary unity into separate beings who search for their "other half," Lawrence outlines a problem of "opening" and woundedness that critics have recognized throughout his oeuvre. Ellmann called Lawrence a "healer" who used his writing to dress personal and universal wounds ("Demon" 186). Kyoko Kondo also has written about the central role of the metaphor of opening in *Women in Love*, and notes that Gerald in that novel experiences opening as a wound.[8] We recognize that the ancient myth essentializes gender to some degree, but it nonetheless resonates with Grosz's claims about intensity, excess, sexuality, and art. Here the refrain—the singing, calling, and answering—acts as a signal to the mate, to the other. Lawrence ends the poem by emphasizing sexuality as the separation and recoordination of bodies: "That which is whole, torn asunder, / That which is in part, finding its whole again through the / universe" (lines 122–124).

In these final moments of Lawrence's text, the link between past, present, and future emerges poignantly. If we had to sum up, we might say that the "far-off" and evolutionarily prior cry of the tortoise vibrates through the speaker in an intensified present that enlivens the speaker's recognition of the shared contingency of the living, and at the same time, illuminates the future processes of becoming in that contingency. The intensely cosmic nature of the final image should be noted: one doesn't find one's complement only in the "other" here, whether human or tortoise. Indeed, one finds one's complement in the "universe," perhaps as that universe or cosmos is manifested in the creatural embodiment of the other. And in this particular poem, the creatural is manifested in the rhythms, the vibrations of life itself as it becomes artistic. As I have mentioned earlier, in relation to Isadora Duncan's futurity, Grosz gives us a sense of this modality when she writes: "art is not simply the expression of an animal past, a prehistorical allegiance with the evolutionary forces that make one; it is not memorialization, the celebration of a shared past, but above all the transformation of the materials from the past into resources for the future" (*Chaos* 103).

It seems fitting to consider the poem itself as an affective becoming that bridges human and animal intensity through a shared vibratory force akin to the voice. One of Grosz's important conclusions is that affects are "man's becoming-other" (*Chaos* 77). By this she means that affects allow the human to "overcome" itself or move outside of itself through "the creation of zones of proximity between the human and those animal and microscopic/cosmic becomings the human can pass through. Affects signal that border between the human and the animal from which it has come" (*Chaos* 77). The rhythm of poetics might provide the most apt literary genre for the shared vibratory experience between human and animal minds, bodies, and being in general to be expressed. In Lawrence's poem, it is the refrain of the animal voice linked to or becoming the refrain of the human poetic voice that demonstrates in full force the voice *of the living*. This generalized vibratory power connects the narrator to the tortoise through a deep and almost seamless vibration by the poem's end. As is often the case for Lawrence, his work refuses to cordon off the mind from the rest of the corpus, and he delves into the bodilyness and embeddedness not of the human or animal, but of the living in general. Thus "Tortoise Shout" performs, in a sense, the interpenetration of cosmic intensities in which all creatures participate.

When discussing Lawrence's "becoming-tortoise," Deleuze and Guattari note, "Lawrence is another of the writers who leave us troubled and filled with admiration because they were able to tie their writing to real and unheard-of becomings" (*Plateaus* 244). In fact, Deleuze often frames his attraction to modernist writers such as D. H. Lawrence, Virginia Woolf, and Franz Kafka through the lens of exceptional talent. But this Deleuzian attraction to modernists should be explained not by the radical "genius" of these individual artists, but more productively by the eruption of animality in a post-Darwinian era and the particular becomings-animal that era cultivates. As I have outlined in earlier work, modernist literature exhibits humanism's intensified engagement with the discourse of species partly in response to the crises that Darwin's and Freud's theories set in motion in the late nineteenth and early twentieth centuries (*Stalking*). Thus, Deleuze's attentions to modernist becomings are owed in some measure to the particularities of modernism's heightened attunement to the species axis. When Deleuze and Guattari single out Lawrence's "becoming-tortoise" as exemplary of affective deterritorialization, we recognize the centrality of modernist literature's becomings-animal in Deleuze's broad theoretical framework. What has been less recognized in discussions of Deleuzian modernism is the coincidence of dancing with moments of inhuman becoming. Dance as a practice of visceral, embodied transformation might be understood as particularly creatural or inhuman among the arts. If dance is the most "animal" aesthetic form, and if Deleuze views the arts as being haunted by animality, then moments of inhuman dancerly becomings in modernist literature can be considered charged minoritarian zones of metamorphosis.

Dancing remains one of the more interesting yet critically underexamined elements of D. H. Lawrence's writing, despite the recurrence of dancing as a variation or refrain in modernist becomings. The relation between dancing and becoming highlights questions of movement, perception, the bodily, and the improvisational that put pressure on the species boundary and render it more porous. A Deleuzian understanding of art as having its roots in inhuman forces allows us to make sense of the well-known, yet undertheorized, moments in *Women in Love* when both Gudrun and Birkin dance. Gudrun's scene in particular, where she dances with a herd of cattle, calls for a careful parsing through a Deleuzian lens. Rather than some "expressive" or symbolic activity, these moments in Lawrence's novel should be understood as becomings-imperceptible/animal that link creativity to an inhuman sexuality, and that access a vibratory energy connecting living beings with cosmic capacities, just as in the tortoise poem. Lawrence's Deleuzian dancing is another "lapsing out" or line of flight into the inhuman;[9] it also parallels modern dance's emergent experimentations with the possibilities of the body that I discussed in relation to Duncan in the previous chapter. Dancing in Lawrence, as in Nietzsche, has a strong affiliation with philosophy in that both writers seem to emphasize the relinquishing of outmoded, humanist templates and to enact what William Connolly might call the "teleosearching" for new concepts, concepts in Deleuze's sense.[10] Thus, dance as a minoritarian art form should occupy a more pivotal status in critical discussions of Deleuzian modernism.

In scholarly analyses of Lawrence's work, moderate attention has been given to Anna's dance while pregnant in *The Rainbow*, but a number of critics also have treated the question of dance in *Women in Love*. It is also interesting to note Gerald Doherty's highly self-conscious, almost performative use of the trope of dance in his introduction to *Theorizing Lawrence*.[11] He suggests dance is a metaphor for the kind of thinking that he himself enacts in the book, and that the ideal reader of the book's contents will approach it as through a dance. Doherty seems to trade on the role of dance in Lawrence's work here, which might implicitly signal the importance of the way dance actually functions in much of Lawrence's writing.

One of the first major attentions to dance in *Women in Love* occurs in the Breadalby section, where Hermione convinces Ursula, Gudrun, and another woman to join her in making "a little ballet, in the style of the Russian Ballet of

Pavlova and Nijinsky" (WL 93). Although the reference to dance revolutionary Nijinsky might lead the reader to anticipate something unconventional, the little ballet that the women enact appears rather clichéd and representational, despite a few scenes that move the male onlookers. After the formal "ballet," when the group of friends begin to dance socially, Lawrence provides the novel's first deterritorializing movement through Birkin, who "when he could get free from the weight of the people present, whom he disliked, danced rapidly and with real gaiety. And how Hermione hated him for this irresponsible gaiety" (WL 92). The contessa, who had been the ballet's fourth dancer, watches Birkin and replies, "He is not a man, he is a chameleon, a creature of change" (WL 92). This brief scene already sets up a difference between "traditional" or imitative dance (majoritarian) and an improvisational, excessive movement that is characterized by creatural becomings, and thus a certain minor unpredictability and "schizo" refusal of the Oedipalized (hu)man. Hermione silently mimics the charge, "He is not a man, he is treacherous, not one of us" (WL 92). Birkin's inhuman, rhizomatic coming-to-life in his own capricious dance destroys her, in part because "of his power to escape, to exist, other than she did, because he was not consistent, not a man, less than a man" (WL 92).

As Lawrence leads up to the extended dancing scene in "Water-Party," he emphasizes Gudrun's desire for "life." When Gudrun sits beneath the trees and listens to Ursula singing a German folk song, she has "the yearning come into her heart" (WL 165). In contrast to Ursula who "seemed so peaceful and sufficient unto herself, sitting there unconsciously crooning her song, strong and unquestioned at the centre of her own universe," Gudrun feels herself "outside" (WL 165). She not only feels external to Ursula's attentions, however. More pointedly, the text describes her as a nonparticipant in the living: "Always this desolating, agonized feeling, that she was outside life, an onlooker, whilst Ursula was a partaker, caused Gudrun to suffer from a sense of her own negation" (WL 165). Gudrun interrupts her sister to suggest that she "do Dalcroze" while Ursula sings a different tune.[12] Gudrun's difficulty in making this suggestion is emphasized by her "curious muted tone" and by the fact that Ursula doesn't hear her properly (WL 165). Having to repeat the request reinforces how difficult the movement toward a minor form or experience really is.

Lawrence's reference to Dalcroze not only indicates his awareness of various dance forms that were in circulation in the early part of the century, but it also confirms the negotiation with animality in Gudrun's cattle dance that I will elaborate shortly. Elgin Mellown catalogues Lawrence's grasp of various developments in early twentieth-century music and dance, and reminds us that Hermione Roddice's character is based on Lady Ottoline Morrell, who was a London patron for Diaghilev's Ballet Russes.[13] Mellown suggests that Lawrence "must have known that the motions which Emile Jacques-Dalcroze had evolved to teach music were based on natural gestures rather than the artificial positions of the ballet vocabulary" ("Music" 56–57). He goes on to call the "version" of Gudrun depicted with the Highland cattle "a creature of primitive instincts" ("Music" 57).

Both Mellown and Mark Kinkead-Weekes note the Isadora Duncan-like movements of this scene. Although Lawrence's actual exposure to Duncan's performances is unverified, Mellown suggests that he was influenced by his wife Freida's own "fluid, expressive movements" that were inspired by the experiments in movement taking place at this time ("Music" 57). Moreover, Kinkead-Weekes describes the transition in this scene from rhythmic, "harmonious" movements to something more rhapsodic—and thus more natural or animal—as "like Isadora Duncan, perhaps in Nietzschean/ Dionysiac mood."[14] Thus, Duncan's own engagements with the inhuman and with a Deleuzian emphasis on the vibrational can be productively linked to Lawrence's fictional engagements with dancing.

For instance, Lawrence evokes a Duncan-esque, intensifying experience through Gudrun's rhapsodic dancing, and we can read the rhythmic opening of this scene as performing a Deleuzian transfer of forces:

> Gudrun, looking as if some invisible chain weighed on her hands and feet, began slowly to dance in the eurythmic manner, pulsing and fluttering rhythmically with her feet, making slower, regular gestures with her hands and arms, now spreading her arms wide, now raising them above her head, now flinging them softly apart, and lifting her face, her feet all the time beating and running to the measure of the song, as if it were some strange incantation, her white, rapt form drifting here and there in a strange impulsive rhapsody, seeming to be lifted on a breeze of incantation, shuddering with strange little runs. (WL 166)

Lawrence's first image exaggerates, through the evocation of chains, the weight of the body, and the body's connection to the earth. In contrast to the ethereal and gravity-defying aesthetic of traditional ballet, Duncan's "modern" dance emphasized the weightiness of the body and eschewed more rigid poses such as the arabesque, which as I have noted, she felt contorted the "natural" body. Carrie Preston also has pointed out that Duncan's exposed and full thighs themselves ushered in a new way to experience and represent women's bodies within a dance and political aesthetic at this time.[15] Given other scenes in *Women in Love*—such as Birkin's somewhat masochistic "becoming-plant" episode after Hermione smashes him over the head with a lapis-lazuli stone—it is useful to recall that modern dance has a specific relationship to the earth. As Elizabeth Dempster puts it, "Modern dance has often been termed 'terrestrial' " ("Watch a Little" 224). Therefore, the way in which Lawrence emphasizes the feet just slightly more than the gestures of arms and hands in this segment also contributes to Gudrun's earth-bound, vibrational method. Her feet pulse, flutter, beat, run, and make her body shudder.

Lawrence's evocation of a barefooted, Duncan-like rhythmic stampeding thus highlights the sense of a Deleuzian transmission of earthly forces to human shudderings. Grosz theorizes the Deleuzian role of vibration for the artistic as a kind of *invitation* to the creative. We inevitably partake in the tremor of the rhythmic and the territorial in Deleuze's terms, to be sure, but the vibratory also functions as an incitement to become *more* vibratory:

> Vibration is the common thread or rhythm running through the universe from its chaotic inorganic interminability to its most intimate forces of inscription on living bodies of all kinds and back again. It is vibration that constitutes the harmony of the universe with all its living components, enabling them to find a vibratory comfort level—neither too slow or too fast—not only to survive but above all to generate excess, further vibratory forces, more effects, useless effects, qualities that can't be directly capitalized. (*Chaos* 54)

Gudrun's becoming-inhuman at this initial moment is most clearly registered through Lawrence's rhythmic invocation of a "rapt form drifting here and there" on "a breeze of incantation." Later, when the cattle arrive, those animals will clarify Gudrun's inhuman becoming-artistic. Here, the drift of pulsation, excess, and display works from earth and wind to Gudrun's activations of a strange kind of rapture. So, too, Ursula's singing intensifies the invitation to the vibrational, and she notices "some of the unconscious ritualistic suggestion of the complex shuddering and waving and drifting of her sister's white form" (WL 166). Waving and drifting evoke not only the experimentations in bodily practice that marked the emergence of modern dance, but also the sort of philosophical "teleosearching" for new concepts that Birkin inhabits throughout the novel.

The "unconscious ritualistic suggestion" that Ursula observes is made all the more Deleuzian and Groszian when we investigate the details of Ursula's switch from a German folk song to a spontaneous American tune for Gudrun's "performance." When Ursula finally understands that Gudrun wants to "do Dalcroze," she can't "for her life think of anything to sing" (WL 166). Then Ursula suddenly begins "in a laughing, teasing voice: 'My love—is a high-born lady—'" (WL 166). The Cambridge edition notes for *Women in Love* provide us with the extraordinary information that this chorus comes from the American song "My Gal is a High Born Lady," which was "advertised as 'The best high-class Coon song of the day'" (WL 550). In addition to a trading on perceived black or interracial "suggestiveness" that we might want to trouble here, Lawrence's choice includes an especially animal element of seduction. The editors' notes continue by providing the following excerpt from this popular song: "'My gal is a high born lady, / She's black, but not to[o] shady, / Feathered like a peacock, just as gay, / She is not colored, she was born that way'" (WL 550).

Again, there would be much more to say about the particular calibration of racial and class discourses here,[16] but for the purposes of this discussion, I want to point out that the peacock brings us squarely into an analysis of the aesthetic workings of sexual selection. The peacock is one of nature's most evident examples of the way in which extreme or excessive bodily extravagance attends the dynamics of sexual dimorphism and attraction. The peacock, then, is an especially keen example of the way that sexuality itself requires creativity: "sexuality needs to harness excessiveness and invention to function at all" (*Chaos* 64).

Grosz also emphasizes the bodily and affective nature of artistic experience via Deleuze and insists upon Darwin's assertion that animals have the power of discrimination or taste that is central to aesthetic appeal and choice. "Music, painting, dance, and the other arts," she explains, "are only possible because the power to appeal and enhance seems to reside in regular ways in [animals'] use of colors, sounds, and shapes for the purposes of resonance and intensification. Art is the formal structuring or framing of these intensified bodily organs and processes which stimulate the receptive organs of observers and coparticipants" (*Undone* 135). On some level, therefore, Gudrun's dance with the cattle is already prefigured in Ursula's choice of tunes. Being compared to one feathered like a peacock reinforces the superfluous qualities of an aesthetic engagement that is "suggestive," extravagant, and at least partly outside the human.

Lawrence's initial portrayal of the Highland cattle might best be described as emphasizing their aesthetic properties and their phenomenological potential, no matter how "diminished" that potential may have been considered by the author. The cattle are "vividly coloured and fleecy in the evening light, their horns branching into the sky, pushing forward their muzzles inquisitively, to know what it was all about. Their eyes glittered through their tangle of hair, their naked nostrils were full of shadow" (WL 167). As mentioned above, vivid coloring is an essential element of animals' bodily excess within the lexicon of sexual selection. Moreover, the image of horns "branching into the sky" emphasizes the aesthetic nature of secondary sexual characteristics in their precise sexual role within the dynamics of enticement. In other words, the horns are, evolutionarily speaking, a good example of Grosz's idea that sexuality must be creative to be itself. This, coupled with the image of inquisitive muzzles and glittering eyes, sets us up to read the cattle as an audience who attempt to discern or distinguish the aesthetic power of Gudrun's performance.

When Gudrun suggests that the cattle are "charming," therefore, the charm is not *merely* sexual. Or rather, it is sexual in a much richer register than we typically assert in critical discussions of Lawrence and sexuality. The cattle are not only or even primarily metaphorical stand-ins for men or male sexuality. Rather, they are charming because they invite Gudrun into an embodiment of a "mating" dance that is not only about sexuality, to be sure, but also is as much about the becoming-artistic of the human through vibrational excess and a Deleuzian harnessing of *inhuman* forces. Gudrun's desire to perform a Deleuzian dance with cattle is clearly linked to all the characters' experiments in living and in being, to their attempts to experience themselves as self-overcoming, to use a Nietzschean phrase. When Lawrence writes of Gudrun that it was "evident that she had a strange passion to dance before the sturdy, handsome cattle," the phrase "strange passion" would seem even more relevant than the descriptors "sturdy, handsome" (WL 167). This strange passion parallels Birkin's own variations on the "grotesque step-dance" (WL 168) that I will discuss shortly.

Another way of thinking about this would have us emphasizing the "strangeness" of the very peacockian excess that all creatures inhabit when becoming-intense, becoming-other, and becoming-artistic. Thus, I would want to elaborate upon one of my earlier claims about Lawrence, namely, the claim that we ought to read sexuality in his work as an important component of a larger recuperation of animality for the human subject in modernism.[17] Inhuman becomings in Lawrence also exhibit vibrational shudderings of the creative, which open us to the emergence of difference or the new. These becomings privilege movement or change, which not only signals the significance of dance in Lawrence's thematics, but also helps to clarify Birkin's search for new concepts and his distaste for static or clichéd mores or ideas. Thus, Gudrun's "strange" dance in the novel functions as a kind of template for the inhuman becoming-excessive that Deleuze and Grosz locate as foundational for aesthetic intensities and that Lawrence makes central to so many of his literary–philosophical explorations.

The role of inhuman forces in Gudrun's "becoming" cattle is registered, in part, by Lawrence through the power of electric currents. The second major description of Gudrun's dancing is more Duncanesque than the first, incorporating the terms "unconscious sensation," "uncanny," "fluctuations," "hypnotised" (WL 167–168).[18] Central to this second description is the line, "She could feel them just in front of her, it was as if she had the electric pulse from their breasts running into her hands. Soon she would touch them, actually touch them" (WL 168). Andrew Harrison discusses the linguistic and thematic role of electricity in the novel as it relates to Lawrence's entanglements with Futurism. He analyses the way that *Women in Love* "places the overwhelming emphasis not on strict chronological verisimilitude but on the psychological shifts which accompanied electrical modernization."[19] Harrison notes that the connection between Gerald and Gudrun is dangerously "magnetic" throughout the text (WL 120) and that in relationships with Gerald the "violent electrical vocabulary does not work up to a new awareness of impersonality, opening up new insights and new forms of symbolism, as it had for Ursula in the final pages of *The Rainbow*. Instead it recounts a form of destructive discharge that there is no getting beyond" ("Electricity" 18). In contrast, Harrison suggests, Birkin and Ursula are distinguished by "their ability to 'earth' or 'ground' the current through their polarity" ("Electricity" 19). Moreover, for them, "an articulate channeling of electrical energies results in a creative kind of closed circuit" ("Electricity" 19).

For Gudrun it is the cattle, it is animality that is "grounding" her own "electric" energies, enabling a circuit that is specifically trans-species or inter-species. I want to read electricity in this moment as a force that enables Gudrun's "communicative or contagious" becoming (*Plateaus* 238). Electricity functions in Lawrence's scene as the conduit of inhuman or cross-creatural forces.[20] When re-examining the details of Deleuze and Guattari's language in the opening of "1730: Becoming-Intense, Becoming-Animal, Becoming-Imperceptible" in *A Thousand Plateaus*, their introduction of the concept becoming-animal trades on electric capacities: "there is a circulation of impersonal affects, *an alternate current* that disrupts signifying projects as well as subjective feelings, and constitutes a nonhuman sexuality" (*Plateaus* 233, my emphasis). To parrot Deleuze and Guattari's own discussion of the 1972 film *Willard*: in the Lawrence scene, "it's all there." Gudrun's becoming does not "proceed by resemblance" because she is ultimately inventing her own dance with the cattle, improvising her line of flight from the human (*Plateaus* 233). Moreover, the herd of cattle instantiates precisely the multiplicity, proliferation, or pack that Deleuze and Guattari, perhaps problematically, install at the heart of such alliances (*Plateaus* 233).[21] Gudrun's "electric" becoming also "forestalls attempts at professional, conjugal, or Oedipal reterritorialization" (*Plateaus* 233), which is what makes Gerald's interference in her experience so traumatic and violent. Because Gudrun, if we are to believe Deleuze and Guattari, is partaking in "involution," which is specifically not regression, and which is specifically creative: "Becoming is involutionary, involution is creative" (*Plateaus* 238). Thus, Gerald's interdiction obstructs what can be seen as a core modality of Gudrun's creative, or we might say "energetic" living or being.

We ought to see this sort of involution in the works of modernists such as Lawrence, Woolf, and Kafka as native to that era *because* of the post-Darwinian specificity of humanism's crisis vis-à-vis the animal. This helps to explain why modernist writers occupy a block, a peopling, a band of intensity in Deleuze's *own* writing. The heightened awareness of our deep historico-evolutionary connection to other animals in the early twentieth century produces precisely the kind of "very special becomings-animal" that Deleuze and Guattari locate in the vampire block from the 1700s (*Plateaus* 237). What's surprising is that they don't overtly identify their own theorizing of the modernist block of becomings-animal but tend to frame it through the veneration of individual authors. That tendency is a rather ironic valorization of the personal, what might be described as a sort of slippage into arborescent thinking about individual "genius," rather than a recognition of the particular assemblage of human animalities in the modernist moment.

Returning to the scene, the fact that Gerald puts a halt to Gudrun's "communion" with the cattle has always called readers' attention to the importance of her "strange" dance with the cattle. That dance is clearly a valuable experience of becoming-other and becoming-imperceptible that Gerald cuts off, and it seems that Gudrun is never able to recapture this kind of redemptive "grounding" in the inhuman. It is true that one can read certain moments in Gudrun's dance as potentially aggressive or even destructive, as when "[a] terrible shiver of fear and pleasure went through her" (WL 168). But I would argue for seeing this scene as, at the very least, fluctuating for Gudrun, and therefore more productively as perhaps the only moment when she approaches the kind of grounded, creative balance that Birkin and Ursula are able to achieve more regularly. Not only is the experience of becoming one that profoundly dislocates our normative sense of self, but creative sexuality also involves "dangerous" excesses of the body and of identity that can unsettle and disrupt. In Deleuze and Guattari's terms, "love itself is a war machine endowed with strange and somewhat terrifying powers" (*Plateaus* 278). That said, the critical tendency, as evidenced in Ken Russell's 1969 film adaptation of the novel, is to highlight a sadistic strain in Gudrun's relation to the cattle. But it is only *after* Gerald stops her that she turns decidedly aggressive with these animals, rushing "sheer upon the long-horned bullocks" who snort in "terror" and run off (WL 169–170). Not long afterward, she strikes Gerald, in the first violent moment of their relationship.

I want to examine a few additional details of Gudrun's "rapt trance" (WL 167) before moving on to a discussion of Birkin. A slightly longer quotation of Lawrence's second major description of the dance will help here:

> [She] went in a strange, palpitating dance towards the cattle, lifting her body towards them as if in a spell, her feet pulsing as if in some little frenzy of unconscious sensation, her arms, her wrists, her hands stretching and heaving and falling and reaching and reaching and falling, her breasts lifted and shaken towards the cattle, her throat exposed as in some voluptuous ecstasy towards them, whilst she drifted imperceptibly nearer, an uncanny white figure carried away in its own rapt trance, ebbing in strange fluctuations upon the cattle. (WL 168)

The above discussion of creative sexuality sheds light on a reading of Gudrun's lifted and shaking breasts. Again, the "mating dance" here is about more than just mating. It is also inherently about excess, display, taste, and discernment in Gudrun's becoming-cow as creative involution. This scene also reminds us of Deleuze and Guattari's admonition that becomings-molecular in sexuality *are* becomings-animal but have "no need for bestialism" as such (*Plateaus* 279). And in this case, we see the discernible wading toward the indiscernible, as Gudrun drifts "imperceptibly nearer" the cattle. Deleuze and Guattari continue to explain that the rites of sexuality are "not so much a question of making love with animals. Becomings-animal are basically of another power, since their reality resides not in an animal one imitates or to which one corresponds, but in themselves, in that which suddenly sweeps us up and makes us become—a *proximity, an indiscernibility* that extracts a shared element from the animal far more effectively than any domestication, utilization, or imitation could" (279). Thus, the contrast between Gudrun's erotic and inventive "cowing" and Gerald's protective fears and claim to ownership, "they're my cattle" (WL 170), is all the more pronounced here, as is the troubling of domestication on both the gender and species fronts.

Moreover, Lawrence's phrase, "drifted imperceptibly nearer," not only emphasizes the "approach" of human to animal, but also draws attention to the specificity of dance practice in his text's working out of deterritorializing lapses. In their discussion of becomings intense, animal, and woman, Deleuze and Guattari suggest that all these transformations are "rushing" toward "becomings-imperceptible. The imperceptible is the immanent end of becoming, its cosmic formula" (*Plateaus* 279). They continue to outline the linked "three virtues" of imperceptibility, indiscernibility, and impersonality, elaborating how one can slip between and grow in the midst of things (*Plateaus* 280). Movement becomes central to this set of questions: "Movement has an essential relation to the imperceptible; it is by nature imperceptible. Perception can grasp movement only as the displacement of a moving body or the development of a form. Movements, becomings, in other words, pure relations of speed and slowness, pure affects, are below and above the threshold of perception" (*Plateaus* 281). Although the dancing body is not equivalent to pure affects, we can nonetheless extract valuable insights from the claim that movement has "an essential relation" to the imperceptible. If perception cannot grasp movement "in itself," to some degree, if perception can only register the mutations of forms that themselves are constantly shifting and reassembling, then dancing ought to be understood as a privileged modality for becomings. Gudrun's becoming-cattle vis-à-vis dance delineates a becoming-imperceptible/animal that—given modern dance's "grounding" of dance practice in the bodily and earthly, and the heightened negotiation with animality in this period—is precisely to be understood as a modernist becoming that moves beyond the threshold of humanism's "perception."

One of the potentially gendered ironies of the novel is that Birkin, rather than Gudrun, more reliably models the kind of dancerly becomings-imperceptible that produce a certain privileging of the rhizomatic across Lawrence's text. The way that Birkin mirrors Gudrun, to some respect, in the "Water-Party" scene, after he and Gerald come upon the two women in their "reverie," might be read as partly departing from what Mellown describes as a stylistic differential between a feminine and masculine way of moving in the unpublished novel, *Mr. Noon*. There, Lawrence seems to associate the feminine with the fluid and "soft," the masculine with a jerky and "rigid" comportment ("Music and Dance" 56–57). Birkin's movements, however, are repeatedly described as "loose" in this scene. Moreover, Lawrence explicitly evokes the vibratory in his calibration of Birkin's dancing, as seen through Ursula's perspective: "Yet somewhere inside her she was fascinated by the sight of his loose, vibrating body, perfectly abandoned to its own dropping and swinging, and by the pallid, sardonic-smiling face above" (WL 169). What further unites their movement styles can be described as an irreverence toward the major or molar, an attendant "madness," and a surfing of inhuman sexuality that re-emerges later in the novel. Here, as Birkin moves in and out of his abandonment, his "grotesque step-dance" in which "his body seemed to hang all loose and quaking in between, like a shadow" (WL 168169), he responds to Ursula's assertion that "we've all gone mad" with "[p]ity we aren't madder," and a sudden kissing of her fingers (WL 169). He puts his face near hers here, and would have kissed her again a few moments later "had she not started back" (WL 169). There's a way in which Birkin seems able to recapitulate, or at least emulate the "animal" mating dance here *with* Ursula, whereas Gudrun seems only able to perform it with the cattle.

Similar entanglements between animality, inhuman sexuality, and what Lawrence understands as the impersonal characterize one of the more critically noteworthy scenes between Birkin and Ursula near the novel's conclusion. In the "Snow" chapter, when both couples dance energetically with the German travellers at their inn, Gerald's "powers" are construed as destructively violent, while Birkin's frightening provocations are ultimately entertained and engaged by Ursula. Moreover, Gerald's animal dancing is treated metaphorically; the young girl he partners with is "in his power, as if she were a palpitating bird, a fluttering, flushing bewildered creature" (WL 412). When describing Birkin, Lawrence moves away from proper metaphor and toward the metamorphic that Deleuze associates with the minor and with becomings. Birkin the dancer is described through Ursula's perspective this way: "Clear, before her eyes, as in a vision, she could see the sardonic, licentious mockery of his eyes, he moved towards her with subtle, animal, indifferent approach" (WL 412). The proximity of animality and indifference, or impersonality, in Birkin's dancing marks an opening onto immanence in Birkin and Ursula's subsequent sexual engagement that exceeds both Oedipalized subjectivity and the parameters of a socially locatable Act. Ursula muses afterward:

> She winced.—But after all, why not? She exulted as well. Why not be bestial, and go the whole round of experience? She exulted in it. She was bestial. How good it was to be really shameful! There would be no shameful thing she had not experienced.—Yes she was unabashed, she was herself. Why not?—She was free, when she knew everything, and no dark shameful things were denied her. (WL 413)

The vacillations among "bestial," "herself," and "free" tend to trouble the human/animal divide, just as the challenging of the concept "shameful" in this segment contests notions of the civilized or proper. When articulating his views on immanence, Deleuze identifies those near death and small children, but his description seems to resonate with Ursula's freedoms above: "The life of the individual gives way to an impersonal and yet singular life that releases a pure event freed from the accidents of internal and external life, that is, from the subjectivity and objectivity of what happens: a 'Homo tantum' with whom everyone empathizes and who attains a sort of beatitude. It is a haecceity no longer of individuation but of singularization: a life of pure immanence, neutral, beyond good and evil."[22] It is Birkin's "animal" dancing, his impersonal antimetaphorical becoming-imperceptible, that functions as an opening for Ursula's moment of immanence.

Dancing demarcates the improvisation of the human animal in Lawrence, where becoming-imperceptible, movement and change, and "electric" self-overcomings are privileged as templates of creative living and as precursors for the emergence of new concepts and new ways of being. Gudrun's becoming-cow stages an inhuman aesthetic mating dance that registers all the "classic" markers of Deleuze's becomings, and all the intensities of Grosz's vibratory emergences: it therefore wildly exceeds a "symbolic" battle of the sexes and should be read as privileging the becoming-excessive located at the heart of aesthetic intensities. Similarly, Birkin's slack and ridiculous jigging prefigures his own "beastly" becomings with Ursula, where their enactment of an inhuman sexuality moves early twentieth-century codes of the "human" outside of that which is discernibly human. Such moments, in addition to the resonating cry of tortoise and human, call our attention not primarily to the "admirable" radicality of Lawrence's individual genius, but rather to the intense assemblage of human animalities in modernism.

3

Woolf's Floating Monkeys
and Whirling Women

Virginia Woolf's relation to animals and animality has become a significant chord in the score of recent Woolf criticism. The emergence of animals in Woolf criticism, however, was slightly delayed given the way that other modernist writers like D. H. Lawrence became the subject of animal studies analyses a few years earlier.[1] This modest interval might be explained by the fact that the relation to animals in Woolf's work is characterized by a certain indirection. In other words, it is often the captive or domestic animal that does the "work" of species discourses in Woolf; her animals are usually subject to some human system of classification or constraint.[2] If compared to Lawrence in this respect, Woolf's menagerie provides an interesting point of departure from his. Lawrence's work certainly catalogues moments of seizing or striking at the animal, because that work often records the ambivalences of the human confrontation with non-human animals and with the human's own inhuman qualities. But the captive animal appears less often in Lawrence; he is, to some degree, more focused on the wild or semiwild nonhuman creature. Woolf, on the other hand, tends to engage with the caged or "humanized" animal much more frequently. The quantity of new critical work on *Flush* nicely testifies to this propensity in Woolf's oeuvre.[3]

Certain biographical anecdotes regarding animals ought to be acknowledged at the outset of this discussion. As Bonnie Kime Scott documents, Woolf and her extended family often used varying animal nicknames, including "Apes, Sparroy (a sparrow monkey blend), Kangaroo and Wallaby for Virginia . . . Chipmunk for Clive Bell, Dolphin for Vanessa" and a host of others.[4] I will return to the fact that Woolf played "mandrill" to Leonard Woolf's "mongoose" later in this chapter (*Hollow* 155). Moreover, Woolf's nephew, Quentin Bell, discusses Woolf's relation to dogs in his biography of her, when he suggests that a cocker spaniel named Pinka—given to her by Vita Sackville-West—was the "original" of Flush.[5] Bell goes on to describe Woolf's general attitude toward dogs, claiming that she was "fascinated by all animals but her affection was odd and remote. She wanted

to know what her dog was feeling . . . and perhaps the dogs were no more inscru-
table than most humans. *Flush* is not so much a book by a dog lover as a book by
someone who would love to be a dog" (*Biography* 175).

Dogs have figured prominently in new animal theory investigating Woolf's
fiction, and the garden functions as a kind of corollary to the home: a human-
controlled, semidomesticated space where people engage with the "natural."[6]
Both the canine and the horticultural in Woolf are figures rife for various
slippages between domestic/wild, human/animal, cultivated/free. There has
been another, minor strain of attention to the zoo in Woolf's imaginary.[7] Richard
Espley, for instance, frames the zoo as an arena in which Woolf resists certain
assumptions about animal qualities that humans might share because of an
evolutionary continuum. Woolf's work often does focus on a kind of animal
domestics, though in my view, this focus can enumerate the ways animality gets
contravened or stalled, bottled up or even transferred into "human" activities. To
depart slightly from Espley, who argues that Woolf's interest in animals often is
limited to a concern with "proper classification," I want to suggest that Woolf's
indirection about animality functions as a kind of feint that can mislead readers
into thinking that her engagement with species questions is more metaphorical
than metamorphic.[8] In fact, there are more than a few becomings in Woolf's
work, becomings that not only disturb a sense of order but that produce value
precisely through certain intense becomings-animal.[9]

In two of her works, specifically the Nurse Lugton story and her novel *The
Waves*, creativity is decoupled from the verticality of the human "genius." A kind
of bioaesthetics emerges in these narratives through the becoming-animal of
writing and through the becoming-artistic of one character's creatural modes of
living. Reading aesthetics through a posthumanist framework in these narratives
thus enables an incisive view, beyond the feint of Woolf's animal indirection,
onto the enlivenment of animality at the heart of Woolf's artistic vision.

Enlivened Animals

Virginia Woolf's children's story about Nurse Lugton depicts a woman whose
stitched figures come alive whenever she falls asleep. Lugton sews various animals onto a curtain; they activate after she dozes off and are then returned to their
"frozen" positions on the drapery when Lugton awakens. The tale has been most
famously known for its discovery in 1963 at the British Museum by Mr. Wallace
Hildick, amid the manuscript notebooks of *Mrs Dalloway*. That story was titled
Nurse Lugton's Golden Thimble by Leonard Woolf, and was published by Hogarth
Press in 1966.[10] Perhaps less well-known is the discovery of a second, revised
version of the story in the 1980s at King's College Library, Cambridge.[11] Thus,

as Kristin Czarnecki points out, we know that Woolf revisited her tale, reworked it, and gave it a name, *Nurse Lugton's Curtain* ("Unravelling" 7). This revised version was published in 1991 by Harcourt, with accompanying illustrations by Julie Vivas.[12] In the foreword to the original, 1966 Hogarth Press book, Leonard Woolf claims that the "story appears suddenly in the middle of the text of the novel, but has nothing to do with it" (*Thimble*: foreword). This assertion practically begs for a critical response, precisely because Leonard Woolf makes the counterintuitive claim that the story appears *in the center* of the *Mrs. Dalloway* manuscript yet has "nothing" to do with it.[13]

This seemingly benign story, however, is not just central to an interpretation of a single Woolf novel, but it also reveals something fundamental about Woolf's understanding of aesthetic principles. Those principles are specifically Deleuzian in that they ground the artistic in the animal and inhuman. As I already have noted, Deleuze and Guattari ask whether "art begins with the animal" and suggest that "art is continually haunted by the animal" (*Philosophy* 181, 182). Woolf's story might be said to literalize this continual haunting of aesthetic practice by animals or animality.

Indeed, I agree with Czarnecki, who maintains that "Woolf confronts the creative process head-on in the story" ("Unravelling" 20), as opposed to avoiding it, as other critics have claimed. What is more, this shadow text reveals something foundational about Woolf's views regarding a writer's relationship to the inhuman. The Lugton tale catalogues an awareness of the way that a writer's aesthetic powers are profoundly linked to becomings that are animal in nature. Moreover, the specific becoming-other/becoming-animate of the prosaic curtain suggests a vital materialism in which matter cannot be cordoned off from the forces of life itself. In the wake of such recognitions, the formerly exceptional human creative genius must be recast from its "verticality" and placed on a horizontal plateau of bioaesthetic forces.

Despite Leonard Woolf's emphasis on a thematic distance between the children's tale and *Mrs Dalloway*, critics have worked to read the texts together and to understand how they might exemplify both a thematic and a psychological or temperamental reciprocity. Geneviéve Sanchis Morgan's 1997 essay goes a long way toward linking the metaphorical work of the children's story with the themes of Woolf's novel, what Morgan calls the "obvious interrelations between the two" that have to do with "Woolf's development as a writer and as a modernist [being] predicated on her negotiation of domestic material."[14] Her essay renders both texts, therefore, intellectually serious. Among several insightful corollaries that Morgan describes is that between sewing and writing. Convincingly, she makes the case that "if sewing is a metaphor for writing, or art making, then the nexus of the two stories implies that the key to changing reality lies within the grasp of the artist's needle and pen" ("Unmanning" 101).

Sayaka Okumura elaborates on this theme and calls the knitting Nurse Lugton "a version of the author herself" and Woolf's "self-caricature" or "self-portrait."[15]

If sewing is a metaphor for writing in Woolf, then this modest, critically un-heeded children's story might be seen as a key of sorts into Woolf's own un-derstanding of her creative practice. This possibility may be all the more likely because Woolf wrote the tale for children. As I discussed in relation to Isadora Duncan, Diana Fuss's "border identities" for humanism—animal, thing, child—and Le Guin's observations remind us of the age-old alliance between children and animals, beings whose liminal status troubles the "integrity of the human" (*All Too* 5). Framing this narrative for children allows Woolf to be less rigid or prescriptive in her artistic and high modernist expectations of herself, as a stylist and a thematic innovator. She can play with the analogue between sewing and writing more easily, without censoring her own conclusions, or judging them as "childish" or naïve. That is, she can work in a space that is generically removed from the all-too-human, internalized censor that demands respectable, elaborate themes in the serious-minded novel.

Czarnecki takes up the question of just how "child-friendly" the story re-ally is, a question that has provided occasion for some rather pointed critiques of Woolf's text as being too serious for children.[16] Skeptical of such critiques, Czarnecki argues that the second version, revised by Woolf, "manifests a focus on children rather than adults" ("Unravelling" 12). Perhaps counterintuitively therefore, the first version of the story often reveals the deep philosophical contours of Woolf's creative vision more clearly. In other words, Woolf's tech-nical revisions for the child reader occasionally work to dilute the more striking or radical elements of this narrative. For that reason, I often refer to the *Thimble* version (1966) rather than the *Curtain* version (1991).

The opening page of *Nurse Lugton's Golden Thimble* usefully sets the stage for considering questions of the posthuman, animality, and the vibratory:

> She had given one great snore. She had dropped her head, thrust her spec-tacles up her forehead, and there she sat, by the fender with her thimble on her finger, and her needle full of cotton, snoring, snoring—on her knees, and covering her apron, a large piece of figured blue stuff. The an-imals had not moved until—one, two, three, four, five—Nurse Lugton snored for the fifth time. Ah! the old woman was asleep. The antelope nodded to the zebra; the giraffe bit off a leaf of the tree. For the pattern on the stuff was this: all the animals in the world were trooping down to the lake and the pagoda, and the boat and the bridge to drink. (*Thimble* 5)

Woolf begins her tale with a snore (in the later version Lugton is asleep at the opening, and the snoring is downplayed). The nurse had given a *great* snore: Woolf commences this "childish" story with the provocations of vibration. Deleuze and Guattari begin their chapter on the refrain in *A Thousand Plateaus* with a child and vibration: "A child in the dark, gripped with fear, comforts himself by singing under his breath. . . . The song is like a rough sketch of a calming and stabilizing, calm and stable, center in the heart of chaos" (311). Deleuze and Guattari's additional examples on this page are of a female child and a woman, but not of a grown man. Perhaps the most clichéd case of the "universal" artistic (albeit this universal often is limited to the human) is the mother humming to her infant.[17] The genre of the children's book, as I already have claimed, may allow Woolf to make more explicit these elementary forces of creativity. Children, women, mothers, nurses are expected to rock, sing, sew, and play circle games. They have cultural permission to make primal refrains (ring around the rosy) a mainstay of their daily play and ritual.

When Grosz theorizes the Deleuzian role of vibration for the artistic, she discusses the movement from rhythm to refrain to music as "nothing but *vibration*, resonance, the mutual condition both of material forces at their most elementary levels, and of music at its most refined and complex" (*Chaos* 54). "What is transmitted and transmuted throughout this vast evolution," she maintains, "is nothing but vibration, vibrations in their specificity, vibrations as they set objects moving in their wake" (*Chaos* 54). As I have discussed in the previous chapter on Lawrence, the vibratory not only connects human life to the inhuman, but Grosz figures vibration as an *invitation* to become more creative. The story's opening with one great snore signals a provocation to creativity through vibration, and this provocation involves a necessary becoming-inhuman. We can apprehend this necessity through the broad thesis of bioaesthetics: Art cannot be understood as exclusively human if it is fundamentally about excesses and displays that we share with other animals. In this story, the inhuman becoming-enlivened of art is manifested specifically through animality and, I want to suggest, places animality at the center of Woolf's own artistic universe.

Although it may seem peculiar at first to emphasize Lugton's snoring as Deleuzian vibration, Woolf dwells upon this activity in a text that occupies only six short pages: She accentuates these tremors, which seem almost to penetrate and shake the animals "awake." By enumerating Lugton's snores, "one, two, three, four, five" (*Thimble* 5), Woolf emphasizes the rhythmic and pulsating intensities that resonate from and through bodies, that incite the aesthetic and ultimately get transferred from bodies to proper works of art. Grosz describes how the forces of the universe connect the arts to one another through sensation: "Deleuze suggests that this is because there is indeed a common force shared by all the arts and the living bodies that generate sensations out of material forms that derives from the universe itself. This is precisely vibratory force—perhaps the vibratory structure of subatomic particles themselves?—that constructs sensations as neural reactions to inhuman forces" (*Chaos* 83). Indeed, Deleuze and Guattari note, "Sensation is excitation itself, not insofar as it is gradually prolonged and passes into the reaction but insofar as it is preserved or preserves its vibrations" (*Philosophy* 211). Lugton's snoring inaugurates the story with an invitation to a becoming-artistic, an initiation of aesthetic emergence through rhythm and vibration.

The opening snores are accompanied by a symbolic beheading and a disavowal of the specular, that challenges the centrality of the human in terms of aesthetics, authorship, and creative "vision." This disavowal is highlighted in the Grant painting that serves as the frontispiece for the Hogarth Press edition (see Figure 3.1). When Nurse Lugton drops her head, she relinquishes

Figure 3.1 Duncan Grant. *Nurse Lugton sleeping upright in her chair.* © [2017] Artists Rights Society (ARS), New York / DACS, London.

the reign of the Enlightenment *cogito* in which human rationality—or in this case human "genius"—is the source of artistic production. Moreover, as she pushes her spectacles up her forehead, she also specifically renounces a humanist "vision." This moment reminds us of Freud's claim in *Civilization and Its Discontents* that the acquisition of human identity coincides with the process of "organic repression," whereby man replaces the olfactory with the specular in his sensorium. In that text, Freud imagines early man's transition from a quadruped to a biped stance and the various results of this rising up from an animal way of being. Walking upright brings about the rejection of formerly stimulating smells—particularly blood and feces—and the consequent transition from an olfactory mode of sensing to a visual one. Moreover, organic repression performs a disavowal of the inhuman and thus thwarts the possibility for becomings. Deleuze and Guattari's discussion of desire as lacking a *subject* rather than an object acknowledges this operation: "it is, rather, the *subject* that is missing in desire, or desire that lacks a fixed subject; there is no fixed subject unless there is repression."[18] Lugton's spectacles represent the dependence upon and, indeed, the sharpening of that most human visuality, which helps maintain the static subject. When she removes them, she relinquishes a humanist way of perceiving and being. That, and her vibratory snoring, are answered with the activation of animality in the story. Once the animals realize Lugton has closed her eyes, which they ascertain from the five snores, they come alive.

Deterritorializing Human Creativity

A significant difference between the original and revised texts is that in the first, Woolf discusses the pattern on the curtain in universal terms. This moment appears on the very first page of the Hogarth Press story. After the initial animation of antelope nodding to zebra and giraffe biting a leaf off the tree, Woolf writes: "For the pattern on the stuff was this: *all the animals in the world* were trooping down to the lake and the pagoda, and the boat and the bridge to drink" (*Thimble* 5; my emphasis). In the later version, Woolf economizes to "all the animals began to toss and prance" (*Curtain* [3]). The obvious difference here is that in the second version "all" refers only to the animals on the drapery, while in the first version Woolf marshals animality as such by using the phrase "in the world." This revision marks an understandable whittling down of what Woolf may have considered "excess" in her original text. But having all the animals in the world galvanised in an image of creativity clarifies my claim that Woolf reveals in this text how her artistic practice has its roots in the inhuman. That is, if the curtain serves as a placeholder for creativity, and Woolf figures it as harboring the activation of animality itself, then we can make more extensive claims about Woolf's own relation to inhuman aesthetic forces.

I have discussed in the previous chapter the idea that animals have the power of discrimination or taste, a power that is central to aesthetic appeal and choice. Grosz goes even further in her theorizing around this set of questions to speculate that sexual selection as Darwin outlined it is the "most elementary form of discernment or taste," and may be understood as "the evolutionary origin not only of all art, but of language use and intelligence more generally" (*Undone* 136). The idea here is that the protocols of sexual selection may produce and fine-tune "processes of perception and reception . . . intelligence, communication, and collective living" (*Undone* 136). Whether or not one agrees with these more catholic claims, Grosz's discussion of enhancement, bodily intensification, and taste locates aesthetic behaviors and discernments well outside a limited human purview. In the broadest terms, then, Woolf's story reveals to us the evolutionary underpinnings of artistic experience, emphasizing the human's deep ontological coincidence with animality. At its most basic, her writing and creating are linked, stitched we might insist, to animal forces, to the rhythms and affects that are shared not just by humans but by the living in general.

The images in both versions command our attention, especially because they represent other artists' renderings of a text that, in my view, is primarily about creativity. The 1966 Hogarth Press book includes illustrations by Duncan Grant, who was known for his rich use of color. It is unfortunate that the black and white renderings of his pictures eliminate that element of his work. In contrast, the contemporary version of the story (*Curtain*) is illustrated in bright watercolors by Julie Vivas, and it includes more than double the number of images that we find in the 1966 text. Because the images are not reproduced in color here, I encourage readers to seek out the text itself for a full appreciation of Vivas's paintings. One striking fact about Grant's comparatively spare set of images is that the curtain is only represented in two of his six illustrations, while animals are represented in five. In fact, after the initial image of Nurse Lugton dozing in her chair, every Grant illustration includes animals.

Grant's second (see Figure 3.2) and third illustrations are composed only of animals that seem to hover in their own space, which suggests a dreamlike quality—a place "free of constraints" ("Unravelling" 9) that critics have associated with the text itself—and in which cross-species interactions occur "peaceably."[19] As I will discuss further, the liminal state between waking and sleeping is a prime condition in which becomings can occur. In these Grant images, we see giraffes, zebras, rams, leopards, elephants, birds, bears, and monkeys. In the

Figure 3.2 Duncan Grant. *The animals of Millamarchmantopolis.* © [2017] Artists Rights Society (ARS), New York / DACS, London.

third image, an elephant seems to merge with an ostrich, perhaps suggesting a dynamism and instability of the block of animality itself that also reflects the border-crossing between human and inhuman creativity. The dreamlike image of an elephant-ostrich hybrid suggests the constant mutation, improvisation, and ultimate species instability that are hallmarks of Darwin's theory of evolution, though these qualities are rarely associated with his concept of species even today. Grosz reads Darwin's account of the unfurling of life itself through a Bergsonian/Deleuzian durational force. She emphasizes that Darwin "develops an account of a real that is an open and generative force of self-organization and growing complexity, a dynamic real that has features of its own which, rather than simply exhibit stasis, a fixed essence or unchanging characteristics, are more readily understood in terms of active vectors of change."[20] Grosz goes on to detail Darwin's "quite peculiar, and thoroughly postmodern, account of origin" as it impinges on the idea of species (*Time* 23):

> Origin is a consequence of human, or rather, scientific taxonomy, a function of language. Origin is a nominal question. What constitutes an origin depends on what we call a species, where we (arbitrarily or with particular purposes in mind) decide to draw the line between one group and another that resembles it, preexists it, or abides in close proximity with it. . . . A species is an arbitrarily chosen set of similarities that render other differences either marginal or insignificant. Species are a measure, an incalculable, nonnumerical measure of significant differences. (*Time* 23)

For these reasons, Grosz claims that, in the "durational unfolding" of evolution, "what evolves are not individuals or even species, which are forms of relative fixity or stability, but oscillations of difference" (*Time* 24). If the image of an elephant-ostrich dismantles our conventional sense of species distinctions in this story, that dismantling only confirms the way in which creativity or the aesthetic sensibilities deterritorialize the human via animality.

That specific deterritorializing of the human as Creator is perhaps most keenly registered in the images of monkeys that Duncan Grant contributes to the original Hogarth Press edition of the story. The first of these appears on the second page of the text, in the initial animal conglomeration in which the creatures seem to float about unanchored. The monkey in this illustration (see Figure 3.2) is almost distressingly hybrid in its oscillation between human and animal features. It appears "monstrous" or uncanny, with the legs and feet of a monkey, and the head and arms of a human. Particularly strange and even difficult to articulate is the way in which the monkey seems to have a human hairstyle, as if this animal woke up and groomed itself with a comb and hair oil. If hair is a residual reminder in humans of their "beastly" prehistory,[21] then the taming of the monkey's hair through styling proves especially captivating in our discussion of aesthetic framing. In a fascinating, and apparently unconscious, visual translation, Vivas renders a similarly coiffed monkey in the 1991 *Nurse Lugton's Curtain*.[22] On the third page of text, as the animals begin to climb off and away from the "blue stuff"—the material of the curtain—one of six enlivened and descending monkeys is drawn in profile and seems to have a cap of human hair (see Figure 3.3). That particular monkey also has unusually humanlike hands compared to the other monkeys in the text, whose hands and feet are more webbed.

Figure 3.3 Illustrations by Julie Vivas from NURSE LUGTON's CURTAIN by Virginia Woolf. Illustrations copyright © 1991 by Julie Vivas. Reprinted by permission of Houghton Mifflin Harcourt Publishing Company. All rights reserved.

Like other monkeys envisioned in Woolf's broader fictional universe, the coiffed one in the original edition seems to hold a nut at which it gazes.[23] Its thoughtful contemplation of the object in its possession renders the monkey all the more "human" and all the less "animal," as the creature almost appears to be reading a text. If, as Georges Bataille suggests, our development of tool-use as a kind of transcendence of the object subtends the "human" participation in symbolic systems, then this monkey's consideration of its nut places it at least in a liminal space between animals, who are erroneously considered tool-less, and humans, at the zenith of technological manipulation.[24] Grant's portrayal of this hybrid creature reminds the reader with an almost shocking force that she, too, is a primate with an object in hand to contemplate, the very children's book she is reading at that moment. This implicit analogy figures taste and discernment within a dizzying *mise en abyme* produced by the interchangeability between nut and book, between "animal" and "human."

Monkeys also figure prominently in the fifth and penultimate illustration of the Hogarth Press edition. Probably the most surreal of Grant's images in the text, this one depicts the imaginary Queen of the fictive town, "Millamarchmontopolis," where the animals roam for their pleasure and to secure food and drink while Nurse is sleeping. The Queen in Woolf's story has come to town in her palanquin and sits reposed, in her regalia. Hovering bizarrely just in front and above her in Grant's image is a cluster of seven monkeys (see Figure 3.4). Although some of the monkeys' faces and heads are obscured, a few nonetheless suggest pensive

Figure 3.4 Duncan Grant. *The queen in her chariot.* © [2017] Artists Rights Society (ARS), New York / DACS, London.

examination. Moreover, the monkey most in the picture's foreground holds a proverbial nut. If Woolf as conventional artist can be understood as residing in the "trappings" of the Queen's highly symbolic and humanist personage—one with a crown that circumscribes and ornamentalizes the "rational" or conceptual lodged in the head—then we must also reckon with her attendant horde of floating monkeys. Indeed, the Queen of modernism (and of high modernism) is nearly surrounded by monkeys, and their hovering suggests that her own imaginative sources are animal rather than royal. This image, perhaps more than any other in the 1966 text, elucidates a replete, Woolfian becoming-animal/artistic.

At this juncture in the story, Woolf has emphasized how the awakened animals freely range over Nurse Lugton's apron, despite the fact that in her waking life Lugton is terrified of even "a little beetle" (*Thimble* 11). That Woolf chooses to depict the animals crossing freely from the curtain right onto Lugton's apron powerfully accentuates an intimacy or familiarity with nonhuman creativity that comes only when the strictly conscious or rational mind is relaxed. Some critics have asserted that the story's reliance on a sleeping state suggests Woolf's dread of the unconscious creative forces at work in her own psyche. For instance, Hodgkins discusses Lugton as Woolf's double and as an "image of the creative female unconscious," but also argues that the association connotes "a fear of its author, that of the artist who wants to avoid confronting the creative process lest its products die in their amber" ("Children's Books" 361). Similarly, Michelle Levy suggests that Woolf's description of Lugton as not seeing the awakened animals amounts to an "alienation from the animal world" and a kind of "anthropocentricity" ("Shorter" 148). Perhaps a more useful way to read the question of conscious and unconscious here is to see the drifting into an unconscious state in the story as the submerging or relinquishing of the humanist self, the "ego" that attempts to cordon itself off from the natural and affective. That is, when Lugton enters an unconscious or semiconscious state, the edicts of organic repression diminish and the affective forces of becoming are triggered. Thus, when the head drops, and the glasses are pushed away, Lugton opens herself to the inhuman creative forces that are less accessible to the "waking" self. The snore signals Lugton's letting go of the impossibly reified and carefully maintained "human," and the ushering in of a world in which the human has a participatory relationship with the animal, natural, and material worlds. It is important to put this process in a Deleuzian context. In his late discussions on immanence, as I mentioned in Chapter Two, Deleuze refers to the dying figure whose individual life "gives way to an impersonal and yet singular life that releases a pure event freed from the accidents of internal and external life, that is, from the subjectivity and objectivity of what happens," and he discusses small children who "are infused with an immanent life that is pure power and even bliss."[25] And it is such a liminal subject, fading between waking and sleeping awareness in Woolf's story, that is best equipped to demonstrate the human's interlacing with the other-than-human.

Another monkey that requires attention in these stories is the mandrill. In both versions, Woolf includes a litany of animals just after she declares officially that they had begun to move. Grant does not represent the mandrill; he uses only chimplike monkeys throughout the Hogarth Press version. Vivas, on the other hand, depicts an almost Biblical parade of animals (reminiscent of the Ark story) at this point in the narrative (see Figure 3.5), illustrating each of the creatures that Woolf mentions in the passage: "First went the elephant and the zebra; next the giraffe and the tiger; the ostrich, the mandrill, twelve marmots and a pack of mongeese followed; the penguins and the pelicans waddled and waded, often pecking at each other, alongside" (*Curtain* [9]).

The mandrill is an especially interesting case for my argument not because mandrills are the world's largest species of monkey, but rather because they are the most vibrantly colored. Notably, Charles Darwin wrote in *The Descent of Man* that "no other member in the whole class of mammals is coloured in so extraordinary a manner as the adult male mandrill (*Cynocephalus mormon*)."[26] Most descriptions of mandrills emphasize the male's brilliant coloration, with a red stripe down the middle of the face and ridged blue muzzle. The "rump" is strikingly saturated with bright pinks, blues, reds, and purples. Indeed, the mandrill seems almost alien in its pigmentation. In Grosz's terms, such extreme coloration would be understood as a particularly incisive example of the way that sexuality itself requires creativity: "sexuality needs to harness excessiveness and

Figure 3.5 Illustrations by Julie Vivas from NURSE LUGTON's CURTAIN by Virginia Woolf. Illustrations copyright © 1991 by Julie Vivas. Reprinted by permission of Houghton Mifflin Harcourt Publishing Company. All rights reserved.

invention to function at all" (*Chaos* 64). Additionally, the mandrill exhibits one of the most pronounced cases of sexual dimorphism in the primate world, where males and females are radically asymmetrical in their physical appearances. For Grosz, such divergence specifically links, in a rather surprising philosophical lineage, the work of Darwin and Luce Irigaray around the crucial Deleuzian question of difference:

> Darwin insists that sexual bifurcation, the division of species into (at least) two sexes, is an evolutionary invention of remarkable tenacity and value, for it multiplies difference *ad infinitum*. Irigaray's conception of nature as the differentiating and differentiated condition of subjectivity . . . remains consistent with Darwin's conception of sexual selection—the division of species into two sexes, two different morphologies, and with it the advent of sexuality and sexual reproduction, and the generation of ever-new (genetic and morphological) characteristics and qualities, ever more morphological or bodily differences. (*Undone* 104)

Thus, the mandrill is an especially significant animal in Lugton's creative universe, because it is a primate whose bodily apparatus testifies to the evolutionary, though not exclusively adaptive, investment of living beings in the "spectacular performance" of creative sexuality (*Undone* 125).[27]

Grosz's broad discussion of difference *as such* is too complex for me to rehearse here, but it partly elaborates Deleuze's notion that difference is "something that distinguishes itself," and that "is made, or makes itself."[28] Grosz's assertion that "difference is the generative force of the universe itself, the impersonal, inhuman destiny and milieu of the human, that from which life, including the human, comes and that to which life in all its becomings directs itself" becomes a useful way to read the animality in and of Nurse Lugton's story and Woolf's writerly process (*Undone* 94). The mandrill in this text functions as an exemplar of creative difference that is specifically aimed to reveal the human's species liminality.[29] That is, the excessively bright, almost painterly monkey seems to insist with a shameless intellectual effrontery that—clearly—the creative can never be a strictly human affair. Moreover, in Vivas's illustration, the mandrill, who marches along in the Ark-like procession, is the only creature who stares directly out at the reader. As I have discussed elsewhere,[30] recent work in animal theory has often coalesced around a kind of "primal scene," in which subjectivities that we call human and animal confront one another, retreat, respond, or otherwise intermingle. Perhaps the best known of these is Derrida's naked-in-front-of-cat scene and, subsequently, Donna Haraway's insightful reading of its limitations. Testifying to the centrality of the inter-species look or gaze, Kari Weil begins her recent book about the "animal turn" in critical and cultural theory with Derrida's now well-known proclamation, "An animal looks at us and we are naked before it. Thinking, perhaps, begins there."[31] Weil rightly emphasizes the link between an animal's look and the concept of human nakedness or nudity. "Does a confrontation with and acknowledgment of another animal," she asks, "*expose* us as humans by stripping us of those clothes and thinking caps with which we have claimed to stake our differences from animals?"[32] (my emphasis). In this case, the mandrill's gaze can be read as a direct challenge to our humanist notions about the artistic. The monkey's look strips away aesthetic human exceptionalism by emphasizing the magnificent becoming-artistic of one of man's more proximate primate relatives. That Woolf called herself mandrill and Leonard mongoose, and that Woolf sometimes emphasized the male rump in erotic letters to Leonard, not only results in the gender play that Kime Scott notes (*Hollow* 155), but it also subtly reinforces at Woolf's "personal" level the performative, sexual bioaesthetic excesses that I am suggesting were central to her artistic life.

Similarly, in a subtle but nonetheless striking visual staging of human animality that again seems less than conscious on the part of Vivas, the back-cover image for Woolf's short story cleverly shows Nurse Lugton viewed from the back, as she sits in her sewing chair hard at work. We see the back of her kerchiefed head, the chair rungs and pillow she leans upon. The way that Vivas draws the backs of Lugton's shoes, especially the seam down the center of each heel, makes Lugton's shoes appear entirely hooflike (see Figure 3.6). Lugton seems to enact a becoming-bovine, which takes on a certain fascinating quality if we consider Nietzsche's claim about reading, art, and the ruminative that Weil cites at the outset of her book: "One thing is necessary above all if one is to practice reading as an *art*. Something for which one has almost to be a cow and in any case *not* a man: *rumination*" (*Thinking Animals* qtd. in epigraph, Nietzsche's emphasis). The point here is that if Lugton is Woolf's alter-ego, then this would seem to be the only visual image of a Woolf-as-writer figure becoming-animal in all of Woolf's oeuvre. Combined with the mandrill's confrontational gaze, the becoming-ruminant of Vivas's final Lugton illustration may be prodding us to ask if the becoming-animal/artistic of the writer does not also invite or compel the reader into a similar trans-species engagement.

This Fold

Okumura makes the important suggestion that Lugton's curtain ought to be understood in terms of textuality. She writes, "Nurse Lugton is sewing a curtain, the description of whose pattern occupies the story's text. Her textile is equated to the author's text" ("Women Knitting" 175). Reading the curtain as creative

Figure 3.6 Illustrations by Julie Vivas from NURSE LUGTON's CURTAIN by Virginia Woolf. Illustrations copyright © 1991 by Julie Vivas. Reprinted by permission of Houghton Mifflin Harcourt Publishing Company. All rights reserved.

materiality itself, in a new-materialist or neovitalist register that is indebted to Bergson and Deleuze, pushes these concepts about textuality even further. In this connection, Derek Ryan's recent focus on Woolf's "cotton wool of daily life" as an entry point for connecting her work to new materialist ideas is highly relevant.[33] To start, consider the curtain's most basic, "architectural" qualities. It is a large piece of fabric that is draped and folded over Lugton's lap. As she works, portions of the fabric are revealed and manipulated, while other portions are inevitably hidden. There are the active vectors being stitched, and in the many folds and creases that remain unworked or latent, there is the virtual, waiting to be actualized. The undulating folds of Nurse Lugton's curtain, coupled with its becoming-animal that serves as engine of the entire story, suggest an almost uncanny enactment of the active and creative force of enlivened matter. Thus for

Bergson, the incalculable creativity of organic life exists, which "we cannot in any way subject to a mathematical treatment" and which exhibits "continuity of change, preservation of the past in the present, real duration—the living being seems, then, to share these attributes with consciousness.... [And] life, like conscious activity, is invention, is unceasing creation."[34] Moreover, Deleuze outlines the virtual as a self-differentiating source for life's actualizations:

> The three requirements of a philosophy of life are as follows: (1) the vital difference can only be experienced and thought of as internal difference; it is only in this sense that the 'tendency to change' is not accidental, and that the variations themselves find an internal cause in that tendency; (2) these variations do not enter into relationships of association and addition, but on the contrary, they enter into relationships of dissociation or division; (3) they therefore involve a virtuality that is actualized according to the lines of divergence; so that evolution does not move from one actual term to another actual term in a homogeneous unilinear series, but from a virtual term to the heterogeneous terms that actualize it along a ramified series.[35]

Grosz remarks upon these concepts: "Each [Bergson and Deleuze] distinguishes life as a kind of *contained dynamism*, a dynamism within a porous boundary, that feeds from and returns to the chaos which surrounds it something immanent within the chaotic whole: life as a complex fold of the chemical and the physical that reveals something not given within them, something new, an emergence, the ordered force of invention" (*Undone* 27; Grosz's emphasis). The folds of Lugton's curtain are more than suggestive of such revelations.

Deleuze insists upon the inseparability of life and matter in his discussions of the fold: "Organic matter is not, however, different from inorganic matter (here the distinction of a first and a second matter is irrelevant). Whether organic or inorganic, matter is all one."[36] Grosz also reminds us that, in Bergson's terms, materiality is characterized by repetitions or "near-repetitions" (*Undone* 29): "The material world is that which is capable of unrolling or unfolding what has been already rolled or folded, that is, caused: it is the inevitable unwinding or unfurling, the relaxation, of what has already been cocked and set, dilated, in a pregiven trajectory" (*Undone* 29). Thus, the folding and unfolding of Lugton's curtain not only conjures the latency of the unknown that marks the possibility for the new and unexpected, the creative, but it also gestures toward the regularity with which the material world maintains itself.

If we remain within a Bergsonian framework for a moment more, we can consider how the animals' coming alive from the folds of the curtain might be read as the functioning of *élan vital*. Jane Bennett suggests that the "task of *élan vital* is to shake awake that lazy bones of matter and insert into it a measure of surprise" (*Vibrant* 78). What is more, Bennett recalls that the task of this vital spark is to "increase the *instability* of material formations" (78; Bennett's emphasis). This indetermination associated with the creative, what Bergson calls "a perpetual efflorescence of novelty," also may explain Lugton's trepidation at confronting the animals while she is fully conscious.[37] In other words, the creative does involve the incalculable, to use Derrida's terminology, and so Lugton or Woolf's disquiet about this unfolding can be appreciated rather than characterized as retrogressive.

In broader terms, Woolf's particular framing of a becoming-animal through the material or textual in this children's story supports a new materialist (or vital materialist, in Bennett's terms) understanding of the relation between life and matter. The curtain—which would have traditionally been understood as inert or frozen matter—self-generates activity or force. This activation is nicely emphasized in Vivas's dancerly illustration of the creatures "flashing" back to the cloth near the end of the story (see Figure 3.7). The fluctuation between a "living" state characterized through nonhuman animation and a kind of dormancy—in which the waking Lugton "caught the animals, and froze them" (*Thimble* 15)—might best be understood as modeling the dynamics of material life itself: as Grosz asserts,

> Life is always on the verge of returning to the inorganic from which its
> elements, its very body and energies, are drawn. Life and matter cannot,

Figure 3.7 Illustrations by Julie Vivas from NURSE LUGTON's CURTAIN by Virginia Woolf. Illustrations copyright © 1991 by Julie Vivas. Reprinted by permission of Houghton Mifflin Harcourt Publishing Company. All rights reserved.

in this tradition, be understood as binary opposites; rather they are divergent tendencies, two different directions or trajectories inherent in
a single whole, matter as undivided, matter as it includes its "others"—
life, ideality, connectivity, temporality. (*Undone* 32–33)

The becoming-life or animation of the curtain cannot be separated from the curtain itself, although Lugton's sleeping state does suggest that humans are perhaps not ordinarily attuned to this coincidence of life and matter. Grosz carefully
explains that in Bergson's view "life" cannot be understood as a separate or special force that is distinct from matter: "The common impetus life carries within
it is that of *materiality itself*, the capacity to make materiality extend itself into the
new and the unforeseeable" (*Undone* 33; Grosz's emphasis).

More pointedly, Grosz reiterates this idea when she insists, "Life is that tendency, *in matter* itself, to prolong, delay, detour, which means that matter, 'an undivided flux,' is as alive, as dynamic, as invested in becoming as life itself" (*Undone*
35). Woolf's text provides a perfectly double-edged example of this dynamic flux
in that Nurse Lugton is stitching, writing, creating, thus participating in the activation or the becoming, but also the material or corporeal "body" or vessel
of that activity—the curtain—becomes more than itself semispontaneously,
activates *itself* through a vibratory animation to take on a "vitality." Moreover, it
is crucial to read this seemingly paradoxical, double activation as a recognition
that human creativity is linked to inhuman creativity. That is, the intricacies of
weaving, writing, painting, and so forth, are not without a space of profound
overlap with the becoming artistic of animals and plants, and even more primitive forms of life. Grosz puts this overlap in fundamental terms when she clarifies
how we ought to understand the "unity of life." It is not that life can be connected
through some genetic web or ecosystem, but rather that

> all life is equally pushed—in its originary emergence from the "prebi-
> otic soup" of chemical elements through to the vastly variable forms of
> life that have existed and exist today—by a temporal, or evolutionary,
> impetus to vary itself, to capitalize on its material conditions, to differ.
> The unity of life is not an end, a final harmony or cohesion, but the
> beginning, the impetus all of life shares with the chemical order from
> which it differentiates itself, and which it carries within it as its inherited
> resource. (*Undone* 33).

In a traditional reading, the curtain itself might be understood as a proverbial
"blank slate" in materialist terms. In Woolf's story, however, that interpretation must be recalibrated, for the curtain is anything but blank in Deleuze's
terms. In other words, one might initially want to read the fabric as one would

read the "canvas" of a painting—an inert substrate upon which art or creativity will be superimposed. But the becoming-animal of the "blue stuff" suggests that such a reading would be erroneous. I am tempted to speculate about how Deleuze himself would have framed the curtain had he been familiar with Woolf's story in the way he was familiar with *The Waves*, for instance. If, according to Cliff Stagoll, a Deleuzian plane of immanence can be understood as "a surface upon which all events occur, where events are understood as chance, productive interactions between forces of all kinds,"[38] might Deleuze have recognized Woolf's curtain as such a plane? Might he have interpreted Woolf's curtain as, in his and Guattari's words, "a section of chaos" that gives "*consistency without losing anything of the infinite*" and that harbors "variable *curves* that retain the infinite movements that turn back on themselves in incessant exchange, but which also continually free other movements which are retained" (*Philosophy* 42; Deleuze and Guattari's emphasis).[39] While Deleuze and Gauttari refer here to concepts in the realm of philosophy, Woolf's plane in the Lugton story might be understood as referring to her own, or any artist's, creative concepts and the movements and variations, indeed, the enlivened manifestations that they undergo. The suggestion in the story of an ongoing repetition of varying becomings-animal during Lugton's waking and sleeping intervals invites this comparison. That is, the reader understands that this "cycle" of waking craft and sleeping enlivenment, this rotation of animal becoming and dormancy, will continue ad infinitum. As Stagoll explains further, a Deleuzian plane "represents the field of becoming, a 'space' containing all of the possibilities inherent in forces. On this plane, all possible events are brought together, and new connections between them made and continuously dissolved" ("Plane" 205). Again, the fluctuation between creative activity and creative dormancy in Woolf's story has a distinctly Deleuzian resonance.

The operative dynamism of the curtain on a systematic level also invites us to read Woolf's text through what Rosi Braidotti calls an "affirmative" ethics of biopower. Rather than focus unduly on *thanatos* or the questions of mortality and suffering in contemporary philosophy, Braidotti notes that we ought to consider the "generative powers of *zoē* and to turn to the Spinozist political ontology defended by Deleuze and Guattari"[40]:

> Death is overrated. The ultimate subtraction is after all only another phase in a generative process . . . . For the narcissistic human subject, as psychoanalysis teaches us, it is unthinkable that Life should go on without my being there. The process of confronting the thinkability of a Life that may not have "me" or any "human" at the center is actually a sobering and instructive process. I see this postanthropocentric shift

as the start for an ethics of sustainability that aims at shifting the focus toward the positivity of *zoē*. ("Life Itself" 212)

What other than the *generative* power of *zoē* is portrayed in Woolf's story, in which it is the Life of nonhuman animality that subtends "narcissistic" human creativity? Indeed, the illustration Vivas created to span pages thirteen and fourteen of the *Curtain* text (if it were enumerated) is a biopoetic image par excellence (see Figure 3.8). Viewed from above, as if from an aerial perspective, animals dip their heads to drink from a lagoon. We see only their backs, each demarcated halfway, like cells preparing to divide. The landscape is represented almost as if sliced on a molecular level, with trees spreading out like microbial pili or flagella. The half-circular image, with cellular and microscopic overtones, seems to reference the power or creative potential of *zoē* itself. It is an extraordinary image at the center of a book about a woman's creative sources in that it embeds her aesthetic powers in inhuman, biological forces.

What Braidotti calls the postanthropocentric shift is indeed what Deleuze often theorized as the impersonal. Grosz describes this decentering of the traditional conceptualization of human life:

> Deleuze seeks to understand life without recourse to a self, subject, or personal identity, or in opposition to matter and objects. He seeks something impersonal, singular, that links a living being, internally, through differentiation or repetition, to elements and forces that are

Figure 3.8 Illustrations by Julie Vivas from NURSE LUGTON's CURTAIN by Virginia Woolf. Illustrations copyright © 1991 by Julie Vivas. Reprinted by permission of Houghton Mifflin Harcourt Publishing Company. All rights reserved.

nonliving. This is what links the concept of life, for him, to becoming-animal, to the Body without Organs, and to immanence rather than to transcendence, the human, or the organism. He is interested in the non-living tentacles that extend themselves into the living, the provisional linkages the nonliving and the living form to enable the living to draw out the virtualities of the nonliving; that is, to enable the nonliving to have a life of their own. (*Undone* 35–36)

The tentacles of the inhuman are not only evident in the cellular image described above, but the impersonal link to "nonliving" forces is powerfully evident in the Vivas illustration that represents Lugton's face as a mountain. Near the end of the story, Lugton is conflated with the landscape: "They could see her, from their windows, towering over them. She had a face like the side of a mountain with great precipices and avalanches, and chasms for her eyes and hair and nose and teeth" (*Curtain* [23]). Vivas draws Lugton's enormous head as partially submerged in the earth, with the sinews of her neck bleeding and blending right into the foothills of the landscape (see Figure 3.9). It is as though her body itself *is* the earth, and her head, putatively the most "human" and "rational" portion of her body, can only be partially separated from the forces of the earth. This image recalls Annie Leibowitz's photograph of Rachel Rosenthal, buried neck deep in the desert (Rosenthal is the subject of Chapter Four). But Vivas can take the concept of merging even further because she blurs the distinction between

Figure 3.9 Illustrations by Julie Vivas from NURSE LUGTON's CURTAIN by Virginia Woolf. Illustrations copyright © 1991 by Julie Vivas. Reprinted by permission of Houghton Mifflin Harcourt Publishing Company. All rights reserved.

Lugton's neck and the descending ripples of the mountain terrain in her water-color depiction.

What we find in this story, then, is aesthetic enlivenment as that which takes place beyond the personal, beyond the egotistical, and beyond the human. Art is understood as the becoming-other of life itself, as the perpetual and recurrent emergence of difference, and as something having its foundation more in a latent animality than in a waking humanity. If Nurse Lugton's sewing is figuratively linked to Virginia Woolf's writing, then this "minor" children's story persuades us to place the becoming-artistic of animality at the heart of Woolf's aesthetic practice. Moreover, the seemingly unremarkable "blue stuff" of the curtain emerges as the generative, affirmative life force of matter itself. Woolf's tale of "magical" animals and curtains is actually a vital materialist narrative in which humans borrow their creative capacities from the becomings-other, from the differentializing and "excessive" tendencies, of the inhuman.

Rhythms and Refrains

This reading of Woolf's affirmative, inhuman bioaesthetics in her "minor" children's tale allows for a deeply counterintuitive rereading of the characters in her most experimental novel, *The Waves*, which many critics consider to be her masterpiece. Taking my cue from the force of biopower in the Nurse Lugton narrative, therefore, I ask how this well-known novel manifests inhuman rhythmic forces and, ultimately, how Woolf's characters in the novel relate to the vibrational. The latter question might best be framed as investigating how the characters function *as* forces of creative rhythm, manifesting a becoming-artistic. As I will finally suggest, it is Jinny who is most bioaesthetic in this respect. This claim runs contrary to received wisdom about the characters, given that Bernard and Louis are the novel's practicing writers. Indeed, Bernard and Rhoda, in particular, often have been linked to Woolf in a kind of quasibiographical, quasitheoretical register in Woolf criticism.[41] My reading, therefore, reframes conventional views about aesthetic practices and "gifts" in the text.

When I first learned that Woolf's provisional title for *The Waves* was *The Moths*, I was reminded of a well-known dance anecdote about Merce Cunningham, the subject of Chapter Five. In connection with his 1951 dance titled *Boy Who Wanted to be a Bird*, a woman reportedly asked Cunningham after the performance how he could dance without music: He noted that "in this funny, dark little place, a gorgeous moth flew in and began moving in the most spectacular way around the one light. And I just pointed."[42] This evocative anecdote usefully links movement, attraction, and the inhuman to human aesthetic practice, connections I will also forge in this reading of Woolf's novel. Moreover, Derek

Ryan has recently explored the question of posthumanist ethics in relation to Woolf's "The Death of the Moth" and Lawrence's poem, "Snake." His conclusion that both writers at times employ an anthropocentrism "that seeks to follow the snake and the moth in order to find a conception of life that is not centered on human subjects" resonates with my investigations of bioaesthetics in the work of both writers in this study.[43]

The idea that sexual selection lies at the heart of aesthetics is also especially salient to a posthumanist reading of creative becomings in *The Waves*. As I have mentioned, Grosz insists upon understanding nature as *dynamic* rather than static, as something that is always opening toward the new and the future in a process of becoming. She emphasizes that, because animals attract mates through various "vibratory" forces, through color and through dance, through song and cadences, the aesthetic is linked to the workings of sexual difference in evolution. These seductions can be as dangerous as they are pleasurable. As I discussed in the Introduction, Grosz suggests that reproduction does not have to be viewed as the primary telos of these processes. Rather, Grosz speculates that "[perhaps] sexuality is not so much to be explained in terms of its ends or goals (which in sociobiological terms are assumed to be the [competitive] reproduction of maximum numbers of [surviving] offspring, where sexual selection is ultimately reduced to natural selection) as in terms of its forces, its effects . . . which are forms of bodily intensification. Vibrations, waves, oscillations, resonances affect living bodies, not for any higher purpose but for pleasure alone" (*Chaos* 33). So again, we need not see sexuality as biologically "determined" or rigidly heteronormative, but rather as a fluid process of becoming that emphasizes pleasure. I want to repeat, therefore, Grosz's description of creatural, embodied intensities during sexual spectacle: "This calling to attention, this making of one's own body into a spectacle, this highly elaborate display of attractors, involves intensification. Not only are organs on display engorged, intensified, puffed up, but the organs that perceive them—ears, eyes, nose—are also filled with intensity, resonating with colors, sounds, smells, shapes, rhythms" (*Chaos* 66). Thus taste, pleasure, performance, and staging all enter into the aestheticization of the body in sexual selection and evolution: "Art is of the animal precisely to the degree that sexuality is artistic" (*Chaos* 70).

Before discussing details of Woolf's novel, I want to emphasize that the incantatory nature of her text, pointedly represented in her claim that she wrote the novel "to a rhythm, not a plot," makes *The Waves* a particularly important work to examine through concepts of vibration and the refrain.[44] As my discussion of Lawrence emphasized, the refrain is "a kind of rhythmic regularity that brings a minimum of livable order to a situation in which chaos beckons" (*Chaos* 52). In music, for instance, the refrain "wards off chaos by creating a rhythm, tempo, melody that taps chaos by structuring it through the constitution of a territory" (*Chaos* 53). Moreover, Woolf's attention to the waves can be framed alongside the life rhythms and the connection between cosmic and bodily forces that I have theorized in relation to Duncan and Lawrence: "These rhythms of the body—the rhythms of seduction, copulation, birth, death—coupled with those of the earth—seasons, tides, temperatures—are the conditions of the refrain, which encapsulates and abstracts these rhythmic or vibratory forces into a sonorous emblem, a composed rhythm" (*Chaos* 55). In the case of Woolf's novel, then, it is various circuits of vibration, refrains that oscillate between the living and the cosmic, that open life onto excess and the artistic.

Perhaps most apparently, Deleuze's concept of the refrain opens up a reading of the interludes in Woolf's text. These repetitions mark the most overt "natural" material in the work. The interludes attest to the inhuman rhythms, the cosmological forces that in one sense stand outside of narrowly human or conventionally humanist preoccupations.[45] Early discussions of *The Waves* made claims to this effect. Frank D. McConnell's 1968 essay, for instance, calls the interludes "deliberate and highly effective attempts to present a phenomenal world without the intervention of human consciousness, a world of blind things which stands as a perpetual challenge to the attempts of the six monologists to seize, translate and 'realize' their world."[46] Although McConnell is clearly correct in one sense, he goes on to suggest that the very final waves that crash on the shore at the novel's end are "simply and sublimely irrelevant to Bernard, as Bernard to [them]" (CC 83). But the text, I think, does not suggest this kind of final disconnect between the natural world and Bernard's world. It may be the case that Bernard is less connected than some of the other characters. McConnell goes on to characterize the "'nature' of the italicized passages" as "neither the anthropomorphic and sympathetic nature of the pastoral nor its malevolent but equally anthropomorphic contrary" (CC 83). It's here where Deleuze's claims are most helpful, and where concepts of the posthuman open up a reading that need not be trapped by views of nature as either "sympathetic" and sentimentally human or hostile and violently antihuman. Because the refrain allows us to understand how even the human is organized through vibrational patterns that are the most elementary cosmic forces. Although Grosz often uses the musical refrain as her key example, she is aware throughout her discussion that these concepts apply to creativity and life forces in the broadest sense:

> Refrains, then, are rhythmic, melodious patterns, small chants, ditties, that shape the vibrations of milieus into the harmonics of territories, the organization of a wall or barrier. Music is the reverse movement, the liberation of these harmonic and rhythmic patterns from their originating location and their placement into a double movement, both musically, beyond the smallness of the refrain and on, to the song, the tune, the

sonata, the duet, the symphony, other forms of music, genres, and so
on, to forms as yet not even conceivable on the plane of composition;
and spatio-temporally, beyond territory, to individuals, peoples, races,
bodily movements, performances. (*Chaos* 54)

I want to emphasize the permeability or "double movement" that Grosz outlines
here to provide a way to think about the relationship not only between the
interludes and the "regular" text, but also the relationship between the waves
and Woolf's human characters. If the interludes function as a refrain, notice
their relationship to the normative text. The "small" chant or dittie is released
from its "originating location," and there is a vibrational movement between refrain and song. The continued elaboration of this pattern eventually becomes
the symphony. Suzette Henke has written that the novel "might be compared to
a musical symphony, whose theme is introduced in the lyrical interludes, then
fully elaborated via the free indirect discourse of each persona's introspective
soliloquies."[47] The Deleuzian refrain clarifies this analogy.

Interestingly, Patrick McGee notes in his discussion of political dynamics
in the novel that the interludes "make a significant *return of the repressed* in the
main body of Bernard's final monologue. No longer italicized, no longer safely
confined to the margins," he continues, "the voice of the interludes erupts from
within the discourse of the imperialist subject."[48] If the interludes are understood as a kind of refrain, then it would only make sense that they appear and
reappear in the main text. But McConnell's notion that Bernard is utterly indifferent to the waves requires a rejoinder. In an extremely rigid sense, this may be
true, but one of the deep ideological claims of Woolf's novel is, in fact, quite the
opposite. Woolf's characters, albeit to varying degrees, participate in the vibrational forces that the waves monumentalize. The movement of the refrain and its
resonance makes its way into individuals, and these forces are, in fact, the very
roots of aesthetics.

Woolf sets up much of the novel's natural and cosmic terrain in the opening
section, where the six figures are young children. As I have already established,
it is a commonplace that children are "closer" to animals and nature than adults,
and Freud gives us one means of theorizing this idea through his discussion of
organic repression.[49] Sight and sound dominate the lines that introduce the six
characters. Although there are too many impressions to recount here, looking
at a few of them reveals how the aesthetic is already rooted in the oscillations
of the natural world at the novel's opening. The children notice rings that hang
and "quiver" in loops of light, leaves that gather "like ears," "islands of light"
that swim on the grass (*Waves* 9). There is also a distinct emphasis on rhythm
and vibration. Rhoda hears a sound, "cheep, chirp; cheep, chirp; going up and
down" (9). Louis, of course, hears "something stamping," "[a] great beast's foot

is chained. It stamps, and stamps, and stamps" (9). I simply want to take note of the movement and rhythm that characterize Woolf's images. We have phenomena that quiver, gather, swim, stamp, and oscillate in scale.

Louis's much-analyzed vision of himself as a stalk rooted "down to the depths of the world" reinforces the claim that the aesthetic finds its roots in the forces of nature. "I am all fibre," Louis notes, "All tremors shake me, and the weight of the earth is pressed to my ribs" (12). He goes on to claim that he hears "tramplings, tremblings, stirrings round me" (12). Louis is comfortable at this level, acknowledging his participation in the tremors of the earth. What Louis is uncomfortable with, but cannot avoid, is the sexualization of art that Woolf and Jinny, especially, insist upon throughout the novel.

Woolf establishes Jinny's centrality to an earthly or exo-human aesthetic discourse immediately in the novel, and she does this, in part, through an emphasis on sexuality. As readers recall, one of the more emphatic and powerful motifs of the opening pages is the kiss, the kiss that Jinny gives to Louis, that Susan observes and is devastated to behold. Here is Louis's initial narration of the encounter: "She has found me. I am struck on the nape of the neck. She has kissed me. All is shattered" (13). Jinny's version of the kiss highlights, among other things, an energy that connects sexuality with creativity. Jinny was running, rather than standing still; she sees leaves moving, and they go on moving despite the seeming absence of a bird in its nest. She is frightened, running faster and faster, asking "What moved the leaves? What moves my heart and legs?" (13). In these early moments, the power of sexual energy is frightening to Jinny on some level, but she connects, through her questioning, the movement of her own body with the movement of the natural world. By the paragraph's end—after she kisses Louis with her heart "jumping" under her pink frock "like the leaves, which go on moving, though there is nothing to move them" (13)—she seems to accept the spiraling together of force, sexuality, and the impulse to excess, all of which are grounded in nature, animality, and evolution. The paragraph ends with these revealing lines: "Now I smell geraniums; I smell earth mould. I dance. I ripple. I am thrown over you like a net of light. I lie quivering flung over you" (13). The movement of Cunningham's moth seems to be captured in such an image.

Other elements of this passage emphasize the becoming-excessive of the living. Flowers are masterful at evolutionary excess. Why are flowers so eternally a symbol of sexuality? Because in addition to offering up their aromas, they also produce excessively attractive sexual "organs," if you will, that are on display for potentially pollinating insects (and for lovelorn humans to experience). All of this is manifested through a startling range of shape and color. Jinny smells geraniums. And lest we be tempted to read the flowers only in their abstracted sense, Jinny also smells earth mould. Her connection to nature is of the earth, not merely symbolic.

Woolf provides another significant investigation of aesthetics and territory early in the novel when Rhoda is depicted with her basin of petals. She wants "white petals that float" when she tips the basin up (18). She drops a twig in as if it is a raft "for a drowning sailor" and uses a sprig of Sweet Alice to serve as lighthouse (18). Rhoda is creating her own imaginary world, but in a sense more literal than we typically indicate by that phrase "imaginary world." Rhoda's is a tiny earth, replete with the powerful forces of tides and the respite of islands that her own ship reaches. That is, she fashions a miniature world of waves; demonstrating the act of artistic territorializing, she frames her own set of vibrations. This process is most clearly revealed when Woolf writes from Rhoda's vantage: "And I will now rock the brown basin from side to side so that my ships may ride the waves" (19). Rhoda appears to create her own waves in what might be understood as an isolated system. It seems possible that this insulated recapitulation of the vibratory is meant to be contrasted to Jinny's "intertwining" of her own bodily system with the actual forces of the earth, to borrow a concept from Maurice Merleau-Ponty. In other words, Rhoda seems to retreat toward a more artificial and representational world of her own, perhaps because the forces that surround her are too overpowering. Jinny, while initially frightened by those forces, is nonetheless revealed as a character who becomes vibratory, or accepts her own becoming-vibratory.

Words also take on an animal nature in Woolf's opening segments. This development clearly links the literary to the animal in Woolf's experimental text. After a passage in which Louis connects language to social and national distinctions and anxieties, three other characters reflect upon the nature of words. For Susan they are like stones, but for Bernard words "flick their tails right and left as I speak them . . . They wag their tails; they flick their tails; they move through the air in flocks, now this way, now that way, moving all together, now dividing, now coming together" (20). Dogs and birds, some of Woolf's favorite creatures, are used here to once again emphasize movement and a living or bodily quality of language. Garrett Stewart's discussion of Woolf's "stylistic drift" is relevant here: Stewart reminds the reader that Woolf claimed to want to "make prose *move*" as never before in this novel (CC 129). Thus, Bernard experiences a becoming-animal of language that seems parallel to Woolf's vision of language in the text. And this becoming is linked to enunciation for Bernard. "As I speak them," he claims, words flick their tails or move in flocks. Perhaps Woolf uses the image of a pack to emphasize the communal qualities or intertwining qualities of spoken language. As people speak to one another, the words are carried as vibratory units that connect body to body. Add to this Jinny's claim that the words are "yellow and fiery" and we have language that takes on a Jackson Pollock quality: it moves, it is full of color. It dances; it splashes. In the 2000 film *Pollock*, directed by and featuring Ed Harris, Pollock seems to be dancing with paint, and

Woolf's sense of language here seems quite similar. We might say Woolf dances with language.

Given all of this flocking and darting of language, it is useful to recall the relationship between birds, birdsong, music, and art in Grosz's readings of Darwin, and to recognize that movement itself seems crucial to Woolf's aesthetic in the novel. Birds and birdsong are featured throughout the novel's interludes, and thus often figure the inhuman elements of aesthetics. Grosz insists that music did not "evolve through natural selection but primarily through sexual selection" (*Chaos* 35). Music functions in evolutionary terms by creating pleasure and attracting one creature to another. In this sense, for Darwin, "it is perhaps birdsong that most clearly reveals the sexual nature of song, the productive role of sexual selection in the elaboration of the arts, and the mutual entwinement of the arts of decoration, performance, staging, and so on, with each other" (*Chaos* 36). Birdsong marks territory, highlights skills in the singer, and attracts and mesmerizes other birds and creatures of other species. It also emphasizes emotion and marks the cultural acquisition of skills that are not reducible to instinct (37–38). Grosz makes an important clarification when she explains, "my claim is not that the bird influences the human, but that the songbird (and the songs of whales) accomplishes something new in its oratory, a new art, a new coupling of (sonorous) qualities and milieus that isn't just the production of new musical elements . . . but the opening up of the world itself to the force of taste, appeal, the bodily, pleasure, desire—the very impulses behind all art" (39). Here is one of Woolf's descriptions of birdsong, from one of the novel's interludes:

> In the garden the birds that had sung erratically and spasmodically in the dawn on that tree, on that bush, now sang together in chorus, shrill and sharp; now together, as if conscious of companionship, now alone as if to the pale blue sky. They swerved, all in one flight, when the black cat moved among the bushes, when the cook threw cinders on the ash heap and startled them. Fear was in their song, and apprehension of pain, and joy to be snatched quickly now at this instant. Also they sang emulously in the clear morning air, swerving high over the elm tree, singing together as they chased each other, escaping, pursuing, pecking each other as they turned high in the air. (*Waves* 73–74)

It's not that Woolf's description replicates precisely a Darwinian vision of birdsong, but rather that the passage emphasizes elements such as the elaboration of emotion, the role of pursuit or sexual play, and the movement of natural musicalities, or as Grosz explains, "the playing out of a certain number of musical themes . . . to create natural sonatas, love songs, requiems" (*Chaos* 39).

In a later interlude, Woolf's description emphasizes even more clearly the "forcefulness" or excessive quality that attends the becoming-artistic of the animal and natural worlds. Woolf also stresses the coloration of birds, a sexual/ artistic quality addressed by Darwin:

> In the garden where the trees stood thick over flower-beds, ponds, and greenhouses the birds sang in the hot sunshine, each alone. One sang under the bedroom window; another on the topmost twig of the lilac bush; another on the edge of the wall. Each sang stridently, with passion, with vehemence, as if to let the song burst out of it, no matter if it shattered the song of another bird with harsh discord. Their round eyes bulged with brightness; their claws gripped the twig or rail. They sang exposed without shelter, to the air and the sun, beautiful in their new plumage, shell veined or brightly mailed, here barred with soft blues, here splashed with gold, or striped with one bright feather. They sang as if the song were urged out of them by the pressure of the morning. They sang as if the edge of being were sharpened and must cut, must split the softness of the blue-green light . . . Now and again their songs ran together in swift scales like the interlacings of a mountain stream whose waters, meeting, foam and then mix, and hasten quicker and quicker down the same channel brushing the same leaves. (*Waves* 109)

A passionate song bursts out of the creature, with enough power to "shatter" the tune of a fellow crooner. Or more powerfully, the song is represented as the "edge of being . . . sharpened" and ready to cut. This particular image, of being itself as a knife slicing through creation, is especially provocative because it emphasizes a kind of sculpting or carving out of new energies and ontologies through a creative and sexually competitive activity.

Making Life

Such inhuman forces can be connected to the novel's human characters by examining how they function *as* forces of creative rhythm, or *in relation to* forces of creative rhythm. And interestingly, it is Jinny who attracts one most in this respect. Jinny seems most vibrational, and ultimately then, perhaps most creative or artistic, in the posthumanist sense. As I mentioned earlier, Jinny is rarely imagined as creative or artistic in Woolf criticism. In fact, she is often reduced to the bodily or sexual, and has famously been labeled a prostitute in Jane Marcus's postcolonial reading of *The Waves*.[50] More recently, Henke characterizes her as having manic passions and as one who "carelessly flits like a moth," and whose activities amount to restless modes of escape ("Ontological Trauma" 135).[51] These readings of Jinny overlook her significance as a character. We need to think more deeply about Jinny, aesthetics, and the forces behind Woolf's waves.

Jinny (like Susan) possesses a "natural happiness" that others clearly envy in the novel (*Waves* 201). She is characterized by undulating movement and her connections to movement, by the bodily as such and her attraction to materiality, and by an awareness of and appreciation for "qualia," or qualitative experiential states. What I am calling Jinny's "totemic fantasy" in *The Waves*, the vision that seems to characterize her in the novel's terms and that recurs throughout the text, is important for a consideration of her character. In the novel's second "chapter," Jinny muses, "for winter I should like a thin dress shot with red threads that would gleam in the firelight. Then when the lamps were lit, I should put on my red dress and it would be thin as a veil, and would wind about my body, and billow out as I came into the room, pirouetting. It would make a flower shape as I sat down, in the middle of the room, on a gilt chair" (34). At first glance, this musing might be characterized as superficial, concerned with conventional notions of female beauty and fashion. One might even be tempted to spurn Jinny's attention to sexual attractiveness, secretly scolding her for catering to heteronormative definitions of women's beauty and sexual availability. These temptations lead many readers to view Jinny as "shallow." But the aesthetic-evolutionary aspects of Jinny's fantasy ought not be overlooked. Normally, in winter, we cover ourselves with heavy clothes, but Jinny wants a dress that is "thin as a veil" and billows about. This detail suggests a more intimate connection between Jinny's body and the dress; it moves with her, it reveals her physicality even in winter, it is part of her "energetic field" in some sense, vibrating right along with her. And consider the final image of this totemic passage in relation to the dress: "It would make a flower shape as I sat down, in the middle of the room, on a gilt chair." Again, here, the flower serves as a signal of the excessive, sexualized nature of aesthetic force. The flower-dress envelopes Jinny, presents her in a performative gesture to her audience of onlookers. She is indeed center stage in this pirouetting presentation of self, and from the perspective of bioaesthetics, performance is a central element of animal aesthetics. Moreover, the gilt chair suggests that Jinny's earthly, passionate becoming-flower is nonetheless accomplished through her attention to couture, in what must be a drawing-room of sorts. High-art or culture finds its roots in nature's excesses, and one is reminded of Donna Haraway's recent discussions of "naturecultures."

Jinny's sensibilities are revealed in connection to affect and movement, and she explicitly links her sense of aesthetics or creation to the inhuman—to animality, the floral, and even to birdsong. In one passage that occurs near the center of the novel, when the characters are in their thirties, Jinny articulates what I would call one of the deep ideological premises of the text that has to do with creative forces manifested through what seem to be wildly divergent natural and cultural arenas: "In one way or another we make this day, this Friday, some by going to the Law Courts; others to the city; others to the nursery; others by marching and forming fours. . . . The activity is endless. . . . Some take train for France; others ship for India. Some will never come into this room again. One may die tonight. Another will beget a child. From us every sort of building, policy, venture, picture, poem, child, factory, will spring. Life comes; life goes; we make life. So you say" (176). There is much to say about this passage, especially in terms of the role of the mundane in relation to art, a theme addressed repeatedly in Woolf's work and in Woolf criticism. I want to note the final suggestion: we make life. This seemingly "straightforward" claim in Woolf's text is utterly salient to our thesis. We don't make art, or literature. We don't live life or experience life. We make life. We create life. Could Jinny be recognizing the becoming-artistic of life itself in its inhuman manifestations?[52] The paragraphs that follow this moment suggest as much.

In the next passage, Jinny links her "bodily" attunement with her *Umwelt* (or life-world)[53] to movement and change in a specifically animal register. She seems even to reject a kind of representational or symbolic relation to the world around her. "[W]e who live in the body," she begins, "see with the body's imagination things in outline. I see rocks in bright sunshine. I cannot take these facts into some cave and, shading my eyes, grade their yellows, blues, umbers into one substance. I cannot remain seated for long. I must jump up and go. The coach may start from Piccadilly. I drop all these facts—diamonds, withered hands, china pots and the rest of it, as a monkey drops nuts from its naked paws. I cannot tell you if life is this or that. I am going to be buffeted; to be flung up, and flung down, among men, like a ship on the sea" (176). The cave seems to be Woolf's metaphor for a reductively symbolic or conceptual aesthetic that transmutes too drastically the qualities of various colors. This kind of creativity, the overly representational, proves stagnant for Jinny; it requires too much sitting or stillness. Like a monkey, she "drops" facts and moves into the crowd where she can join the larger forces of the people, to be "flung" about like a ship on the sea.

Once Jinny has entered "the fray," she essentially inhabits the process of sexual selection, with all the elements of taste, attractiveness, battle, territory and marking that originate in the animal world and reveal to us the fundamentals of art:

> For now my body, my companion, which is always sending its signals,
> the rough black 'No,' the golden 'Come' in rapid running arrows of
> sensation, beckons. Someone moves. Did I raise my arm? Did I look?
> Did my yellow scarf with the strawberry spots float and signal? He has

broken from the wall. He follows, I am pursued through the forest. All is rapt, all is nocturnal and the parrots go screaming through the branches. All my senses stand erect. . . . We are out of doors. Night opens; night traversed by wandering moths; night hiding lovers roaming to adventure. I smell roses; I smell violets; I see red and blue just hidden. (177)

Here, the pedestrian scene is suddenly transfigured into one that takes place in the forest at night. Jinny, like a monkey in the previous passage, is now surrounded by screaming parrots, pursued by her mate. Her scarf signals in yellow and red wisps, like a bird's bright coloration. In fact, later in the passage, she generalizes the scene's meaning by explaining that she hears the "crash and rending of boughs and the crack of antlers as if the beasts of the forest were all hunting, all rearing high and plunging down among the thorns" (177). "One has pierced me," she continues, "One is driven deep within me" (177). The significance of territory in Deleuzian terms emerges in these renderings. As Deleuze and Guattari explain, the artist is "the first person to set out a boundary stone, or to make a mark. Property, collective or individual, is derived from that, even when it is in the service of war and oppression. Property is fundamentally artistic because art is fundamentally *poster, placard*. As Lorenz says, coral fish are posters. The expressive is primary in relation to the possessive" (*Plateaus* 316). Grosz helpfully glosses this concept by explaining that the "boundary is not self-protective but erotico-proprietorial: it defines a stage of performance, an arena of enchantment, a mise-en-scène for seduction that brings together heterogeneous and otherwise unrelated elements: melody and rhythms, a series of gestures, bows, and dips, a tree or a perch, a nest, a clearing, an audience of rivals, an audience of desired ones" (*Chaos* 48). And if there is any doubt about Jinny's experience, the following sentences near the end of this passage seem incontrovertibly to link her sensibilities to the becoming-artistic of the animal and inhuman worlds: "Now let us sing our love song—Come, come, come. Now my gold signal is like a dragon-fly flying taut. Jug, jug, jug, I sing like the nightingale whose melody is crowded in the too narrow passage of her throat" (*Waves* 177).

Life, movement and affect continue to be crucial for Jinny in the novel, perhaps most pointedly in the coming to fruition of what I called her "totemic fantasy" earlier in this discussion. Woolf signals or hails this fantasy's manifestation not only when she begins the scene with the phrase "Here are gilt chairs in the empty, the expectant rooms . . . " but even more bluntly when later in the passage she has Jinny claim, "This is what I have dreamt; this is what I have foretold. I am native here. . . . This is the most exciting moment I have ever known" (101–102). Just as the earlier fantasy indicated, the moment is a social one dominated by "taste, appeal, the bodily, pleasure, [and] desire" (*Chaos* 39). It is also especially compelling because of the central role that movement and dance play in it. Jinny has arrived after dark at what seems to be a socially respectable dance hall. She describes her prepared self in sensory and artistic terms throughout the passage: "My silk legs rub smoothly together. The stones of a necklace lie cold on my throat.... All is exact, prepared. My hair is swept in one curve. My lips are precisely red" (*Waves* 101). And once again, in what would seem a specifically "cultural" milieu, where men are checking their ties and pocket-handkerchiefs, Woolf provides an extremely organic description of Jinny's state of mind or of being: "I now begin," she claims, "to unfurl, in this scent, in this radiance, as a fern when its curled leaves unfurl" (102). She continues in this scene to characterize herself as a plant that is rooted, but yet flows: "I flutter. I ripple. I stream like a plant in the river, flowing this way, flowing that way, but rooted, so that he may come to me" (102). Dance may represent the most perplexing of artistic forms to those who attempt to separate aesthetics from the bodily. In its way this is an obvious claim since for dancers the body *is* the instrument. The "formal" execution of forces, speeds, qualities, and shapes all must be rendered by the body. As I have suggested in my chapter on Duncan, dance helps us think about the vibrational in its specificity as bodily, and about the body's response to and participation in forces and qualities that are clearly more-than-human. In Jinny's totemic fantasy come true, dancing to music with her partner among the gilt chairs seems to frame a moment of the becoming-artistic of her life. Once she has settled on her chosen male, they begin their dance:

> Now with a little jerk, like a limpet broken from a rock, I am broken off: I fall with him; I am carried off. We yield to this slow flood. We go in and out of the hesitating music. Rocks break the current of the dance; it jars, it shivers. In and out we are swept now into this large figure; it holds us together; we cannot step outside its sinuous, its hesitating, its abrupt, its perfectly encircling walls. Our bodies, his hard, mine flowing, are pressed together within its body; it holds us together; and then lengthening out, in smooth, in sinuous folds, rolls us between it, on and on. (103)

The "figure" here can be read as a frame; it functions to cordon off a "space" of sexual performance in which the life forces of two bodies interact in a creative duet. The framing created by the music and dance seems clearest when Woolf writes, "it holds us together; we cannot step outside its sinuous, its hesitating, its abrupt, its perfectly encircling walls" (103). For Jinny, then, it makes sense that dance, the most bodily of aesthetic practices, figures so prominently in her totemic moment of becoming-artistic. Jinny is, after all, the one who spins, and pirouettes, and flutters. Her attraction to dance emphasizes the active force in art, the affective, that which resists hardening into concepts.

Thus, Jinny is positively tied to or actively participating in the vibrational. As the scene above demonstrates she *makes life itself artistic*; she is in herself, in the unfolding of her own life or being, perhaps the most creative character in *The Waves*, if we understand the artistic as the opening up of life itself to rhythm, desire, and excess. And if we understand the artistic to have its roots or its tentacles well beyond the human. Moreover, when Louis is described as having known little "natural happiness," it becomes clear that Jinny functions as his foil. The formally or conceptually artistic in this text are potentially less creative than Jinny, who some suspect may be a call girl.

These readings of the artistic pertain to one of Bernard's observations, a statement that reveals his own recognition of Jinny's mode of being: "We are creators. We too have made something that will join the innumerable congregations of past time. We too, as we put on our hats and push open the door, stride not into chaos, but into a world that our own force can subjugate and make part of the illumined and everlasting road" (146). But the creations here are hardly restricted to human worlds. Rather, the creative force that Woolf reveals, especially in characters like Jinny, opens the human onto its own participation in the inhuman. Woolf's work, despite certain indirect engagements with animality, understands that force, intensity, art, and movement connect the human, the animal, the earth, and the cosmos, within intense vibrational refrains.

4

Strange Prosthetics: Rachel Rosenthal's Rats and Rings

Rachel Rosenthal's complex and extensive body of performance work, spanning from the mid-1970s to the mid-1990s, often circulated around the human desire to control nature, and the concomitant quest to maintain a rationalist or masculine position of superiority through that domination of the nonhuman world. Her interest in humans' ethical relationship to nonhuman animals, and in humans' own animality, is in perfect keeping with these broader thematic emphases. Rosenthal included live animals and addressed animality most explicitly in her 1982 and 1985 pieces, *Traps* and *The Others*, respectively. Moreover, her 1987 performance *Rachel's Brain* foregrounds the problem of the human's constitutive imbalance, or the colocation of high-order cognition and organic, corporeal animality. I should also note that dance was an important part of Rosenthal's history. She took ballet lessons as a child and even danced in Merce Cunningham's junior company in the late 1940s and early 1950s.[1]

Although critics have discussed Rosenthal's use of animals on stage with some frequency, there has been almost no scholarly consideration of her unconventional book *Tatti Wattles: A Love Story* (1996). This text's illustrations, in particular, suggest that Rosenthal understands her creative process itself to be other than human, to be affectively more linked to animality than to humanity proper. Moreover, the intense animal orientation in the book's images is accompanied by a powerful tendency to efface the human, thus "unmasking" human creativity as having animal origins. In this respect, the *Tatti* illustrations reveal even more about Rosenthal's aesthetic engagement with animality than her performances, which explicitly address the species boundary.

In the years just before the 1985 piece *The Others*, Rosenthal included her rat named Tatti Wattles in three performances. Those appearances of Rosenthal and Tatti on stage, in addition to the media attention she was garnering in the 1980s as an artistic persona (who carried Tatti with her nearly everywhere), helped to cement the centrality in Rosenthal's performance work of the human relationship to nonhuman animals. In subsequent years, she spoke repeatedly about her commitment to animal issues. Moreover, Rosenthal announced upon her retirement from the stage in 2000 that she would dedicate her remaining years to animal rights activism and visual art (mostly painting). One current website wraps up its summary of Rosenthal's epic career with these lines: "Rosenthal's work centers around the issue of humanity's place on the planet. She is an animal rights activist, a vegetarian, and companion to two outstanding dogs: a white Siberian hybrid called Sasha, and a puppy of unknown origins called Fanny."[2]

In a 1994 interview with Alexandra Grilikhes on the topic of "taboo subjects," Rosenthal claims: "I've always been more identified with animals than with people. The pain of animals was and is so real to me that I feel it physically in my body."[3] Later in the same interview, she discusses her planning for the piece *The Others,* in which scores of animals and their human companions populate the stage while Rosenthal examines our use and abuse of nonhuman animals.[4] When recollecting her preparations for that performance, Rosenthal explains that she had always sent money to humane organizations but requested they not send her literature because she "knew that reading the literature would make me ill" ("Taboo" 75). In order to stage the piece, however, she later realized she had to look at such material:

> Finally I decided, 'I have to look at this.' For the piece I started to read the literature about the way animals are abused, treated, exploited, totally objectified—as if they are not sentient beings and lack feelings—and it had so strong an effect on me that I contracted myasthenia gravis, a disease which is the result of severe emotional shock. Right now the disease, which I've had since 1985, is in remission, thank goodness. Doing the piece was painful and difficult because it not only brought out all the ways we oppress and torture animals, but there is a whole section in which I become the animal. ("Taboo" 75)

The affective and identificatory transfer in this inter-species moment of empathy may come as a surprise.[5] Rosenthal had contracted a chronic and semipermanent disease, ongoing for ten years at the time of the interview, from her extended study of animal suffering.[6] Her physical body seems to have registered or absorbed the trauma that nonhuman animals are subject to in contemporary life, in a kind of somatic exchange. Rosenthal's corporeal response is an acutely pointed example of what Derrida calls "the possibility of sharing the possibility of this nonpower [with animals], the possibility of this impossibility, the anguish of this vulnerability, and the vulnerability of this anguish."[7] Such a radical affective openness to animal life, in conjunction with Rosenthal's frequent thematizing of the species boundary in her work, suggests that Rosenthal may be one of the most animal-identified performers on record.

Rosenthal's performative investigations of the human relationship to other animals have received a modest amount of critical attention, perhaps most notably in H. Peter Steeves's exquisitely experimental essay, "Rachel Rosenthal Is an Animal."[8] The essay takes the form of a dramatized conversation, where Steeves uses excerpts from Rosenthal's works and imagined responses by figures like Socrates and Phaedrus[9] to explore the sensibilities in Rosenthal's oeuvre that frame animality in performance as more than a symbol of the human. While commenting on Robert Rauschenberg's piece "Monogram," which featured a taxidermied goat inside a rubber tire,[10] Steeves explicitly argues that, unlike this work, Rosenthal's work goes beyond a modernist aesthetic that denies "that there is a context that comes attached to all production" (RRA 5). "The truly postmodern animal," he continues, "is neither paraded on stage as a naïve symbol of some human fable, nor is it placed before us as if it could possibly mean nothing, as if the artist is somehow beyond or outside the web of culture, language, symbol, etc. that makes the appearance of art possible" (RRA 5). As opposed to performance acts like Ralph Oritz's decapitation of live chickens on stage,[11] Steeves argues that

> Rosenthal and her nonhuman performing partners are always and utterly different. Tatti Wattles was not a trained rat doing tricks. Tatti Wattles was not put on stage as a sign for human disgust or fear. Tatti Wattles was not presented as meaning *nothing*, as a thing, as 'a rat.' Instead, Tatti Wattles was acknowledged as animal, as human, as vermin, as rodent, as friend, as lover, as a ham, as feared, as fearful, as brave, as creative, as Rachel, as Tatti, as performer. (RRA 6)

The final moments of *Traps* (1982) help to clarify Steeves's claims here. As Rosenthal circles the stage with Tatti on her shoulder, projected images of her caressing and combing him appear on the screen behind her. The two creatures proceed around the stage as Rosenthal picks imagined fruit for her and Tatti to eat, a symbol of possible hope based on "untapped sources of tenderness and affection in the world."[12] Rosenthal's mocking of evolutionary progress in the piece, and such claims that she is "nothing but a dance of particles . . . mysteriously connected to every other particle in the universe" (*Traps* 91) combine to emphasize Tatti's status as a companion or coparticipant in the moment of the performance, rather than as an overly manipulated symbol of Rosenthal's thematics.

Tatti already has functioned as a kind of fulcrum for discussions of Rosenthal's relationship to animals in performance. Despite those discussions, however,

Rosenthal's book *Tatti Wattles: A Love Story* has received almost no critical attention in performance studies, animal studies, or feminist studies.[13] I want to examine this book in part because of the contrast it provides to Rosenthal's experience of becoming ill after reading about animal suffering. In fact, this text (published in 1996) seems to function in a curative manner. Rosenthal's production of the illustrations for the Tatti book appears to have served as a healing mechanism that also produced an exploration of her general relationship to bioaesthetics. Thus, *Tatti Wattles* helps me to address the question of Rosenthal's aesthetics as such in relation to animality, rather than addressing the contours of specific performances or specific Tatti appearances on stage. In other words, while Steeves has powerfully drawn attention to the "posthuman" stage presence of Tatti as an individual, in his singularity, I want to examine Rosenthal's aesthetic practice *itself* in relation to animality. The book devoted to Tatti helps me do that.

Tatti Wattles is an unconventional, esoteric text that functions as part memoir, part elegy, and part didactic reflection on the contemporary plight of nonhuman animals in a postcapitalist culture. The book's written text constitutes a fascinating and intense description of Rosenthal's emotional connection to her rat companion.[14] Early in the book, Rosenthal recalls Tatti: "You were a beautiful little creature, Tatti Wattles. I want to tell this to the world. For the world knows your kind as enemy, vermin, anonymous flesh pool used in abominable laboratory experiments, or as food for snakes. I have known you as an individual and I want to open people's eyes to you as an individual—for it is only when we see others as unique, precious, and irreplaceable that we will be ready to assume our full humanity."[15] The written text is characterized by such commentary, and by a tender retelling of Tatti's life with Rosenthal. On the other hand, the illustrations, all drawn by Rosenthal, speak to a much broader vision of Rosenthal as artist, and to questions of aesthetic inspiration, specifically. The illustrations are also incredibly bizarre and surreal. In one, Rosenthal's evacuated heart or breast area is occupied by a large rat; in another, rats enjoy a traditional picnic just outside a tunnel-like structure that looks like the entrance to a large stomach. But many of these curious depictions suggest that Rosenthal views her performative practices as being deeply connected to the inhuman. Thus, I want to consider how the pictorial component of Rosenthal's unusual book may address the relationship between animality and aesthetics in a way that was not necessarily the focus, or intentional topic, of the book.

The disjunction or productive tension between the written text and the visual components might best be understood through the work of Julia Kristeva on the semiotic. That is, the drawings in the book appear to express a *choric* quality that "precedes evidence, verisimilitude, spatiality, and temporality."[16] They don't "make sense" in terms of the signifying economies to which we are accustomed.

The drawings seem outrageous and fantastical, to be sure, and I want to emphasize their pre-verbal or extra-verbal, supplementary relationship to the written
text. Rosenthal explains near the end of the book that these drawings are based
on visions she had during shamanic workshops in which she was involved after
Tatti died. The shamanic seems perfectly aligned with the semiotic on some level,
because it deals with the "other than rational" or the prerational, the mythic, the
animist.

Although the primary subject of *Tatti Wattles* is the undeniably meaningful
and personally potent companionship Rosenthal experienced with Tatti, I want
to suggest that the subtext of the book circulates around the way that animality
subtends Rosenthal's self-identification as an artist as such. This subtext is
presented performatively, through the book's illustrations, both the major, color
illustrations and the more minor black and white drawings. The images also are
marked by Rosenthal's "auto-graphy" as a mover or dancer, by alimentary motifs,
by the concept of mediation, and by the taming of human exceptionalism. These
elements in Rosenthal's "vision" of her artistic practice, self, and process are repeatedly aligned with animality, specifically with the rat (as individual) and rats
(in general).

Creative Becomings

The cover image of *Tatti Wattles* sets the stage for these inhuman markers of
animality (dancing and the alimentary, for instance) in Rosenthal's aesthetics.
Rosenthal titled this image "Rats Show Me a Heart in the Upper World," and the
cover is technically a detail from a larger work (see Figure 4.1). Most striking and
unconventional are this cover illustration's two main figures, occupying both the
upper left and lower right quadrants of the cover and thus dominating the visual
space. In the upper left floats a large and traditionally drawn heart shape that in
its formal outline could be taken straight off a Hallmark greeting card, and in the
lower right is a dancing Rosenthal figure. The heart shape is even made to radiate
or shine like a hyperconventional children's graphic might, with white beams
emanating from its lower portion. But the viewer is immediately struck by the fact
that the gray-colored heart is composed of a mass or swarm of rats. It's a startling
juxtaposition, because the pastel pinks, purples, and greens in the illustration's
other clusters of images suggest an almost cotton-candy, dreamlike world of play
or fairytales. The gray rats floating in their buoyant, solar heart shape, seem to
shed light on the rest of the scene's objects. Despite this centrality and planetary
benevolence, the viewer is never quite able to reconcile the rat motif with the elfin
pastels that define the rest of the illustration. If one were to try counting the rat
bodies in the gray heart motif, they would surely number near a hundred.

Figure 4.1 Rats Show Me a Heart in the Upper World. Illustrations by Rachel Rosenthal.
© Rachel Rosenthal Trust.

The swarm of undifferentiated rodents in the book's cover image enacts precisely the pack, multiplicity, or proliferation that Deleuze and Guattari identify
as central to becomings-animal. Indeed, their discussion in "1730: Becoming-
Intense, Becoming-Animal, Becoming-Imperceptible" begins with an analysis of
becoming-rat in the film *Willard,* and they go as far as claiming that "every animal
is fundamentally a band, a pack" (*Plateaus* 239).[17] This Rosenthal figure on the
book's cover can thus be understood as highlighting a becoming-animal of the

performing body. Rosenthal seems to be dancing an artistic overcoming of the human in the image. That is, through its depiction of Rosenthal's relation to a rat multiplicity, as I will continue to describe, the illustration suggests that her *performative* identity is more animal than human. Although Rosenthal has said she is personally more identified with animals than humans, as I noted earlier, these illustrations reveal a similar, posthumanist quality within her creative practice.

The instability of the species boundary in the image is further highlighted by the analogous movement of the rat tails and Rosenthal's scarf. The emphasis on movement is crucial here, given that the dancing body itself, as I have discussed in earlier chapters, would have a privileged relation to Deleuze and Guattari's becomings imperceptible, animal, and intense, because movement is "by nature imperceptible" and thus signals transformation or metamorphosis (*Plateaus* 280). Rosenthal's dancerly images also give us a particular purchase on Deleuze and Guattari's insistence that "*becoming is a verb* with a consistency all its own; it does not reduce to, or lead back to, 'appearing,' 'being,' 'equaling,' or 'producing'" (*Plateaus* 239; my emphasis).

Rosenthal not only crafts this autobiographical figure through an unmistakable image of dancing, but she also emphasizes mediation or channeling. Standing on one foot with the other leg raised in an anterior sagittal, parallel *attitude*, the Rosenthal figure looks toward the heart as her pink scarf flutters back and upward. While the figure's face is turned toward the rat-heart, her arms and hands are outstretched like the scarf in an ecstatic and energetic line that moves *away* from the rats and toward the viewer. One of the more fascinating elements of the illustration is that this torsion or tension seems to signal precisely how the relation to animality is not only elegiac in this text, but it is also a relation that manifests itself through Rosenthal's artistic praxis. That is, Rosenthal figures herself as a kind of aesthetic *medium* in this image, torqueing an inhuman artistic message toward the viewer.

I already have discussed a Deleuzian understanding of the vibratory as a common force that is infectious, almost viral across the arts. The idea of the artist channeling a vibratory, cosmic force appears in various ways across artistic commentaries. For instance, the experimental German composer Karlheinz Stockhausen in his wildly unconventional 1968 "score" for musicians *Aus Den Sieben Tagen (From the Seven Days)* writes to the player in his section, "Litany":

> I do not make MY music, but only relay the vibrations I receive; that I function like a translator, that I am a radio.
>
> . . .
>
> Now comes the difficult leap: no longer to transmit man-made signals, music, tintinnabulation, but rather vibrations which come from a

higher sphere, directly effective; not higher above us, outside of us, but higher IN US AND OUTSIDE.[18]

This fragment from Stockhausen surely functions as an artist's statement in the most catholic sense, as well as in the most Deleuzian sense.

Mediation, in Stockhausen's sense, undergoes a radical transvaluation via animality in Rosenthal's cover image. While Stockhausen seems to locate the source in the air, or the "spheres" in a more traditional sense, he insists that the source is "in" us, reinforcing a notion of the vibratory that connects human to nonhuman. He suggests further that the "higher sphere" is not "higher above us," thus calling into question certain hierarchies of being often associated with the cultural. But Rosenthal goes further, for the source in the cover image is clearly animal. Rosenthal is depicted as transmitting, passing along, the vibratory power of this source through her aesthetic practice. Moreover, I want to suggest that the practice of performance art itself may present a particularly rich case of the self-transformation that Grosz associates with the affective, with the way that the human "overcomes itself" through certain nonhuman becomings (*Chaos* 77). Grosz is interested in the "virtual conditions by which man surpasses himself and celebrates this surpassing . . . *by making himself a work of art*, by his own self-conversion into a being of sensation. Affects are man's becoming-other, the creation of zones of proximity between the human and those animal and microscopic/cosmic becomings the human can pass through. Affects signal that border between the human and the animal from which it has come" (*Chaos* 77; my emphasis). Although Stockhausen to some degree makes himself a work of art, he nonetheless uses external instruments for his channeling.

Rosenthal's practice has been described by Bonnie Marranca as "autobiology," and Marranca is quick to point out that "performance art is primarily a solo form *made on the body of the performer*" (my emphasis).[19] Marranca's concept of the autobiological clarifies why Rosenthal has figured herself as a dancer throughout *Tatti Wattles*. In other words, for the dancer, the body itself is the medium, the body itself or biology itself inhabits the sensations, the vibratory, the forces of the earth and the cosmos, the affective. And if affects link us to the animal from which we have come, then Rosenthal's attribution of aesthetics to the animal in its specificity confirms her performance practice as a kind of autopoiesis of the post-Darwinian human, the human that experiences and negotiates the episodic resurgence of animalities "within" itself.

This kind of celestial debunking in the cover image of *Tatti Wattles* happens not only through the ratty nature of the solar "source" of aesthetic inspiration, but also in a much less overt image, the purple clouds. Rosenthal's clouds are, in fact, so intestinal in their appearance that the viewer must work very diligently to recognize that they are meant to represent clouds in this psychic landscape. What they clearly resemble is, again, intestines. Thus, the cover signals an alimentary motif at the heart of her aesthetic dynamic. Moreover, the flapping scarf only intensifies the delineation of movement in this figure. It seems to function as a tail, as Rosenthal's tail. The images appear to posit a central connection between tails and movement, creativity, and the intestinal. I will return to the tail later in this discussion. For now, I want to focus on the alimentary in Rosenthal's iconography, a theme that functions as a reminder of the human's own animality in her work.

Food has been a principal question in Rosenthal's performance work. Moira Roth notes that throughout much of her adult life, Rosenthal was aware of "her weight problem and her obsession with food."[20] For her piece *Soldier of Fortune,* Rosenthal was photographed eating seven-course meals at seven high-end Los Angeles restaurants (Tatti joined her for some of these meals). Una Chaudhuri, in her critical commentaries on Rosenthal's work, skillfully turns her attention to carrots, eggs, and cake as they have been used on stage in various pieces, also highlighting the importance of food to Rosenthal's work.[21] Perhaps Rosenthal's most piquant treatment of the alimentary occurs in *Rachel's Brain* (1987). This iconic piece features as its central prop a head of cauliflower as brain. And it is the irreconcilability of rational and animal that constitutes the cauliflower's traversing emblematic power in this performance work. The opening scene of the piece, in which Rosenthal plays Marie Antoinette, evokes the image of the severed or isolated head in order to emphasize a specifically Cartesian disavowal of that which is not cerebral. The lengthy monologue in this scene begins with the line, "I am the flower of the Enlightenment!"[22] (RB 116). The disavowal of animality in its specificity is not far behind as Rosenthal croons, "My head, hovering over a cloud of talcum powder, is neatly sev- / ered from the beast. I am a higher human! . . . I am a thought machine! / Je pense donc je suis. / La tête c'est moi. / My head is me" (116). She goes on to gloss the body as "the others below" (116), a phrase that cleverly references her own earlier piece *The Others,* which has as its overt theme the violent disavowal of animals and animality at the center of human culture.

When Rosenthal proffers a cauliflower "brain" as edible human flesh in *Rachel's Brain,* the ironic play on symbolic cannibalism proliferates in a nearly uncontrollable refraction of meanings and their dismantling. Eating brain itself gives the lie, in a radically superlative manner, to the notion of the *cogito* as disembodied human presence, and it does so in a supremely materialized and abjected register. Rosenthal's performance soon makes it clear that the oh-so-precious brain is not only edible, in her performative universe, but it is also passable as excrement. Indeed, Rachel's highlighting of the passage of brain into waste product suggests that the highest of human functions is "shit." In other words, she casts profound suspicion on the humanized subject through this particular alimentary segment of the performance.

It is not uncommon for artists to frame their creative practices in scatological terms. James Joyce may be most famous for such tropes of creativity.[23] Although the passages in *Rachel's Brain* aren't necessarily focused on the creative process itself as scatological, the intestinal image on the cover of *Tatti Wattles* does suggest a certain centrality of the alimentary in Rosenthal's vision of her creative life. Perhaps what compels in Rosenthal's case is the way that the alimentary cannot be cordoned off from an ethical recasting of our relation to other animals. Her performance work suggests a link between recognizing our own bodily vulnerability and recognizing the need to respect the bodily integrity, fragility, and suffering of nonhuman animals. Thus Rosenthal's commitment to vegetarianism and her animal rights activism seem relevant here, within the framework of her general recalibration of humanist values.

Faces, Tails, and Footprints

A clear ethical recasting of human preeminence is represented in the illustration "Reunion with Tatti in the Lower World" [*Tatti* 6] (see Figure 4.2). In the "Reunion" illustration, the human is dwarfed by a giant rat, and the dwarfing does not partake of any seeming distortion, miscommunication, disciplinarity, or redirection. Rather, the dwarfing of the human is figured as an enriching and even ennobling moment that takes on spiritual overtones. This image accompanies the very first page of Rosenthal's written text, in which nearly every sentence begins with "I loved" and goes on to describe some quality or element of Tatti or Tatti's behavior. The image is, again, startling in its extremely unconventional depiction of the rat, who is historically viewed as a pest or an instrument in scientific experimentation—an object to be killed or subjected to testing. On page seventeen of *Tatti Wattles*, Rosenthal writes a mock-up of the horrified reaction her reader might have to this rat memorial. It reads, in part, "Rats are dirty. / Rats are mean. / Rats bite. / Rats bring on the PLAGUE! / Rats are pests. / Rats are vermin. / Rats eat babies. / **RATS!** / Rats are to be exterminated!" (*Tatti* 17). And despite this conventional view of rats, we have the "Reunion" image in which an enormous Tatti stands towering over Rosenthal in what can only be described as an attitude of benign munificence.

As is typical of these images (and which I will discuss further), the Rosenthal figure in the "Reunion" image is only visible from the back, so we see the profile of her famously bald head, an adorned ear, and no real facial features. Moreover, Rosenthal's head is more figurative than literal, with an abstract ear but no other details that would give it individuated form. Tatti, however, who stands with his

Figure 4.2 Reunion with Tatti in the Lower World. Illustrations by Rachel Rosenthal.
© Rachel Rosenthal Trust.

front visible, is drawn in great detail, comparatively. His white belly shows, his large eye peers down at Rosenthal, his facial features are clear, with nose and whiskers specifically rendered. In other words, the effacement of the human in this image is directly correlated to the excessively detailed facial presence of the rat. There can be no doubt that this rat is depicted as some sort of muse, an inspirational figure, a kind of beatific presence. Tatti is clearly portrayed as imparting something valuable to the receptive Rosenthal figure, whose arms are outstretched in a receptive partial embrace.

Moreover, the two visual extensions that one notices coming away from the circular frame of this particular illustration mark out a space of animality. First, on the lower left, what begin as flowers seem to morph into animal tracks, rendering the trace of animal footprints just below the Rosenthal figure's own shod feet. Given that Tatti's foot-paws are bare, the image suggests that Rosenthal's artistic signature is rather what I will call a "poditure," more animal than human, more of the foot than the hand. In other words, Rosenthal's mark is subtly realigned away from Heidegger's handedness, with all of its troubling anthropocentric presumptions that I have outlined in other chapters. In Rosenthal's image, the identifying mark is disassociated from the hand and redirected toward a more "bestial" and "a-human" footprint as artistic autograph. Second, the very large tail that extends off Tatti's body carries the snaking, alimentary energy that we have already seen in the cover image. This tail turns the entire circular illustration into a kind of primordial, amoebae figure that is propelled or moved by Tatti's tail. Even though the two figures in the illustration are standing still, the overall image is characterized by movement because of the placement of the tail. We might even want to link the intestinal and the tail-like in these two early images in *Tatti Wattles*. In very broad terms, Rosenthal's artistic and ethical project seems to be partly premised upon the recuperation of animality as it is signaled by the alimentary and an affinity for the tail, all of which suggest that her performative aesthetics are characterized by a Deleuzian becoming-animal.

Strange Prosthetics

In what is nearly the physical center of Rosenthal's book, there is a kind of centerfold, the only two color illustrations that are exhibited side by side, so that the text is exclusively visual. The two drawings featured here may arguably be the most visually pleasing, as well, from a traditional pictorial viewpoint. (see Figures 4.3 and 4.4) For my purposes, they are the most compelling in terms of the question of bioaesthetics.

When considering the two central illustrations side-by-side, it is important to notice that they seem to represent Rosenthal in two complementary moments of creative practice. In the first, titled "Planting Rats in a Rice Paddy. They Grow into Big Trees Filled with Parrots," [p. 38] she seems to be planting "seeds" of artistic knowledge. As the title indicates, the seeds are rats. Here, the self-portrait is characteristically drawn from a posterior angle, and Rosenthal's face and most of her head are obscured. She is leaning over, barefooted, with a rat in her right hand that she prepares to plant. The activity or agency of the rats is notable in this image. Even though they are quite small in scale, they look and lean in various directions, sniff and "gesture" with forearms in ways that clearly emphasize their individuality. Their gestures also echo the dancerly way in which rats are depicted on the inside front and back covers of the book: There, Rosenthal's

Figure 4.3 Planting Rats in a Rice Paddy. They Grow into Big Trees Filled with Parrots.
Illustrations by Rachel Rosenthal. © Rachel Rosenthal Trust.

small sketches of rats include a few of them leaping. Another compositional element of the drawing accentuates animals' bioaesthetic capacities: Rosenthal
keeps the trees in the picture completely white so that the coloration of the birds
is set in sharp relief. And while three of the colorful birds are sitting on tree limbs,
four larger parrots are depicted in flight, mostly with fully spread wings and even
with exaggerated feather spans. The movement of the creative creatures is a

Figure 4.4 Catching Gold Rings with a Rat, on Top of a Needle Formation Made of Rats.
Illustrations by Rachel Rosenthal. © Rachel Rosenthal Trust.

dominant visual element in the composition of the drawing, and complements
the movement of the Rosenthal figure on the opposite page, which I will now
address.

In the second illustration, Rosenthal appears to be interacting with the creative knowledge planted and "grown" in the first. In one sense, therefore, the
Rosenthal figure is slightly more passive in the first image, and then becomes

more agential in the second. Rosenthal names the second illustration, "Catching Gold Rings with a Rat, on Top of a Needle Formation Made of Rats" [p. 39]. It has a Seussian quality with its giant sun in the background, needle-like mountains as landscape, and quirky figuration of Rosenthal. Shaped here, once again, as a dancer with one leg lifted, this Rosenthal figure is balancing on a demi-pointe relevé. The precarious balancing on top of the needle suggests risk, and a kind of poise in moving beyond the conventional or expected. It also should be linked to the idea of transferability, which I will come to in a moment.

One of the most remarkable facets of this second center illustration is the fact that Rosenthal's extended right arm and hand "catch" a gold ring not through their own powers, but through the powers of the rat that she holds. Indeed, the rat in her right hand takes on a prosthetic quality, and at first glance it genuinely appears to be an extension of her reaching arm. There are more than a few noteworthy points about this prosthetic rat/hand. Although recent work on the prosthetic often forgets the distinction, it is nonetheless true that a classic prosthesis is an *artificial* substitute for the original organ. In this case, we have a living animal acting as hand or reaching appendage for/with Rosenthal. Interestingly, then, the fact that this "substitute" is also a living, discreet creature would seem to make the human-animal boundary even more porous in Rosenthal's supplementary iconography.

David Wills reminds us that prosthesis in a broad sense "treats of whatever arises out of that relation, and of the relation itself, of the sense and functioning of articulations between matters of two putatively distinct orders: father/son, flesh/steel, theory/fiction, translation/quotation . . . nature/artifice, public/private, straight/limping, and so on."[24] In this case, the ostensibly distinct orders are animal and human. Rosenthal's reaching rat/hand obviously troubles our received ideas about the unbreachability of the species barrier. Moreover, Wills's discussion of both the grammatical and anatomical prosthetic and its emphasis on transfer gives us a way to further understand Rosenthal's tipping posture in this image:

> The significance and effect of transfer is not something subsequent to a given prosthesis but rather what occurs at its beginning, as its beginning. Prosthesis occurs as a rapid transfer. . . . One could posit for it another type of beginning in the conjugational disjunction—the dysfunctional syntagmatic transfer—of a peculiarly irregular Latin verb, *ferre* (to bear; past participle *latum*), doing double duty in a hermeneutic gesture that relates and refers everything back to a series of shifts, bringing discourse back to a fact of being borne, to a point of weight transfer. . . . from leg of flesh to leg of steel, it is necessarily a transfer into otherness, articulated through the radical alterity of ablation as loss

of integrity. And this otherness is mediated through the body, works through the operation of a transitive verb—*movere, ferre*—signifying first of all something carried by the body. (*Prosthesis* 12–13)

My point about the image, therefore, is that Rosenthal's specific bodily position in this illustration—balanced on demi-pointe, one leg in the air, precariously leaning off the tip of the rat-needle into space—serves precisely to accentuate the idea of transfer inherent in the prosthetic as such. The image suggests that a cross-species transference is at the heart of Rosenthal's aesthetic vision. Rosenthal's creative agency is not merely augmented by the rat, but the rapid transfer of "catching" is both hers and the rat's. They function as coeval. And as in the "Reunion" image discussed earlier, the rat here as extension and first feeler suggests an animal primacy in the affective register for artistic work or perception.

Cary Wolfe addresses animality and the prosthetic in his discussion of the potential interlocking concerns of animal studies and disability studies. The most well-known example of this line of inquiry is Wolfe's discussion of the blind person with a guide dog. This prosthetic relation between human and nonhuman animal has historically framed the animal as a mere object that "ables" the blind person. But Wolfe counters that we might better understand this relationship as constituting "a shared trans-species being-in-the-world constituted by complex relations of trust, respect, dependence, and communication" (*Posthumanism* 141). In his larger discussion of trends in disability studies, Wolfe emphasizes the problematic critical focus on ability, activity, and agency, while countering that we are obliged to address the shared finitiude and passivity of the living in general, what Derrida discusses repeatedly in his later work on the suffering and passion of the animal. Susan McHugh elaborates upon these claims in her extended discussion of the guide dog and "power sharing among differently embodied agents" (*Narrating Across* 64).

The "Rings" illustration posits a shared *creative* agency between Rosenthal and the rat, so that the complex relations of trust and dependence that Wolfe and McHugh theorize would clearly apply here, albeit in an artistic and performative register. Wolfe analyzes the prosthetics of subjectivity itself at some length in *What is Posthumanism?*[25], and I want to suggest that Rosenthal's image thematizes the prosthetics of *creativity* itself. This creative prosthetics involves the human being off-balance and reaching "beyond" itself, across the species barrier. What can the rings represent if not aesthetic projects, fulfillments, inspirational cues or insights? Rosenthal shares this creative reaching and dancerly negotiation of artistic process with the rat.

The combination of eulogy in the text with bioaesthetic images also provides a commentary on one of the central theoretical debates in animal theory at this moment: the emphasis on *thanatos* versus *bios* that I raised in the Introduction. Rosenthal's book as a whole was written as a kind of elegy to Tatti after his death. Indeed, the first several pages are a blow-by-blow recollection of Tatti's death and Rosenthal's own feelings of guilt and anguish at his passing. On the other hand, the illustrations speak to his power or agency in the artist's creative life. Rosenthal's book can, therefore, be said to acknowledge that we share with animals both our mortality and our vitalistic becoming-other through creative and artistic life forces.

Ornamental Animality

I want to end this chapter by considering one of the black and white sketches in *Tatti Wattles*. This sketch [p. 29] (see Figure 4.5) most clearly illustrates what I have identified as the hallmark effacement or erosion of the human and the concomitant visual plenitude of the rat throughout the book. Specifically, the outline of Rosenthal's head, characteristically viewed from the back, is absolutely sparse. A single line is traced from right shoulder all the way around, demarcating a bald head, hint of brow and cheekbone, and chin. The left ear is similarly minimalist, given no additional features other than what makes it most sparingly recognizable as an abstract ear. Attached to this effaced figure of the human head *through the earlobe* is Tatti, the rat figure. Tatti is illustrated with comparatively immense detail. His fur is depicted, his eyes and nose, his whiskers—all these features are meticulously rendered. Indeed, the whiskers around Tatti's eyes are drawn to provide a sense of his individual character or disposition. Rather than illustrate human specularity in this text, Rosenthal elides human looking and repeatedly highlights animal vision.

In fact, in the image that accompanies the title page of the book, "Rats Approve the Tatti Book During the *Snakes in the Eyes* Journey," Rosenthal's own eye sockets are occupied by two snakes that emerge and intertwine just in front of her forehead (see Figure 4.6). In the upper-left corner of this picture, a large rat peers down toward Rosenthal, and other rats scrutinize small versions of the Tatti book itself. The animal gaze seems to replace or coincide with the human gaze in some of Rosenthal's images. This shared vision is usefully contrasted with Derrida's staging of his confrontational and shameful being-seen by an animal, "caught naked, in silence, by the gaze of the animal . . . I have trouble repressing a reflex of shame," which I have discussed in the Duncan chapter (*Animal That* 3–4). Rosenthal surely experiences the animal's gaze as a self-illuminating force in these images, but perhaps the "laying bare" of the human is experienced without the emphasis on shame for her.

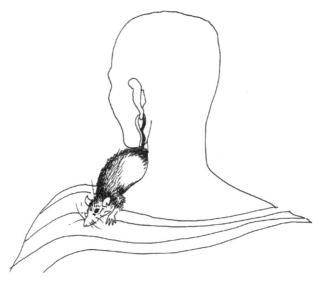

Figure 4.5 Illustrations by Rachel Rosenthal. © Rachel Rosenthal Trust.

Figure 4.6 *Rats Approve the Tatti Book During the* Snakes in the Eyes *Journey.* Illustrations by Rachel Rosenthal. © Rachel Rosenthal Trust.

Moreover, Tatti metaphorized as earring gets to the heart of this discussion of animality and the artistic. Tatti in this portrayal is ornamental embellishment and aesthetic adornment, but in a radically atypical manner. The use of *dead* animals, animal skins, animal bones, and animal furs is highly conventional across cultures, and rehearses what Derrida would call the logic of sacrifice at the core of human practices of adornment.[26] Wearing fur, for instance, is charged with the violent and erotic message of dominance and of the destruction of another being for the sake of fashion.[27] In Rosenthal's drawing, the rat is living and sniffing the air, investigating: The rat is agential and appears to be acting out his own desires. This rat is far from Bataille's subject-turned-object in order to calm human fears about our own objectification.[28] Indeed, the particular mechanism of attachment between rat and human is fascinating in this illustration. Tatti's tail is looped through Rosenthal's ear, just as the post of an earring would be. The tail, an appendage that induces intense ambivalence in the human, moves through Rosenthal's own flesh and then comes back around to "close" the loop. In other words, there is no part of the tail left hanging or open in the illustration; the somatic connection or interimbrication is rendered as whole or complete, suggesting corporeal unity. Rat and human seem inseparable, with their flesh intermingled. Indeed, the tail is the more agential force in this arrangement, as it pierces through passive human flesh and forms its interlocking loop. Moreover, the overt inclusion of Tatti as embellishment tends to emphasize Grosz's claim that adornment, display, and excesses of the body are artistic impulses that humans share with nonhuman actants. Although a first impulse might be to read this image as Rosenthal "using" Tatti as a mere tool of adornment, the illustration has an opposing effect. Especially given its effacement of the Rosenthal figure, the sketch seems to place the human "in its properly inhuman context" (*Undone* 21). This image reinforces how Rosenthal imagines or understands her creative powers as more animal than human. She effaces the aesthetic force of the conventionally human artistic "vision" and elaborates animality's role in creative and performative practice.

5

UnCaging Cunningham's Animals

There seems to be an emerging, though still partly veiled, recognition of Merce Cunningham's engagement with animality across his choreographic career. Cunningham died in 2009 after decades of being recognized as one of the most important choreographers in the second half of the twentieth century, and beyond. His works are now restaged regularly, despite his own directive that his company should disband after his death. In a *New York Times* article published in 2017 titled, "Merce Cunningham's Multifaceted Mirror, Held Up to Nature," well-known dance critic Alastair Macaulay remarks that "For over 50 years, Cunningham kept developing the potential of [his] study of zoology" across many works that are called his "nature studies."[1] But after describing a number of pieces that address "flora and fauna," Macaulay ambivalently claims that "it remains curious that Cunningham so recurrently devoted dance poetry to these nature studies" because he lived in an urban environment; yet, Macaulay then insists that Cunningham was deeply influenced by zoos and wildlife documentaries. What Macaulay overlooks, as can be typical of mainstream responses to Cunningham's dances, is the deep strain of bioaesthetic impulses that runs through Cunningham's dance works and his thinking about dance. If we look closely, we can see how Merce Cunningham, despite being repeatedly associated with an "architectural" style of movement, is also very much the inheritor and progenitor of a vibrant animality that has been the focus of this study.

Merce Cunningham and John Cage are generally considered innovators of the post-1950s, postmodern era in dance and music, an era that eschewed narrative or representational forms of art. They have been most critically celebrated for using chance methods in unconventional ways in their creative processes and productions, an element of their work I will return to later in this chapter. It turns out, however, that Merce Cunningham also regularly drew sketches of animals in his personal notebooks, often on a daily basis, for the greater part of his mature choreographic career. Many of those animal drawings were published in 2002, in a book titled *Other Animals*. Despite being viewed as a primarily "structural" innovator in twentieth-century dance, Cunningham also can be seen as an inheritor and subsequent progenitor of the animal eruptions that Isadora Duncan unleashed decades earlier.

Animals have tended to occupy a whimsical role in Cage and Cunningham's creative undertakings, but we ought not mistake that position as nonserious. When talking about the value of music, John Cage often insisted on the primacy of sound. But he also accentuated the importance of being delighted. His emphasis on delight serves to highlight the trans-species role of pleasure in the rhythmic and vibrational milieu of the living in general, which has been the preoccupation of this book. Although animals and animality were not necessarily a constant or primary focus for Cage, what we might call a creatural experience of sound certainly seemed to be. Moreover, in the fashion of J. M. Coetzee's protagonist David Lurie in his novel *Disgrace*,[2] one of Cage's early compositions called "Black Mountain Piece," "considered the first true sixties-style 'happening,' involve[d] piano playing, poetry recitation, record-players, movie projectors, dancing, and, possibly, a barking dog."[3] As Alex Ross explains, this "happening" was performed in the eighteen months or so leading up to Cage's famous piece, "4'33"" from 1952. Thus, animals did surface as agents of sound in his compositional work. In a number of interviews with Cage and with both Cage and Cunningham, Cage's resistance to a conceptual or representational theory of music turns on the valuing of what we might call bare sound, after Agamben. Moreover, the pleasure that he obtains from sound is connected, spontaneously, to animal pleasure, in a particularly revealing interview.

In that interview, recorded in 1991, Cage explains his rejection of a "psychological" understanding of music, wherein music represents feelings or experiences. He insists upon the value of traffic noise in this particular discussion: "What it does is it gets louder and quieter, and it gets higher and lower, and it gets longer and shorter. It does all those things which I've . . . I'm completely satisfied with that. I don't need sound to talk to me."[4] Cage goes on to detail the manner in which people respond to these ideas:

> When I talk about music, it finally comes to people's minds that I'm talking about sound, that doesn't mean anything, that is not inner but is just outer, and they say, these people who understand that finally, say, you mean it's just sounds? . . . Thinking that for something to just be a sound is to be useless; whereas I love sounds just as they are. And I have no need for them to be anything more than what they are. I don't want them to be psychological. I don't want a sound to pretend that it's a bucket, or that it's a president, or that it's in love with another sound. (laughter) I just want it to be a sound. ("another sound")

After describing people's typical responses to his ideas about sounds, Cage invokes Immanuel Kant's idea that laughter and music are two things that don't need to have "meaning": "Don't have to mean anything, that is, in order to give us very deep pleasure," he clarifies. And immediately upon claiming this, Cage turns to his cat, saying "you know that, don't you?" ("another sound"). He then momentarily plays with his cat, who nips at Cage's fingers. Here Cage links human animality to nonhuman animality through the pleasure of bioaesthetic, vibrational forces. This moment is reminiscent of another interview from the film *Cage/Cunningham* by Elliot Caplan. In that interview, Cage insists, "I actually prefer sound to music, and I *like* the sounds that I hear"[5] (my emphasis). Cage again accentuates pleasure, what already exists, and what is not constructed through human artifice.

These encounters with Cage provide useful context for thinking about Cunningham's relationship to animality, both in his own bodily aesthetic, and in his ideas about dance and his immensely influential corpus of choreographed works. Additionally, and crucially, this chapter will examine the little-discussed Cunningham book of drawings, *Other Animals* (2002), in relation to performance pieces such as *Beach Birds* (1991), *Ocean* (1994) (which uses whale and dolphin voices in its soundscape and was inspired by comments about James Joyce), and *BIPED* (1999). Cunningham's cultivation of "pure-dance" and his architectural aesthetic need to be complemented by a study of the way animality runs through his body of work. His propensity for drawing vibrantly colored animals, for instance, links him back to Duncan, who modeled her dance movement on the "free animals." Moreover, specific illustrations in *Other Animals* are remarkably reminiscent of the depictions of animal hordes in Virginia Woolf's *Lugton* tale that I have discussed in Chapter Three. This examination of Cunningham, therefore, allows me to trace the vibratory, excessive impulse of bioaesthetics from modernism to the early twenty-first century, connecting this impulse to a "postmodern" dance artist who is rarely considered in relation to animal theory.

It would seem obligatory at the beginning of this chapter to acknowledge that many critics claim it is "impossible" to write about Cunningham's work.[6] This impossibility often is linked to the way that Cunningham understood dance as that which ought to stand outside of representation, to at least a large degree. Cunningham, like Cage, was "not interested in telling stories or exploring psychological relationships: the subject matter of his dances is the dance itself" according to David Vaughan (MC 1). As early as 1948, Cunningham described dance at a conference at Vassar College as "organized movement in a specified time and space," and stressed that, unlike ballet and other early forms of modern dance, "dance need not, and indeed, should not have a literary meaning" (MC 44). Particularly interesting for our purposes is the recollection from the Vassar discussion that Cunningham felt that "the meaning of dance is in the doing and that it should not try to put across an idea. Dancing for him is a reflection of human behavior in dance form, and because of this it is [in] no way an abstract art" (MC 44). As Vaughan himself explains, "This does not mean that drama is absent, but it is not the drama in the sense of narrative—rather, it arises from the intensity of the kinetic and theatrical experience, and the human situation on stage" (MC 1). I will return to this line about the "human situation" on stage, as that situation seems rather inhuman the moment one begins to look at it closely.

Cunningham and Cage are best known for one of their particular artistic experiments, namely, the use of chance procedures (not pure improvisation). This practice, which has perhaps been critically fetishized to some degree, produced for the two artists' collaborations a kind of "organic" structure rather than a lack of structure or chaos (MC preface). When discussing their process, Cage was also fond of quoting Thomas Aquinas: "art imitates nature in the manner of her operation" ("Searching"). Critical receptions and discussions of Cage and Cunningham's work—like Isadora Duncan's work—have sometimes overlooked the natural in "nature," however, and the animal in its specificity. In other words, discussions of Cunningham's aesthetic commitments and proclivities have tended toward the "mathematical," perhaps in an attempt to associate the seriousness of his artistic innovations with a discourse perceived as serious. As with Duncan, critics may be consciously or unconsciously rescuing these artists from the natural strains that are so prominent in their creative practices.

There is a kind of irony in the valorization of chance as a mathematical framework (rather than, say, an evolutionary or "biological" framework) because Cunningham deeply resisted the all-too-human urge to represent ideas or narratives in a traditional sense on stage. That is, Cunningham was invested in the way that modern dance—in certain forms at least—should undo the overly symbolic or cognitive. It is also germane to note what Edwin Denby and others observed about Cunningham's own dancing body. When Cunningham was a young performer, embarking on his first concerts with Cage, Denby described him in the following manner after seeing Cunningham perform a solo titled *Mysterious Adventure* (January 1945) at the Hunter College Playhouse:

> Mr. Cunningham reminds you that there are pure dance values in pure modern technique. He is a virtuoso, relaxed, lyrical, *elastic like a playing animal*. He has an instinct for a form that makes its point by repetition, each repetition being a little different, and the phrasing of each difference exceptionally limpid. He has a variety of drive and speed which phrases his dances, and better still an improvisatory naturalness of emphasis which keeps his gesture from looking stylized or formalized. (MC 37; my emphasis)

When Denby sees a second iteration of this piece in May of the same year, he writes that Cunningham is presented as a "sort of playful animal creature of fancy," but notes, "There is no mimicry of animal motion in the number, but there is dance illusion of a nonhuman world. It is a difficult and delicate effort to try but an original and serious one" (MC 37).

David Vaughan's book also notes an early piece from 1951 with the title *Boy Who Wanted to be a Bird*. This was a solo on Martha's Vineyard that was set without music. The famous moth anecdote that I mentioned in Chapter Three, in relation to Woolf, is associated with this piece. When a woman asked Cunningham after the performance how he could dance without music, he noticed that "in this funny, dark little place, a gorgeous moth flew in and began moving in the most spectacular way around the one light. And I just pointed" (MC 63). Cunningham's lesson is partly that the human body itself in its living, embodied duration is already and always—by virtue of being creatural—partaking in cosmic vibrations and rhythms amidst the forces of its lived environment. Thus, the dancing body need not be spurred by an outside, forced structure of formal music. Animals doing mating dances are a clear example of this self-activated becoming-rhythmic. The human body also can harness, express, and invent its own bioaesthetic forces and rhythms in connection to itself and the contours of its situated life-world. The title of Cunningham's solo piece, therefore, is especially interesting in its suggestion that nonhuman creatures precede us in such art-inducing capacities, and that dancers especially long for an embodied becoming-aesthetic. Moreover, it is particularly interesting that Vaughn writes, "The solo, about which Cunningham remembers nothing, was never performed again" (MC 63). Might we consider this a particularly Nietzschean moment of animal forgetfulness? Although it is not the only early piece of which Cunningham had minimal memories, perhaps this marks some "originary" half-forgetting that is worthy of note, and that is answered, to some degree, by much later works such as *Beach Birds*, which I discuss below.

The ethos of the Black Mountain Summer School in 1952 that Ross references above as the site of the first "happening" is evoked by Cunningham, who describes that titular piece in the following manner: "Cage organized a theater event, the first of its kind. David Tudor played the piano, M. C. Richards and Charles Olson read poetry, Robert Rauschenberg's white paintings were on the ceiling, Rauschenberg himself played records, and Cage talked. I danced. . . . There was a dog which chased me around the space as I danced. Nothing was intended to be other than it was."[7] The presence of a dog that chased Cunningham around the space, in what can be assumed a nonchoreographed or undirected "role" for that animal, lines up with Cunningham's claims in his essay "Space, Time and Dance" (1952). The final paragraph of that piece is worth citing in full here, which comes after Cunningham's suggestion that his and Cage's innovations allow dance to be "free to act as it chooses":

> For me, it seems enough that dancing is a spiritual exercise in physical form, and that what is seen, is what it is. And I do not believe it is possible to be "too simple." What the dancer does is the most realistic of all possible things, and to pretend that a man standing on a hill could be doing everything except just standing is simply divorce—divorce from life, from the sun coming up and going down, from the clouds in front of the sun, from the rain that comes from the clouds and sends you into the drugstore for a cup of coffee, from each thing that succeeds each thing. *Dancing is the visible action of life.* (MC 67; my emphasis)

Cunningham articulates the dancer as embedded in the rhythms of the material environment, as a creature affected by the circadian rhythms of sun and moon cycles, weather patterns, and the like. Getting a cup of coffee is not best understood as a cognitive decision but as a body's response to changing material conditions in one's lived world. The dancer is not an artifice-seeker but a moving, breathing enactment of life forces that entangle the dancer with the nonhuman and material forces of all other life. This view provides a piquant context for Carolyn Brown's comment upon taking her first master classes with Cunningham in the 1950s (Brown worked as a Cunningham dancer for decades). Brown writes, "Merce gave two master classes. I took both of them. I'd never seen anyone move like that—from such a quiet center, with such animal authority and human passion."[8]

Although Cunningham was intensely opposed to narrative or highly theatrical forms of "expression" in dance, his comments about his work nevertheless link him in important ways to Isadora Duncan and her commitment to nudity that I discussed in Chapter One. From his earliest work as a choreographer, Cunningham disavowed what had been developed by artists like Martha Graham as highly symbolic and emotional figurations in twentieth-century dance. For instance, when discussing the piece *Suite by Chance* in 1953, Cunningham opines, "It was almost impossible to see a movement in the modern dance during that period not stiffened by literary or personal connection, and the simple, direct and unconnected look of this dance (which some thought abstract and dehumanized) disturbed" (MC 69). He goes on in the same passage to claim, "My own experience while working with the dancers was how strongly it let the individual quality of each of them appear, naked, powerful and unashamed. . . . It was unprompted by references other than to its own life" (MC 69). The valuing of nudity and the unashamed liveliness in his individual dancers, and his repeated return to the force and centrality of "life" in his comments, echo Duncan's philosophical commitments that take formal dance in a species-crossing direction, and away from the "deadly" strictures of ballet.

The more-than-human quality of dance in Cunningham's conceptualizing is not accidentally animal; he explicitly links it to the creatural in one of his most important theoretical tracts on dance. In this short essay from 1952, "The Impermanent Art," Cunningham is once again at pains to take dance out of the realm of representation. Dance is not "social relationships" nor "emoting" he insists, but rather is "more primal than that"; it is "energy" a "source of energy" that may be channeled into emotion, but which is not itself emotion (MC 86). Cunningham goes on to call the essence of dance a "bare energy" (MC 86). In the same section of his essay, he discusses the idea that dance must be expressing "images deep within our conscious and unconscious," and claims that "there is no need to push for them" (MC 86). And further, crucially,

> I am no more philosophical than my legs, but from them I sense this fact: that they are infused with energy that can be released in movement (to appear to be motionless is its own kind of intoxicating movement)— that the shape the movement takes is beyond the fathoming of my mind's analysis but clear to my eyes and rich to my imagination. In other words, *a man is a two-legged creature—more basically and more intimately than he is anything else.* (MC 86; my emphasis)

It is worth pausing here to note that Cunningham explicitly connects dancing as that which is "beyond" mental analysis to the basic, earthbound, and creatural fact of human embodiment and morphology. Man is a two-legged creature, more than anything else. Cunningham further decenters the cognitive and champions an embodied "racial" memory, which also may be understood as a species memory. If you "really dance," he claims, "—your body, that is, and *not your mind's enforcement*—the manifestations of the spirit through your torso and your limbs *will inevitably take on the shape of life.* We give ourselves away at every moment. We do not therefore, have to *try* [MC emphasis] to do it. Our racial memory, our ids and egos, whatever it is, is there. If it is there, it is there; we do not need to pretend that we have to put it there" (MC 86; my emphasis).

Cunningham goes to almost extreme lengths in this major essay ("The Impermanent Art") to keep the "natural" at the center of his ideas about dance, despite the fact that his use of chance operations has garnered more attention in critical and cultural discourses than his other philosophical commitments. To that end, he discusses his recently performed "Untitled Solo" and immediately elevates the organic "bones" of the dancing over the use of chance methods:

I choreographed the piece with the use of "chance" methods. However, the dance as performed seems to have an unmistakable dramatic intensity in its bones, so to speak. It seems to me that it was simply a question of "allowing" this quality to happen rather than of "forcing" it. It is this "tranquility" of the actor or dancer which seems to me essential. A tranquility which allows him to detach himself and thereby to *present* freely and liberally. Making of himself such *a kind of nature puppet that he is as if dancing on a string which is like an umbilical cord: mother-nature and father-spirit moving his limbs, without thought.*" (MC 86–87; my emphasis)

Given the way in which Cunningham has been framed as an architectural and sometimes bloodless choreographer, these images of umbilical connection to the natural world—and the dancer as a "nature puppet" that moves "without thought"—are noteworthy. I am suggesting they have been disavowed or ignored to a significant degree in discussions of Cunningham's legacy (although Carrie Noland, whom I discuss shortly, helpfully emphasizes many of Cunningham's "natural" engagements). My point is that these are highly biological and creatural frameworks at the heart of Cunningham's notion of what is "essential" to dance work. In Cunningham's fetal image, the dancer is fed in a primordial, precognitive way by a natural life force. Dancing is inextricably linked to the natural, generative biological world in this most fundamental, raw manner. Dancing is most importantly "in our bones," rather than in our brains.

Carrie Noland's recent work on Cunningham gestures toward a recognition of how animality might be important to an understanding of Cunningham's choreography. Noland is interested in the question of expression or the expressive in Cunningham, and articulates a complex set of interconnections between Adorno's ideas about aesthetics and Cunningham's "practical and theoretical interventions," which she feels can "illuminate more traditional literary and philosophical discourses on the aesthetics of expression."[9] Noland argues that when Cunningham refers to the "human situation on stage," he is (in the 1950s) beginning to differentiate between two kinds of expression. That is, Noland suggests that the human body "is doubly expressive: it can be expressive transitively, in an easily legible, culturally codified way, and it can be expressive intransitively, simply by exposing its dynamic, arc-engendering force" ("Human Situation" 54). Noland links this latter force with what Adorno calls the "proto-subject" and further describes it as "a set of kinesthetic, proprioceptive, weight-bearing, and sometimes tactile problems to be solved" and, also, as an "*embodied response to the present moment,* an embodied response to the utterly unique conditions of existence at one given point in time" ("Human Situation 55).[10]

Elaborating on Adorno's notion in *Aesthetic Theory* of a "primordial senso-rimotor apprehension captured mimetically in art," Noland then connects these concepts to Darwin's "corporeal intensities" or forms of protoexpression ("Human Situation" 56). Part of her detailed work in this segment of her argument is trained on the decoupling of expression from hackneyed or culturally sanctioned gestures, thus Cunningham "trusts that by preventing the conventional sequencing of movements within a phrase (through the application of chance procedures) he will coax dancers to exhibit dynamics that are . . . utterly idiosyncratic . . . radically subjective, we might say, in the sense that they are generated by the singular body of the dancer confronting an utterly unique 'human situation on stage'" ("Human Situation" 57). Here Noland turns to Cunningham's essay "The Impermanent Art" (1952), where he calls dance "more primal" than emoting and links it to a "blatant exhibiting of energy . . . geared to an intensity high enough to melt steel in some dancers" (qtd. in MC 86). Noland connects this corporeal energy to Darwin's discussion of animal "intensities," noting that Cunningham seems to recognize how humans always try to interpret (she uses the term anthropomorphize here) animal behaviors. In Cunningham's resistance of codified movement or sequences, then, according to Noland, "One could even say that Cunningham attempts to de-anthropomorphize our understanding of *human* behavior on stage" ("Human Situation" 58).

Finally, Noland discusses Cunningham's use of the example of wild animals in Disney films who are musically robbed "of their instinctual rhythms" (qtd. in MC 10) to explain why he separates music from choreographic work. She then claims that a kind of sympathetic, mimetic animal signifying, a "set of wild gestures" ("Human Situation" 58), is what Cunningham seems to be after all along. Noland thus significantly privileges animality in her argument when discussing "human" protosubjective expressivity. If we turn to Cunningham's drawings in particular, they help confirm that a very animal kind of "wildness"—however we may want to qualify such a term—is central to Cunningham's aesthetic worldview. He seems to identify or sympathize with animals, all the while perhaps mining (rather than miming) their own aestheticized bodily extravagances and their attunement to evolutionary creativity as part of his choreographic inspiration. I should reiterate that part of my attraction to writing about Cunningham's drawings has been their occasional yet remarkable affiliation with themes or image formats that I've analyzed already in this book. Thus, I'm suggesting an approximate arc or line of affiliation that runs from Duncan's ideas about "free animals," to Woolf's hordes and monkeys, to Cunningham's various images in his notebooks. There are far too many images in Cunningham's book *Other Animals* to describe adequately here, but one of my aims is to highlight at least some that have interesting resonances within this particular investigation, alongside others that call for a bioaesthetic interpretation on their own merits.

In an early segment of *Other Animals*, a notebook page dated 1/9/97 characteristically marks the time, weekday, and weather conditions, but then includes—covering the left margin of the paper from top to bottom—eight small sketches of animals including sharks, rabbits, bats, dogs, and other creatures (OA 14). To the right of these images, Cunningham writes: "What would this diary look like on the internet? A child's scribbles? It doesn't provide info, but a visual mix-up look. Blotch is curled onto a chair. It's cold, snow coming, an inch . . . How to whip oneself together on a dreary Thursday, mid-week stasis"[11] (see Figure 5.1). Cunningham considers the amateur nature of his drawings here, describing them as not fit for public consumption (the Internet). The phrase "child's scribbles" draws our attention for several reasons. First, it is true that Cunningham's handwriting is often unclear and difficult to decipher in the notebooks. Even on this single page, there are a few words that remain very difficult to read. The reference to scribbles thus recalls the "anti-handedness" in Duncan's work, but through a different register. The undoing of clear, abled human handwriting on pages that include animal sketches is itself of interest. But Cunningham surely refers also, if not mainly, to his sketches, or drawings, as scribbles. Either way, the emphasis on childishness is important for reasons that are by now familiar to readers of this book. As I discussed in earlier chapters, Diana Fuss and others identify children and animals as beings whose liminal status unsettles the boundaries of the human. Like Woolf, whose children's story may have permitted her a less rigid or prescriptive artistic exploration, Cunningham is very playful throughout his sketches and notebooks (which he seems not to have anticipated would be published for public consumption). Moreover, since Blotch is the name of a companion animal, then the "blotting" and "blotching" of animal forms in these notebooks seems especially charged with the question of animal energy. The need of "whipping oneself up" to do the work of creative, bodily art-making is perhaps just as animal as human, in a "mix-up" kind of way.

Cunningham further hints at his relation to a bioaesthetics that is characterized by envious approximation and sympathetic borrowing in a notebook page dated 4/25/97. Here he draws a scarlet ibis that takes up a significant portion of the space, writing: "The endangered scarlet ibis, ravishing in color and contour, beset by the evils of jealous humans. What right has it to be so beautiful when we ungainly bipeds must putter on? The morning light on the veranda is rich, gaudy, and glorious. Face the day, pumpkins. Crack the shell the way the chicks do" (OA 42) (see Figure 5.2). This passage implies, with its emphasis on an endangered species, that human destruction of nonhumans is fueled by envy of their artsy bodies, of their "color and contour," the very markers of aesthetic taste that I have been discussing throughout this project.[12] Cunningham even connects the bird's bodily aesthetics to the "gaudy, and glorious" morning sunlight. He figures a variety of human self-loathing and a clumsiness that is specifically linked

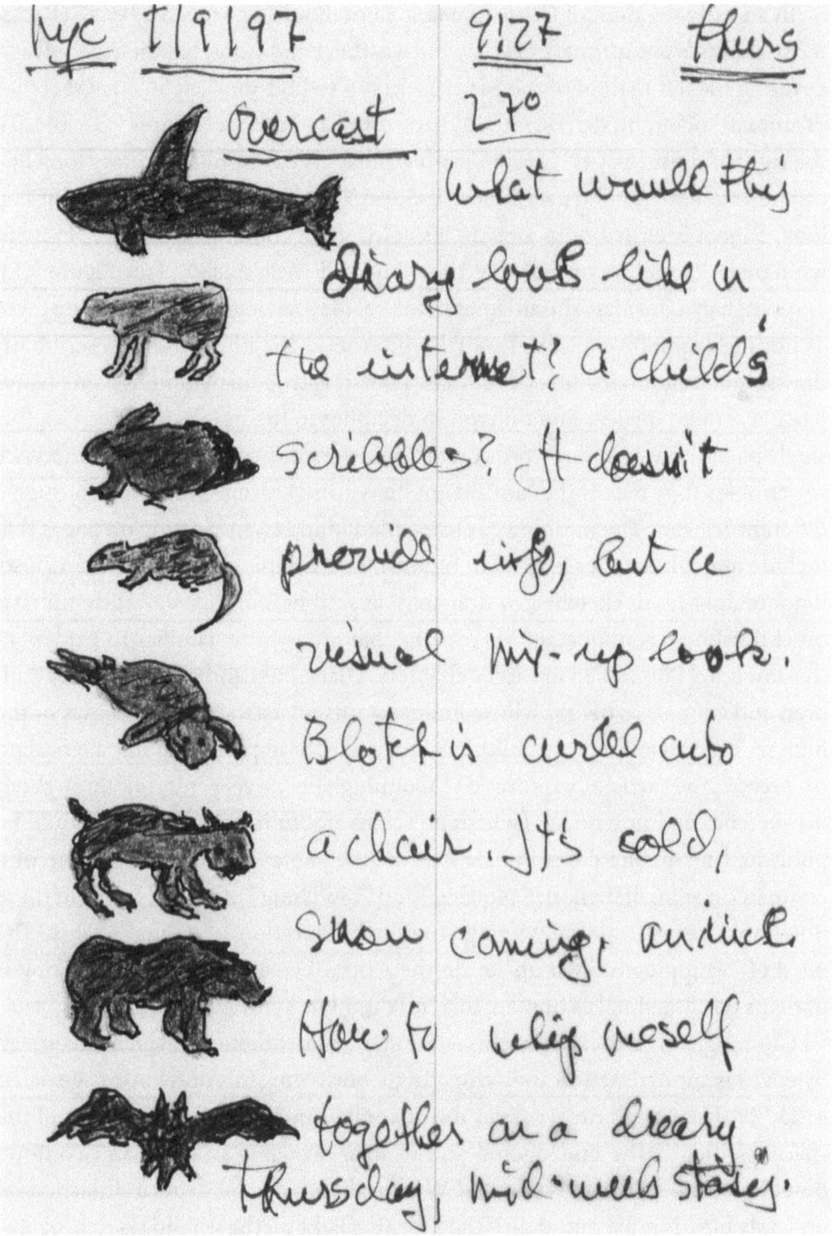

Figure 5.1 Images provided courtesy of Laura Kuhn. ©Merce Cunningham Trust.

to our bipedal stance. Cunningham thus bemoans as an aesthetic hindrance humans' erection from all fours, typically hailed as securing our vertical and specular exceptionalism among the living. Of course, birds are not quadripedal, but Cunningham still ties human awkwardness to that particular stance. Does

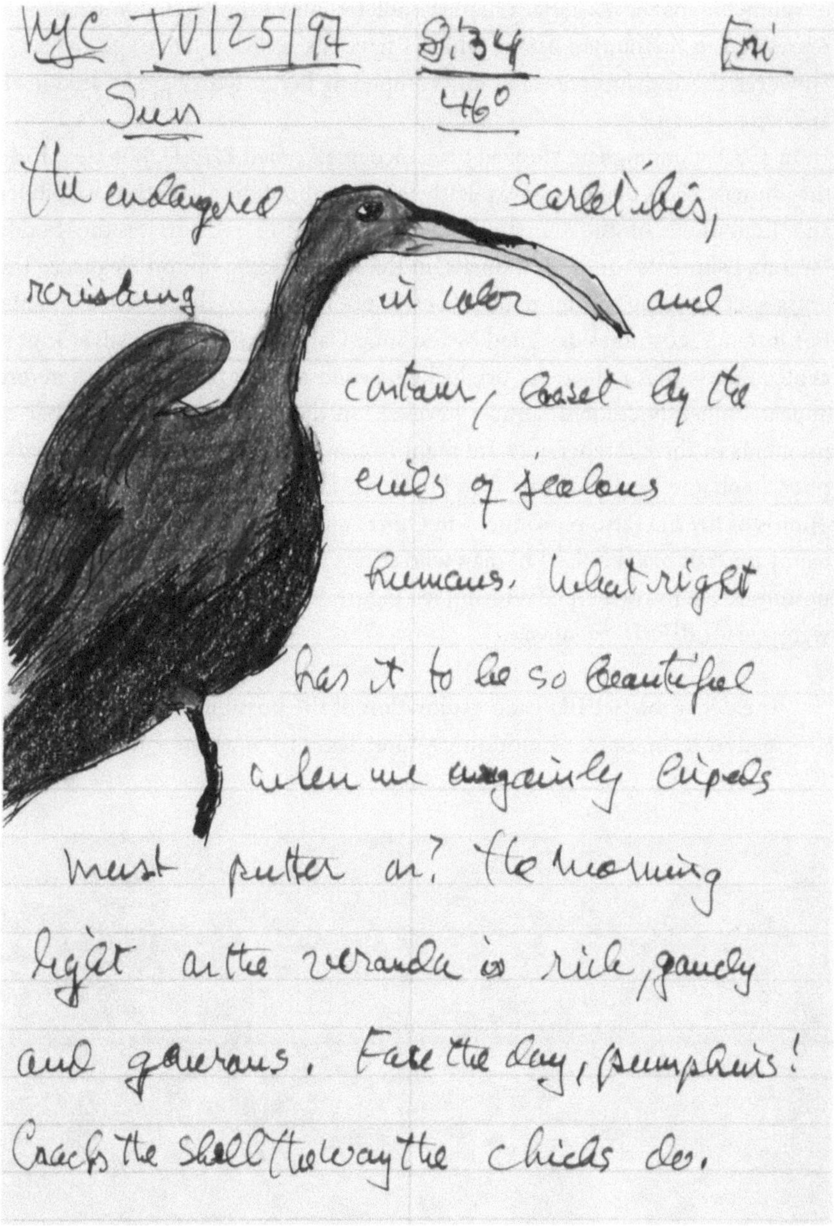

Figure 5.2 Images provided courtesy of Laura Kuhn. ©Merce Cunningham Trust.

the capacity to fly mitigate such awkwardness in birds? Regardless, these brief remarks, at the least, imply that had *Homo sapiens* remained quadripedal, and more "animal," they might have been more graceful and more aesthetically functional in their most basic forms of locomotion. Cunningham's notion of ungainly bipeds recalls certain literary indictments of the "ugliness" of organic repression in the human estate, which I have discussed at length elsewhere.[13] However, these claims are especially compelling because they are located in an aesthetic register.

In 1999, Cunningham showed his dance work called *BIPED*. It is clear from the journals, then, that he was explicitly thinking about the aesthetic possibilities and limitations of the human body, specifically in relation to the bodily "accomplishments" of other animals, in the years leading up to that piece. The cross-species comparison seems reflected in a number of the work's elements. For instance, costumes designed by Suzanne Gallo for *BIPED* are silver irides-cent unitards that reflect the bright lights used for the piece. They therefore appear brilliantly colored, almost jeweled, on the dancers. And a number of moments in the choreography are flight-like, as an image caught by photogra-pher Stephanie Berger reveals (see Figure 5.3). Moreover, another of Berger's photos of *BIPED* (also reproduced in *Other Animals* [OA 57]) provides an un-canny portrait of a digitized human who seems to look down, perhaps in disap-pointment, at its own bipedal form (see Figure 5.4). As the Cunningham Trust webpage for *BIPED* explains:

> The décor for **BIPED** is an exploration of the possibilities of the ani-mation technology of motion capture. The digital artists Paul Kaiser

Figure 5.3 Stephanie Berger © 2017. Copyright belongs to Stephanie Berger. All rights reserved.

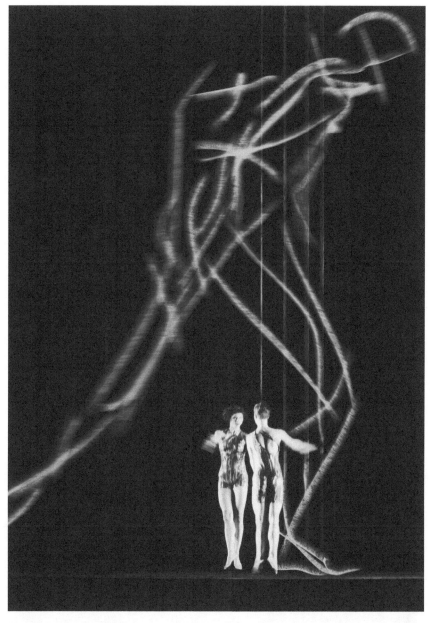

Figure 5.4 Stephanie Berger © 2017. Copyright belongs to Stephanie Berger. All rights reserved.

and Shelley Eshkar collaborated with Cunningham, who, working with two dancers, choreographed 70 phrases that were transposed into digital images. These animated images, as well as abstract patterns (vertical and horizontal lines, dots, clusters), are projected on to a scrim at the front of the stage, behind which the live dancers may be seen. Cunningham also used computer software, DanceForms, to develop the choreography for the dance, which is in a number of sections: solos, duets, trios, and ensemble dances.[14]

I also would suggest that the digital patterns and shapes projected on the scrim for *BIPED* serve as prosthetic, hyperaesthetic qualities for the human forms, in order to exaggerate their bodily becomings. That is, humans do not sport the brightly colored feathers of the scarlet ibis, but the digital projections often appear to "en-feather" and enhance the dancers and their movements, suggesting a more highly elaborated "animal" aesthetic for the dancers' human movement and on-stage creations (see Figure 5.5).

Cunningham's final line on his notebook page about the scarlet ibis (where he discusses cracking the shell like a chick does) is also notable because he likens his self-cultivated motivation to continue doing creative work to the breaking through of some integument by juvenile animal energy and perseverance. We might even consider this comparison an alignment of creative practice with the "instinctual" at its most elementary—instinct as a creatural force that is trained toward embarking upon and enacting life. Yet, it is important to note recent work on instinct that asserts the complexity and noninstrumentality of the instinctual. Brian Massumi, for instance, theorizes instinct in relation to a "supernormal"

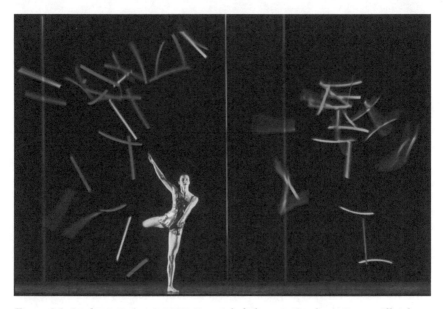

Figure 5.5 Stephanie Berger © 2017. Copyright belongs to Stephanie Berger. All rights reserved.

animal capacity that is dynamic and that "twists the situation into a new rela-
tional variation, *experientially* intensifying it. What is in play is an immanent experiential excess by virtue of which the normal situation presents a pronounced
tendency to surpass itself."[15] Massumi's discussion of the plasticity, rhythms,
and patterns that attend "instinctual" bird behaviors studied by the ethologist
Niko Tinbergen, and his claims that instinct should be understood as the way
"life extends its own activity into objective-event mode," make Cunningham's
egg-cracking analogy nicely translatable to the antiutilitarian spirit of creative
practice ("Supernormal" 12). It is worth reiterating that Cunningham's chick
metaphor for creative work is a far cry from a "conceptual" or cognitive configu-
ration of aesthetic energy or aesthetic process.

Another striking feature of Cunningham's book *Other Animals* is that it
includes several images of multispecies animal hordes, in addition to images
of primates that are particularly liminal in their human-like appearance. These
images reprise a number of questions that I have considered in earlier chapters.
For instance, the animal hordes in Cunningham's book are strikingly similar to
Duncan Grant's portrayal of creatures in the first illustrated version of Virginia
Woolf's story, *Nurse Lugton's Golden Thimble*. As I noted in Chapter Three, I am
interested in the way these images suggest a dynamism and instability of the
block of animality itself that also reflects the border-crossing between human
and inhuman creativity. The appearance of these images in the work of artists
as different as Woolf and Cunningham is noteworthy. Perhaps the horde image
instantiates a kind of creative involvement or involution, an aesthetic attitude,
or practice that post-Darwinian artists can express more explicitly than artists
might have in earlier historical eras. As I have claimed, the dreamlike image
of multiplicity—especially in the details where the boundaries or borders
of individuals merge or are shared in Cunningham's drawings—suggests the
constant mutation, improvisation, and ultimately species instability that mark
Darwin's theory of evolution.

The horde images not only dismantle our conventional sense of species
distinctions but, in doing so, they confirm the way in which creativity or aesthetic sensibilities deterritorialize the human via animality. In other words, in
my reading, human creativity is being situated within a trans-species swarming
here, wherein the human individual, or "subject" (or "genius"), gives way to
oscillations and multiplicities of dynamic, creative living forces in general. These
forces do not simply include animals but have a particular cathecting interest in
animals. There are three major horde images in Cunningham's *Other Animals*
(which suggests that Cunningham may have drawn these with some frequency,
given that only a portion of his drawings are collected in the book). The horde
picture that appears last (of the three) is in many ways the more "radical" and un-
tidy. The first two include animals' bodies or faces that are relatively demarcated,

even though they visually float, hover and merge—to some degree—with the other images. Yet in the final horde sketch, the space is more visually packed with segments and partial renderings of various animals (OA 64) (see Figure 5.6). It is difficult to decipher many of the animal shapes in their specificity, especially from a moderate distance. I submit that this image is highly suggestive of corporeal improvisation, in the way that Noland discusses it. The composition of the picture itself is gestural and has a kind of "wild" visual movement. So, the

Figure 5.6 Images provided courtesy of Laura Kuhn. ©Merce Cunningham Trust.

sketches tend to confirm that animality is indeed at the heart of the innovations in dance practice that Cunningham was undertaking across the twentieth century. The "unofficial" or "doodling" work of both Cunningham and Woolf detail a kind of ontological entangling, a becoming-animal or deterritorializing of the human through a Deleuzian multiplicity of the horde that seems to be part of how they understand their aesthetic engagements.

Another specific deterritorializing of the human as Creator is keenly registered in the image of a moving or dancing monkey that Cunningham pens (OA 56). Just as the monkeys in Duncan Grant's illustrations of the Woolf story are almost distressingly hybrid in their oscillation between human and animal features, Cunningham's monkey appears very weird (to use one of Tim Morton's favorite terms) along species lines, as it does a bipedal dance of sorts (see Figure 5.7). I should note that very few of the images in Cunningham's text include animals that are overtly dancing. But we can compare the monkey to the dancing ostrich on the frontispiece of the book, with its leg and foot outstretched in a kind of arabesque. That is, a few of the images are explicitly dancerly. These may suggest that Cunningham makes dance the animals he views as somehow "closer" to humans or even to human dancers. In other words, the primate is genetically a

Figure 5.7 Images provided courtesy of Laura Kuhn. ©Merce Cunningham Trust.

near-cousin to the human, and the ostrich, in a different way, might be viewed as "lyrical" or graceful simply because of its anatomy. It thus has a dancerly appeal. More generally, these overt images of animal dances in the text suggest that creative forces or creative sources for human dancers and choreographers are not strictly human within Cunningham's imaginary, even if the images seem slightly awkward or "staged." Cunningham's monkey, like the mandrill in the contemporary illustrated version of Virginia Woolf's children's tale, gazes directly outward at the viewer. This is one of the few creatures in Cunningham's *Other Animals* who does so. As I noted in Chapter Three, Derrida and Weil theorize the animal's look in ways that trouble human exceptionalism. In this case, as in the images accompanying Woolf's short story, the monkey's gaze can be read as a direct challenge to our human-centered notions about the artistic.

Other images and their accompanying text in Cunningham's book point up the importance of bodily adornment and extravagance as enactments of performative enticement in sexual selection. Cunningham's "oddly plumed bird" (OA 58) appears with bright yellow feathers in a fringe around its face, drawn as if to evoke lightning or electricity, in a note dated 11/25/97 from Belfast (see Figure 5.8). This image seems clearly to showcase a rockhopper penguin, a bird that has bright yellow feathers emerging from above the eyes and the crown, that are sometimes referred to as "eyebrows" in common parlance. This creature also stares straight out at the viewer in Cunningham's sketch. The notes on this page describe a touring Cunningham's "dreary view" out the window in Belfast, and suggest that the unusual bird might "clear the spirit." Thus, the artistic excess of the animal's body is meant to provide encouragement or a sympathetic "electrification" for Cunningham, the artist. I find this page especially compelling because of the way in which the "electric" yellow feathers of the sketched penguin are aligned with creative inspiration, often traditionally construed as a flash or bolt of light that illuminates the artist's work, path, or process.[16] Therefore, an animal's elaborated, performative body is affiliated with the kind of creative inspiration that is sometimes associated with transcendent or spiritual impulses from "on high"; these impulses are, conversely, often dissociated from the mundane, the bodily, the animal. Moreover, one of the general refrains of these notes is Cunningham's weariness, or melancholy, and his concomitant need to find "spirit" or courage to continue in his artistic and performative work. Cunningham's habitual attention to his "colored animal drawings" (OA 59), as he calls them in a different note from Belfast (dated 11/29/97), seems to provide a spur to continue doing artistic work, particularly dance work that is pointedly *of the body*.

The animal drawings are perhaps most interesting, then, for their "electrifying" or bringing to vibrancy Cunningham's aesthetic forces in a general manner. However, the thread of animality in its specificity, or a creatural, nonhuman

Figure 5.8 Images provided courtesy of Laura Kuhn. ©Merce Cunningham Trust.

force, in his choreographic work is also of interest, yet has received scant critical attention. While I will not attempt an exhaustive discussion of this question across his vast, decades-long oeuvre, I do want to examine *Ocean*, and its precursor, *Beach Birds*, two of Cunningham's "nature studies" that were performed in the 1990s.

John Cage had the idea for the piece that eventually would be performed in 1994 as *Ocean*, but this would not happen until after his death (he died in 1992). The well-known piece *Beach Birds* (1991) was performed instead of *Ocean*, largely because the latter required massive technical framing that took several years to fund and arrange. Conceptually, both *Beach Birds* and *Ocean* were allegedly inspired by Joseph Campbell's comment to Cage that James Joyce's next book (after *Finnegan's Wake*) would have been about water and the ocean.

Cunningham spoke of *Beach Birds* as a piece about birds, people, and rocks (MC 258). He also mentioned flocking as an influence on his choreography (MC 258). Moreover, Cunningham made some whimsical comments about species boundaries in relation to *Beach Birds*. For instance, in an essay called "Dancing—Not Counting," he explained, "It is not meant to be a particular bird, but I used the idea of a bird, and then since dancers are also human beings, I thought I might as well include that" (qtd. in MC 258). *Beach Birds* is interesting as a precursor to *Ocean,* in large part because it is much more representational, and therefore, serves in some ways as a foil to the more broadly or inchoately "in-human" work that we see in *Ocean.* But the earlier piece also raises a few pointed issues in relation to hand and foot that I want to emphasize.

In the film *Beach Birds for Camera* (1993) by Charles Atlas, for which the piece was slightly restaged, the homology between arms/hand and wings saturates the opening frames of the film. In those initial frames, the camera isolates several of the dancers' arms and hands as they cross and hover; these movements are minimal, sometimes nearly imperceptible. This arresting set of micro images immediately places an avian sensibility at the center of the filmic version of the dance work. Moreover, it is difficult to overemphasize the effect of the costuming for this piece, which was designed by Marsha Skinner. The costumes are white leggings, and leotards that are white from the chest down, but black across shoulders and arms, with the most striking feature being that the leotards include black "gloves" for the hands that appear seamless. In other words, there is no visible break in the line from shoulder to arm to hand and fingers—the entire human appendage appears in sleek black continuity.

There is an evolutionary commentary embedded in this set of choreographic and costuming choices in *Beach Birds*, especially as intensified in the filmic version, which emphasize quite sharply the entanglement of the human in a more-than-human world of movement—movement that is housed in, articulated, and "theorized" by Cunningham through particular forms of embodiment. The most specific form of embodiment that I am emphasizing here is limbs. The seemingly idiosyncratic question of limbs appears in recent discussions of process philosophy and the interweaving of human and nonhuman forces and dynamics. William Connolly, for instance, during his discussion of Whitehead's concept of the eternal object and "real creativity in human and nonhuman processes" mentions the "repetition with variation of certain patterns in leaves, wings, and mammal limbs" as patterns that persist in the current cosmic epoch.[17] In this discussion, he is exploring the way different thinkers understand the emergence of the genuinely new amidst systems of relative stability. Connolly considers how Whitehead construes forms or tendencies that resist entropy or tend to cohere in a given epoch of chronotime and comments: "[t]o what extent does the march of real creativity in human and nonhuman processes require eternal objects to sustain them? It seems to me, now at least, that a universe of real creativity could be marked by flexible *tendencies* toward patterns that persist and evolve as the world changes" (*Fragility* 163). Connolly then turns to the idea of "preadaptations," in evolved systems, which set preconditions for the creative development of new functions or abilities (but do not "pre-ordain" those changes). His prime example comes from Brian Goodwin, who suggests that "the wings of primitive birds set preadaptations from which the limbs of animals and humans eventually evolved" (qtd. in *Fragility* 163). This long durational unfolding of creatural extremities over centuries of evolution, from wings to mammal limbs, is particularly interesting because, as I have already discussed, the hand and its agential capacities have tended to be marshaled as a demarcating force of human creativity. But that creativity has its foundations in animal limbedness.

Also compelling here is the way in which the limbs or appendages of the living in general can be seen as both performing—but also marking in a more "representational" mode—the "teleodynamic searching" that Connolly and others have identified as central to the basic organismic creativity (or what Grosz or Nietzsche might call creative self-othering) of all living beings. Connolly picks up the term teleodynamic from Terrence Deacon, who describes living organisms as self-maintaining, correcting, and reproducing.[18] Connolly goes on to conjecture about how organisms affect creative self-transformations in light of work by such figures as Whitehead and Nietzsche. For the purposes of this chapter then, first, Cunningham's focus on wing-like hands in *Beach Birds* can be understood as an embodiment and a figuration of the fact that human "handedness" is indebted to the "wingedness" of primitive birds. The translation of this danced figuration in bioaesthetic terms: human creativity has animal origins. Second, the general accent on extremities in *Beach Birds* (and later in *Ocean*, as I will show), can be read as stressing the process of teleodynamic searching, by which beings "test" the unfolding of their own emergent newness or otherness within the world of becoming, that is, within the way life, materiality, and cultures behave. Put more plainly, the living organism's reaching outward through extremities or limbs both is and represents its morpho-dynamic, creative becoming-other in the world. This, we can say, is a most fundamental creative property of life itself.

The combination, then, of the "un-handing" or "re-winging" of the human that the gloved costume emphasizes, and a number of choreographic choices for the dancers' upper bodies, arms, and hands in *Beach Birds*, creates uncanny interspecies images for the viewer, where the viewer's mind hovers or wavers between seeing the bodies and appendages as human and/or avian. Some of the subtler movements are, not surprisingly, intensified by the film work, which can catch and magnify the slighter gestures of hands, for instance. In the first twenty seconds of the film, the dancers flick their wrist-wings sporadically in quick, surprising, and occasional movements that may be seen as quite representational as they "mimic" the way a bird might shake its wings. This mimicry or becoming, however, is a form of reinscription of the human, enabled partly by costuming and partly by choreography, that resonates with my earlier discussion of handedness and footedness in Isadora Duncan's body of work. If Duncan's commitment to barefootedness is a philosophical position meaningfully linked to animality and to an antihandedness that shapes some of the broader choreographic arcs of twentieth-century modern dance, *Beach Birds* provides a case in point for positioning that long historical arc. Again, both the "disappearance" of the human hand in Cunningham's piece, and its "evo-translation" or involution into a bird wing, can be seen as powerful commentaries on handedness and handiness, and therefore on creativity. These elements of the dance challenge the figuration of the human as superior, in its evolutionary "distance" from the animal.

Perhaps most astonishing is the corollary emphasis on the bare foot in *Beach Birds*. At the eleven-minute mark in the film, one dancer extends a leg forward, at a low angle, and begins to shake the bare foot. The dancer continues this movement, with its entire focus on the vibrating bare foot. Then a second dancer commences the same movement, and soon there are also groups of three dancers facing one another and shaking or trembling an exposed foot. Although there is no doubt that this movement evokes the sudden, lively, and alert movements that we associate with birds as a species, the prolonged emphasis on shaking a bare, extended foot also powerfully conjures Duncan's very early commitment to barefootedness, which I argue resides at the heart of modern dance's emergence as an "animal" form in the early twentieth century. As I suggest in Chapter One, the bare foot opens up the possibility for contact with the earth itself, while the balletic foot, which Duncan viewed as "tortured," can be construed as cut off from earthly pulsations. Cunningham's dancers' prolonged and loose or chaotic foot shakings (the foot is not forcibly pointed or flexed, and each dancer shakes to an idiosyncratic, personal rhythm) evoke an emphatic "vibrant podology" that seems linked to the occlusion or redressing of human handedness and all its attendant ideological effects throughout the dance. In this sense, twentieth-century modern dance's investment in the vibrancy of the bare foot seems to entail a concomitant "undoing" of human handedness and all of the exceptionalism that stems from that bias.

Cunningham and Cage's *Ocean* has taken on a more mythological status than some of his works partly because John Cage died before it could be realized; it, therefore, serves as a kind of last, great achievement of the two artists' epic collaboration. A substantive description is worth quoting from the Merce Cunningham Trust webpage:

> John Cage's original concept of **Ocean**, in 1991, was for a dance to
> be performed in a circular space, with the audience surrounding the

dancers, and the musicians (112 of them) surrounding the audience. It was not possible to realize this project at the time, but a commission for performances in Brussels and Amsterdam in 1994 made it a reality. Andrew Culver composed music according to Cage's concept and David Tudor made an electronic component (*Soundings: Ocean Diary*). Cunningham's choreography was in nineteen sections, using a chance process based on the number of hexagrams in the *I Ching*—64, but owing to the length of the dance this was doubled, 128. This number of phrases allowed for solos, duets, trios, quartets, and group sections. To accustom the dancers to dancing in the round, Cunningham told them "you have to put yourself on a merry-go-round that keeps turning all the time." Marsha Skinner designed unitards in varied colors; at a certain point the women added dresses. Ocean was first performed in May 1994 at the Cirque Royal, Brussels. It was revived in July 2005 in that year's Lincoln Center Festival in New York City. The last performance was in the Rainbow Quarry in Minnesota, September 2008, at which time the piece was filmed by Charles Atlas. (–David Vaughn)

It is important to note here that the sound score used sea mammal and fish sounds, in addition to other sounds from arctic ice, sonar, and so forth. There can be no "last word" on the work *Ocean*, as it represents one of Cunningham (and Cage's, posthumously) most ambitious and technically spectacular pieces. I would like to make some observations about the work that help link Cunningham's "architectural" style to something more "biological" and "animal," in a broad sense. Let me begin by noting that *Ocean* has a piquantly architectural style, the sort of movement that sometimes results in accusations of robotic and "expressionless" choreography.[19] This impression may largely have to do with the rigidity of the dancer's torso and pelvis in the piece, which is especially prominent. At times, the dancers do indeed look strangely like dolls or robots.

In addition to the rigidity of the torso and pelvis, the dancers' limbs and extremities are almost constantly extended and engaged in specific types of open or "receptive" formations. The limbs in many ways take on the action of the dance, while the center of the dancer's body (torso/pelvis) remains relatively static. The limbs seem to become the sensorium of the dancers' bodies in this piece. The arms/hands and legs/feet repeatedly cup, curve, reach, and extend in a manner that suggests the individual "creature" or dancer is exploring its surroundings and examining its possible engagements with its immediate environment, as well as occasionally with the other beings there. In comparison with *Beach Birds*, where the limbs generally remain closer to the body (despite a number of wing-like movements), the dancers' limbs in *Ocean* are especially extended—much more "distal," in dance parlance—as they are near-constantly carving and ranging, outspread as if in ceaseless examination of the organism's surroundings. My reading of the dance would emphasize not overtly "animal" movements in a representational way, but more the engaging in forms of teleodynamic searching that is rendered or enacted in the limbs.

If the ocean serves as the repository of our earliest evolutionary relatives, as housing the life forms from which reptiles and mammals have all essentially come forth, then the limbed teleodynamic searching that characterizes large choreographic plateaus of the piece can be understood as a deeply embodied commentary on the creative emergence and becoming of the human, through its entanglement with the forces of other creatural life. Moreover, the piece also would seem to signal the human's remaining entanglement or shared habitation with those forces and processes. It is, therefore, also appropriate to see the embodiment of teleodynamic searching in the limbed reaching and exploring in the choreography as a rumination on biological creativity, specifically the kind of creativity that this book has been examining. That creativity is an embodied (rather than a primarily conceptual) process of self-organization of entities, attraction and repulsion between entities, and a becoming-complex or becoming-other of beings that are alive.

Although a viewing of the Charles Atlas film of the Minnesota performance of *Ocean* best reveals this limbed searching, some photos of the piece provide an elementary notion of the processes that I describe. A photo of the 2006 production of *Ocean* by Tony Dougherty shows both the limbed searching and the Bacchic head movement in one image (see Figure 5.9). In fact, Cunningham uses this Dionysian head position frequently in the piece, although the body of the dancer does not correspond to Duncan's positions. In fact, in Cunningham's piece, the Bacchic head might even be translated as a further "limbed" creatural exploration or openness of the organism to creative encounters and becomings-other.

Finally, the circularity of the stage lends a cellular quality to the entire undertaking and reminds us of the images in the second illustrated version of Woolf's *Golden Curtain*. At times the work in *Ocean* is highly suggestive of DNA-like processes, as dancers combine and recombine, perhaps evoking "genetic" possibilities, propensities or drives during their teleodynamic dance, though in a way that would eschew notions of predetermined resemblances and would, instead, evoke the unpredictable emergence of differences. In this case, it seems highly productive to think about "chance" in biological or Darwinian terms, in relation to Cunningham's choreography.

I would like to end this chapter by discussing two images, one that comes from the book *Other Animals*, and a second that I found in the New York Public Library of Performing Arts archives. In the first (see Figure 5.10) a bird with a long beak stands off-balance (OA 35), in a way that is reminiscent of the Rachel Rosenthal figure in the "Catching Gold Rings" illustration from *Tatti*

Figure 5.9 Photo: Tony Dougherty.

Figure 5.10 Images provided courtesy of Laura Kuhn. ©Merce Cunningham Trust.

Wattles. Like Rosenthal's image, the balancing bird suggests processes involving creative risk and species-transferability in the aesthetic register. In the casual image from the archive, Cunningham aligned his own signature with the long beak of a bird that looks quite similar to this interstitial bird from the book. Cunningham frequently drew small animal faces next to his signature when writing personal letters or notes. What struck me in this particular image is the suggestion of a nonhanded biosignature of the beak. Here Cunningham seems to associate animal foraging, marking, pecking, and consuming, through the extended "appendage" of the beak, with his own practice of creative marking and foraging—that is, with his ongoing dance work that constitutes his embodied, creatural engagement with the material world.

Afterword

Notes Toward a Bioaesthetic Theory

In the 1991 film *Cage/Cunningham* by Elliot Caplan, many of the pair's long-time artistic collaborators make comments about both artists, and about what it was like to have worked with them, and to have observed them working. Robert Rauschenberg, for instance, discusses the messiness of the way in which he, Cage, and Cunningham would work entirely separately on elements of a piece, to have it all come smashing together in the final product, when it was too late to change much of anything. Rauschenberg's fame in the art world certainly adds to the interest of his comments about chance procedures in the film, but I would propose that it is the comments of a less famous woman in the film that are the most striking. M. C. Richards was a scholar, poet, and potter who taught at Black Mountain College from 1945 to 1951, and was involved in the first "happening" there, which I discuss in the previous chapter. She was part of the "inner circle" of artists working at Black Mountain at that pivotal time in the late forties and early fifties. The footage of her in Caplan's film is not specifically dated, but we can assume it was shot, roughly, in the 1980s. Richards seems to be struggling with her words in this short clip, almost slurring them at times, in a manner I find rather wonderfully contraposed to Rauschenberg's crisp and confident engagement with the camera. Richards also wears a string of flowers around her head in a strikingly "childish" manner that accentuates the natural (she would have likely been in her seventies at the time of filming). In other words, she seems quite "foolish," or "strange," from a conventional perspective, especially in her juxtaposition to the illustrious Rauschenberg. But her "ramblings," which I will partly reproduce here, and which are extremely repetitive and incantatory, accentuate not the cleverness and cutting-edge nature of chance procedures but, rather, an affirmative kind of bioaesthetics that she finds spiritual in its significance:

> [John and Merce] have a particular task in our time . . . to work artisti-
> cally, creatively, with such an *affirming* touch, it's an *affirming* touch in

the work that they do, such an *affirmation of life* . . . [their work is] essentially *life-affirming* in a time when, not only in the arts but in general,
there's this real uncertainty about whether a life will continue or indeed
whether it should continue, or whether the human being is, you know,
is finished. . . . John and Merce are like angels whose life . . . has been
dedicated to this kind of task . . . as if there were something extraordinary at stake.[1]

Richards is a poet: She articulates her ideas in a manner reminiscent of the
refrains I highlight in Chapter Two when discussing Lawrence. She rhythmically
repeats her urgent view of the life-affirming essence of Cage and Cunningham's
creative practices. Richards's formulation bears witness to what I will call a vibrant animalism (in a nod to Jane Bennett's *Vibrant Matter*) that resides at the
heart of bioaesthetics, as I have been framing it throughout this project. Such
a force informs much of Cunningham's work, and the creative practices and
products of the other innovators I have examined in this book. Reiterating, practically stuttering, the value of a haptic and therefore embodied commitment to
life, Richards's very tongue gets in the way, asserts itself, and subtly signals an "en-
mouthed" statement that Bataille's ideas might lead us to call more animal, less
human. Her comments about the affirmation of life mesh with the bioaesthetic
lens I have been applying in this project, in the valuing of a rhythmic, vibrational
affiliation of all creatural creativity. The artists in these chapters draw upon and
harness animal forces as part of their creative becomings-other in writing, choreography, performance, and drawing.

    Richards's stop-and-start, stuttering attempt to describe with words what was
so lively, animated, or pulsating at the center of Cage and Cunningham's work
also literalizes the shimmering, shimmying, dancerly qualities that have been
the major thread running through this study. Her description not only returns
us to the "flocking" of words that Woolf describes in *The Waves*, or to the brave
"nudity" of Duncan, but her enlivened and repetitive description also raises that
very essential question of swerving that Bennett (re)sets at the heart of new materialism or thing-power. Lucretius's primordial swerve, Bennett reminds us, is
an "element of chanciness" residing at the heart of things (*Vibrant* 18).[2] In short,
Richards attends to the animism in Cage and Cunningham's work, and also
provides a new purchase on why chance procedures made sense in their work—
because even matter itself is always dancing in ways that are unpredictable.
Although Althusser called Lucretius's ideas a "materialism of the encounter"
(qtd. in *Vibrant* 18), we could just as easily call them a materialism of the dance.
Creatures, moreover, enliven this dance exponentially, and unmistakably.

    It is also the case that Richards's grave uncertainty about the persistence of
human life, which likely stemmed from Cold War fears of global destruction, has

taken on epic proportions in subsequent decades, as climate change has brought our ever-increasing precarity to the fore in extreme and unprecedented ways. Moreover, as I was finalizing this book, Trump was elected to the American presidency, and new calls to eliminate the National Endowment for the Arts (NEA) and the National Endowment for the Humanities (NEH) began circulating in classic right-wing fashion. In fact, Ann Carlson's performance piece, "Doggie Hamlet," which includes sheep and sheep dogs, has been especially prominent among works recently funded by the NEA that were being pilloried as "undeserving" of support. The Washington Free Beacon, for instance, published a dismissive story on December 20, 2016 (after Trump was elected, but before his inauguration) titled, "Taxpayers Foot Bill for 'Doggie Hamlet.'" Art and human life, art and biological life, dangerous and endangered, increasingly under threat from macro and micro forces. The perceived dangers of art always have been associated with art's "excesses" and art's proliferation of diversities; excessive diversity of forms, views, meanings, materials, ways of experiencing—art's excessive ways of transgressing borders, of swerving out of bounds, of creating hybrids and "dangerous" collaborations. What this study affirms is an ever more radical valuing of art's excesses, because they are the site of a most profound surfeiting of the human itself that is actually ennobling in its effects.

It is time to risk one more border-crossing in our view of art and see it as part of our shared affective becoming-excessive, as a fundamentally noncognitive zone of self-othering that *all* animals engage, not just human animals. Aesthetic becoming is our evolutionary and embodied inheritance, not something we invented with our exclusively human minds (whatever that could mean). Art connects us profoundly to other creatures. The aesthetic capacity *is* animal; it doesn't just approach animals or hold them in its purview. And if this is the case, then we can anticipate wholly new ways of viewing, inhabiting, and understanding our own artistic practices. And we also will have wholly new ways to consider the aesthetic impulses and activities of nonhuman creatures. Although it is true that we live in precarious times, we also must insist upon the affirmative capacity of creatures to invent new "selves," and to harness the forces of the earth and the cosmos in embodied, vibratory aesthetic-becomings. To create a small dance between Bennett's concepts and my own, we must affirm the innovative swervings of creatural excess as life's ongoing embeddedness in bioaesthetics.

Brad Evans recently recapitulated a series of short essay/interviews in "The Stone" segment of *The New York Times* that called upon the role of art in its affirmation of life. The series is dedicated to a critique of violence in the current moment, and even included a piece by Cary Wolfe on the ethical parameters of posthumanism in relation to nonhuman animals. Near the end of Evan's overview piece, he cites his earlier interview with artist and theorist Bracha Ettinger and its emphasis on the "humanity of the arts." Ettinger's work is painfully trained on the suffering of women and children during the Nazi era. Evans writes in this relation that "it is with the arts that we truly enter those most precious and fragile of ethical bonds that foreground the importance of love, compassion, and human togetherness."[3] This is no doubt true, yet Ettinger makes the claim in her earlier essay that "Art . . . like love, appears as a form of fragile communication in which complete strangers can understand one another by resonance, both inside and outside one's close 'community.' One then realizes that humans are part of fragile and shared systems."[4] Although Ettinger's important work is quite different from the kinds of work I have highlighted in this study, I was struck by the way that she emphasizes resonance and strangers, in what *could* be read as a more-than-human "shared system," even if this was not what she intended.

Many discussions of art stress a "humanizing" function and a human community. *Choreographies of the Living* suggests that one of our challenges and tasks for the twenty-first century is to see aesthetics even more broadly as "creaturizing," so that our artistic undertakings—those we have traditionally viewed as exclusive and "elevated"—are framed in ways that truly *resonate with strangers*, in a shared system that is fully more-than-human in all its fragility, but also in all its creative aliveness and improvisation. The transporting power of art, the becoming-intense of aesthetics, the felt vibrations of aesthetic forces, and the taste for certain affect-circulating performances all have their "ancestral" lineage for us in animals' aesthetic engagements. Bioaesthetics thus reminds us that the world of art includes hordes of other creatural actors and living assemblages— and that these beings always have been artistic. And finally, I would submit that all this makes the artistic, in every permutation, even more extraordinary.

NOTES

Front Matter

1. For a riveting artistic meditation on the frustrations of ballet, which also anticipates my discussion of Isadora Duncan's critique of the "deathly" nature of that form, see the video excerpts titled EN PUNTAS, by Javier Pérez: https://vimeo.com/66721776. I would suggest this film also highlights ballet's performance of the feminine. I am grateful to my colleague Edward J. Kerns for alerting me to this work.
2. This was the same installation Cary Wolfe analyzes in his very recent essay. See Cary Wolfe, "Each Time Unique: The Poetics of Extinction," *Animalities: Literary and Cultural Studies Beyond the Human*, ed. Michael Lundblad (Edinburgh University Press, 2017). Michael Pestel created several performances on Lafayette's campus in the fall of 2014 as part of his "living" and changing installation about Martha, the last Passenger Pigeon. Ours was titled "M," and was a collaborative dance and sound event. "M." Michael Pestel and Carrie Rohman. Williams Center Gallery. Lafayette College, Easton, PA. November 11, 2014.
3. This performance was titled "Breach: Left Behind," and was staged in conjunction with Alison Saar's gallery show, "Breach." "Breach: Left Behind." Jessica Warchal-King. Grossman Gallery. Lafayette College, Easton, PA. September 28 and October 1, 2016.

Introduction

1. Gilles Deleuze and Félix Guattari, *A Thousand Plateaus: Capitalism and Schizophrenia*, trans. Brian Massumi (Minneapolis: University of Minnesota Press, 1987), 255. Henceforth cited in the text as *Plateaus*.
2. Elizabeth Grosz, *Becoming Undone: Darwinian Reflections on Life, Politics, and Art* (Durham, NC: Duke University Press, 2011), 2. Henceforth cited in the text as *Undone*.
3. https://www.theguardian.com/music/2010/may/14/lou-reed-laurie-anderson, accessed January 5, 2011.
4. http://www.billboard.com/articles/news/957900/laurie-anderson-plays-concert-for-dogs-at-sydney-opera-house, accessed January 5, 2011.
5. There is also an increasing interest in "formalized" art made by nonhuman animals, and in what is called inter-species art. One well-known example of this interest is exhibited in the Komar and Melamid Elephant Art School Project in Thailand. As my discussion will demonstrate, I am less interested in animals that "mimic" or enact something that we associate with human painting activities, and more interested in how human painting itself can be understood as emerging from creatural engagements that cut across species lines. Discussions of animal "painting" tend to retain a notion of art that privileges the conceptual, rather than the affective and bodily. However, a number of interesting ethical and theoretical questions are explored by others in this relation: see, for instance, Jane Desmond, "Can Animals Make

'Art'? Popular and Scientific Discourses About Expressivity and Cognition in Primates," *Experiencing Animal Minds: An Anthology of Animal-Human Encounters*, ed. Julie A. Smith and Robert W. Mitchell (New York: Columbia University Press, 2012), 95–108.

6. See John Berger, *About Looking* (New York: Vintage, 1992).

7. See Steve Baker, *Picturing the Beast: Animals Identity, and Representation* (Urbana: University of Illinois Press, 1993) and Steve Baker, *The Postmodern Animal* (London: Reaktion Books, 2000).

8. See Steve Baker, *Artist/Animal* (Minneapolis: University of Minnesota Press, 2013). Henceforth cited in the text as *Artist/Animal*.

9. Cary Wolfe, *What is Posthumanism?* (Minneapolis: University of Minnesota Press, 2010), 165. Henceforth cited in the text as *Posthumanism*.

10. Cary Wolfe, "Each Time Unique: The Poetics of Extinction," *Animalities: Literary and Cultural Studies Beyond the Human*, ed. Michael Lundblad (Edinburgh University Press, 2017).

11. Ron Broglio, *Surface Encounters: Thinking with Animals and Art* (Minneapolis: University of Minnesota Press, 2011), xxvi. Henceforth cited in the text as *Surface*.

12. McHugh's observations appear in Susan McHugh, "Art and Animals," *Anthrozoos: A Multidisciplinary Journal of the Interactions of People and Animals* 26, no. 3 (2013): 474. See Giovanni Aloi, *Art and Animals* (London: I. B. Tauris, 2012). Henceforth cited in the text as *Art*. Aloi has also provided important and provocative commentary on animal studies and art criticism in an extended editorial in the online journal *Antennae*. There he discusses several problematic "negative" critiques from animal studies that he suggests are too narrow, in a bid to broaden and complicate the recent lines of interaction between critical animal studies and contemporary art practices and criticism. See Giovanni Aloi, "Animal Studies and Art: Elephants in the Room," Special Editorial, *Antennae* (February 2015): 1–27.

13. Timothy Morton, "Guest Column: Queer Ecology," *PMLA* 125, no. 2 (2010): 275. Henceforth cited in the text as "Ecology."

14. Braidotti, Rosi. "Animals, Anomalies, and Inorganic Others," *PMLA* 124, no. 2 (2009): 526. Henceforth cited in the text as "Anomalies."

15. The proliferation of these critical investigations cannot be fully accounted for here, but the following citations give a sense of the wide-ranging work on "life itself": Jane Bennet, *Vibrant Matter: A Political Ecology of Things* (Durham, NC: Duke University Press, 2010); Eugene Thacker, *After Life* (Chicago: University of Chicago Press, 2010); Timothy Morton, "Guest Column: Queer Ecology," *PMLA* 125, no. 2 (2010): 273–282; Diana Coole and Samantha Frost, Eds., *New Materialisms: Ontology Agency, and Politics* (Durham, NC: Duke University Press, 2010); Melissa Gregg and Gregory J. Seigworth, Eds., *The Affect Theory Reader* (Durham, NC: Duke University Press, 2010); Stefan Helmreich, "What Was Life? Answers from Three Limit Biologies," *Critical Inquiry* 37, no. 4 (2011): 671–696; Gil Anidjar, "The Meaning of Life," *Critical Inquiry* 37, no. 4 (2011): 697–723.

16. Stephen Davies, *The Philosophy of Art* (Malden: Blackwell, 2006), 2. Henceforth cited in the text as *Philosophy of Art*.

17. Davies's book, *The Philosophy of Art*, cited above provides a useful set of overviews and references for such debates.

18. One notable exception to the "mainstream" philosophical view of art as exclusively human has been reinvigorated by Richard Shusterman in his work on pragmatist aesthetics. See Richard Shusterman, *Pragmatist Aesthetics: Living Beauty, Rethinking Art* (New York: Rowman and Littlefield, 2000). Shusterman discusses how analytic philosophy in the twentieth century dismissed the work of John Dewey, whose aesthetics includes a "somatic naturalism" (6). Dewey insisted that the foundations of beauty and art were linked to biology and to processes that are not exclusively human. Although the question of the animal was not Dewey's primary focus, he nonetheless provided a theory of art that saw it as rooted in natural and organic experiences. Yet as I discuss below, Dewey's ultimate claims about art retain an exceptionalist position for most scholars.

19. Stephen Davies, *The Artful Species* (Oxford: Oxford University Press, 2012), 14. Henceforth cited in the text as *Artful Species*.

20. In an interview with Jane Goodall that uses the idea of dance in its title, Paul Waldau and Kimberley Patton ask the primatologist about her witnessing of what she describes as

chimpanzees' experiences of and embodied responses to awe. See Jane Goodall, "The Dance of Awe," interview by Kimberley Patton and Paul Waldau, in *A Communion of Subjects: Animals in Religion, Science, and Ethics*, Eds. Paul Waldau and Kimberley Patton (New York: Columbia University Press, 2009): 651–656.

21. Readers will find Alessandro Giovannelli's edited volume, *Aesthetics: The Key Thinkers*, very useful in reprising, chapter by chapter, the theories of most of the major figures in aesthetic theory. See Alessandro Giovannelli, *Aesthetics: The Key Thinkers* (New York, Bloomsbury, 2012).

22. I first used the term *bioaesthetic* in a 2014 publication to signal a cross-species concept of the aesthetic impulse (Carrie Rohman, "No Higher Life: Bio-aesthetics in J. M. Coetzee's *Disgrace*," *Modern Fiction Studies* 60, no. 3 [2014]: 562–578). My usage of this term counters trends in "neuroaesthetics" that regard all artistic capacities as exclusively human.

23. Here it is important to note a companionate ethics with Susan McHugh's incisive work in her book, *Animal Stories*. As McHugh explains, "stories might be seen as key points of ethical negotiation across artistic and scientific models of species and social life" (14). The implications of my work here are not dissimilar: aesthetic impulses themselves are a point of contact or exchange between human and animal life-worlds. See Susan McHugh, *Animal Stories: Narrating Across Species Lines* (Minneapolis: University of Minnesota Press, 2011). Henceforth cited in the text as *Narrating Across*.

24. Gilles Deleuze and Félix Guattari, *What is Philosophy?*, trans. Hugh Tomlinson and Graham Burchell (New York: Columbia University Press, 1994), 182. Henceforth cited in the text as *Philosophy*.

25. We ought to remain somewhat skeptical of the tendency in Deleuze to associate animality proper with a form of packness, and to thus reinforce the notion that animals are not "individuals" or do not experience a form of self or "subjectivity." The implication that our Oedipalizing of them is purely a phantasm tends to reinforce what Bataille also assumed about animal experience, that "every animal is *in the world like water in water*" (19), and that "there is nothing in animal life that introduces the relation of the master to the one he commands, nothing that might establish autonomy on one side and dependence on the other" (18). Although becomings obviously disrupt certain subjective singularities, they may not be exclusively human. See Georges Bataille, *Theory of Religion*, trans. Robert Hurly (New York: Zone Books, 1989). Henceforth cited in the text as *Religion*.

26. Elizabeth Grosz, "The Creative Impulse," interview by Julie Copeland, *Sunday Morning Radio National*, August 14, 2005, 2. Henceforth cited in the text as "Impulse."

27. Elizabeth Grosz, *Chaos, Territory, Art: Deleuze and the Framing of the Earth* (New York: Columbia University Press, 2008), 2. Henceforth cited in the text as *Chaos*.

28. For a similar emphasis on sexual selection and aesthetic taste from a scientific perspective, see Richard Prum's work on what he calls "the evolution of beauty."

29. The number of scholars from many disciplines I would need to identify here grows exponentially. But a very partial list would include thinkers such as Carol Adams, Giovanni Aloi, Philip Armstrong, Colleen Glenney Boggs, Ron Broglio, Matthew Calarco, Una Chaudhuri, David L. Clark, Marianne DeKoven, Josephine Donovan, Margo DeMello, Erica Fudge, Carol Gigliotti, Lori Gruen, Donna Haraway, David Herman, Kevin Hutchings, Michael Lundblad, Susan McHugh, Robert McKay, John Miller, Richard Nash, Anat Pick, Mary Pollock, Derek Ryan, Nicole Shukin, Karl Steel, H. Peter Steeves, Gary Steiner, Tom Tyler, Paul Waldau, Kari Weil, Cary Wolfe, Wendy Woodward, and others.

30. See Carrie Rohman, *Stalking the Subject: Modernism and the Animal* (New York: Columbia University Press, 2009). Henceforth cited in the text as *Stalking*.

31. The "animality" of the body in a modern dance aesthetic is evidenced, for instance, when Joan Accocella discusses Mark Morris's piece *Behemoth*, and its struggling, gravity-loving bodies. Morris also has been described as having webbed feet. See Joan Accocella, "Mark Morris: The Body and What It Means," in *The Routledge Dance Studies Reader*, Ed. Alexandra Carter (New York: Routledge, 2010), 269–277. Moreover, as I discuss later in this introduction, Deleuze and Gauttari associate "minor" art with a move from metaphor to metamorphosis, which is especially interesting given the embodied realities of dance.

32. For other scholarship on animals in performance, see also Lourdes Orozco, *Theatre and Animals* (Basingstoke: Palgrave Macmillan, 2013); the earlier book Nicholas Ridout, *Stage Fright,*

Animals, and Other Theatrical Problems (Cambridge: Cambridge University Press, 2006); Peta Tait, *Wild and Dangerous Performances: Animals, Emotion, Circus* (Basingstoke: Palgrave MacMillan, 2012); and the recent collection Lourdes Orozco and Jennifer Parker-Starbuck, Eds., *Performing Animality: Animals in Performance Practices* (Basingstoke: Palgrave/ Macmillan, 2015). See also the 2014 volume by Chaudhuri and Hughes described in Note 32. Readers should additionally note that work in biology, such as that done by Karl Von Frisch (who won the Nobel Prize alongside Konrad Lorenz and Nikolaas Tinbergen in 1973) on the communicative function of dancing in bees, has had an important impact on fields such as ethology and biosemiotics. See Karl Von Frisch, *The Dance Language and Orientation of Bees*, trans. Leigh Chadwick (Cambridge, MA: Harvard University Press, 1967).

33. Una Chaudhuri, "Animal Geographies: Zooësis and the Space of Modern Drama," *Modern Drama* XLVI, no. 4 (2003): 646–662. See also her recent expansions of the capacities of this term, zooësis, where she adds the *"valorization"* of animals as a key goal in the volume *Animal Acts*; Una Chaudhuri and Holly Hughes eds., *Animal Acts: Performing Species Today* (Ann Arbor: University of Michigan Press, 2014).

34. Una Chaudhuri, "Queering the Green Man, Reframing the Garden: Marina Zurkow's Mesocosm (Northumberland UK) and the Theatre of Species," *Scapegoat: Architecture/ Landscape/Political Economy*, Issue 2: Materialism (2011): 6–8.

35. Professor Desmond's lecture can be accessed at https://www.youtube.com/watch?v=4JdXXb_-zc4. Video recording published on January 26, 2017; talk given on October 25, 2016, Dance Studies Colloquium, *Moving Across Species Lines*, Temple University.

36. I am using the term *creatural* throughout this study, following David Herman's recent explanation for and adoption of a shift from the term *creaturely*. Opposing Eric Santner's notion of a creatureliness that circulates around human exceptionalism, Herman identifies a strain of discourses that Anat Pick adopts and suggests the new term: "The slight semantic shift from *creaturely* to *creatural* . . . is meant to indicate [an] alignment with the second of these two strands of discourse, in which the status of being a creature, subject to the requirements of the surrounding environment, the vicissitudes of time, and the vulnerabilities of the body, emphasizes the fundamental continuity between humans and other animals" (3); see David Herman, *Creatural Fictions: Human-Animal Relationships in Twentieth- and Twenty-First-Century Literature* (New York: Palgrave Macmillan, 2016). My study emphasizes the creative capacities that are continuous between species, and it thus further emphasizes a link between the creatural and the creative itself.

37. Rosi Braidotti, *Transpositions: On Nomadic Ethics* (London: Polity, 2006), 40. Henceforth cited in the text as *Transpositions*.

38. D. H. Lawrence, *Birds, Beasts, and Flowers* (Santa Rosa, CA: Black Sparrow Press, 1995), 127.

Chapter 1

1. Max Eastman, "Isadora Duncan is Dead," in *Isadora Duncan: Twenty-Four Studies by Arnold Genthe* (New York: Mitchell Kennerley, 1929), 37–40, 39. Henceforth cited in the text as *Twenty-Four*.

2. Isadora Duncan, "The Dance of the Future" [1909], in *Art of the Dance*, ed. Sheldon Cheney (New York: Theatre Arts, 1969), 55. Henceforth cited in the text as *Dance*.

3. Isadora Duncan, "Notes for a Lecture," *Irma Duncan Papers*, archived at the New York Public Library for Performing Arts.

4. I emphasize Duncan's writings in this chapter to elucidate her engagements with animality and the inhuman. Duncan spent a great deal of time writing about her practice, in part, because her own "revolutionary" ideas and performance style created such a disruption in perceived notions of formal dance. Although it is important to keep the dancing body itself in view, as much as possible, in discussions of dance, it is also important to value the intellectual production of a figure like Duncan. In fact, it is necessary to take seriously what Duncan wrote about the body and the body in motion, and not just value what she did with her body in motion. Max Eastman insisted upon this emphasis when he claimed that Duncan was "not only a supreme artist endowed by nature with momentous power and the exquisite gift of retaining it—she was also a mind and moral force" (*Twenty-Four*). Moreover, because Duncan

was never filmed, analyzing her actual performances proves especially challenging. Given the lack of a Duncan film archive, it seems particularly important to value her ideas and writings, alongside her choreographic legacies.

5. As my argument will make clear, I am linking ballet to a symbolic and "all too human" body while suggesting that modern dance performs the "animal" or organic body in a way that was unprecedented for "high" Western aesthetics before the twentieth century.

6. As Carrie Preston reminds us at the outset of her chapter on Duncan, the sculptor Laredo Taft suggested Duncan was "all the muses in one," and many other artists including Auguste Rodin and Abraham Walkowitz created images of her. Preston also suggests that Duncan performed feminism in important ways. See Chapter Four in Carrie J. Preston, *Modernism's Mythic Pose: Gender Genre, Solo Performance* (New York: Oxford, 2011). Henceforth cited in the text as *Mythic*.

7. See Preston, *Mythic* 253.

8. For instance, Elizabeth Dempster has claimed that "Duncan's vision of the dance of the future presumes an unproblematic return to a body of untainted naturalness and to an essential purity which she believed was fundamental to women." See Elizabeth Demster, "Women Writing the Body: Let's Watch a Little How She Dances," in *Grafts: Feminist Cultural Criticism*, ed. Susan Sheridan (London: Verso, 1988), 51. Dempster also suggests that Duncan's vision of dance may be "complicit with the concept of 'natural' sexual difference," which Dempster views as extremely problematic (51). Other important critics, such as Mark Franko, occasionally have relied upon the view of Duncan as "essentialist" in her equation of woman and nature. See especially Chapter One in Mark Franko, *Dancing Modernism/Performing Politics* (Bloomington: Indiana University Press, 1995). Henceforth cited in the text as DM. It may be interesting to reconsider the image of the nymph, once a species analysis of Duncan's work is in place.

9. See Preston's discussions of Hansen and North's work, *Mythic* 59–60.

10. See, for instance, Margo Norris, *Beasts of the Modern Imagination*; Carrie Rohman, *Stalking the Subject: Modernism and the Animal*; Jeffrey Mathes McCarthy, *Green Modernism*.

11. For instance, the essay collection Alexandra Carter and Rachel Fensham, *Dancing Naturally: Nature, Neo-Classicism and Modernity in Early Twentieth-Century Dance* (New York: Palgrave, 2011) includes an array of insightful analyses of the "natural" in early twentieth-century dance, yet despite various attentions to Duncan in the book, there is no discussion of animality in Duncan's discourses.

12. I want to clarify that I do not view this chapter as a "corrective" to Preston's important work, or to McCarren's scholarly insights. Rather, I see it as complementing the rehabilitation of a complex and critically important Isadora Duncan for modernist, feminist, and performance studies.

13. See Ann Daly, *Critical Gestures: Writings on Dance and Culture* (Middletown: Wesleyan, 2002), 246–262. Henceforth cited in the text as *Gestures*.

14. Una Chaudhuri elaborates Morton's notion of such an ecology as one that "proposes a post-Romantic view of nature that vigorously deconstructs the nature/culture binary of traditional environmental thought and assumes an interdependency among life forms, rejecting the view of organisms as bounded, holistic entities." Una Chaudhuri "Queering the Green Man, Reframing the Garden: Marina Zurkow's Mesocosm (Northumberland, UK) and the Theatre of Species," *Scapegoat: Architecture/Landscape/Political Economy*, Issue 2: Materialism (2011): 6. Moreover, the "vibratory" in Duncan's work is fruitfully connected to Jane Bennett's work on vibrant matter. In fact, when Bennett describes a vital materialism as articulating "the elusive idea of a materiality that is *itself* heterogeneous, itself a differential of intensities" where "there is no point of pure stillness, no indivisible atom that is not itself aquiver with virtual force," we ought to think of Isadora Duncan, and of Eastman's characterization of her as an elusive animal, which serves as the epigraph to this chapter (*Vibrant* 57). Jane Bennett, *Vibrant Matter: A Political Ecology of Things* (Durham, NC: Duke University Press, 2010). Henceforth cited in the text as *Vibrant*.

15. I took a master class in Duncan technique with Lori Belilove of the Isadora Duncan Dance Foundation (IDDF) at Franklin and Marshall College, February 26, 2014. Belilove is Founder and Artistic Director of the Foundation and considered a premier performer and teacher

of Duncan's choreographies. She studied with Anna and Irma Duncan, and with second-generation Duncan dancers such as Julia Levien. All references to her teaching refer to this class.

16. Duncan often noted that her interest in Greek culture was driven by the Greeks' valuing of nature.

17. The Institute was cofounded in 1977 by Maria-Theresa Duncan and Kay Bardsley.

18. Jeanne Bresciani, telephone interview. January 26, 2014. All quotations from Bresciani refer to this interview.

19. D. H. Lawrence, *Women in Love*, ed. David Farmer, John Worthen, and Lindeth Vasey (Cambridge: Cambridge University Press, 1987), 168. Henceforth cited in the text as WL. The title of the 1996 book *D. H. Lawrence: Future Primitive* also reinforces the overlap between Duncan and Lawrence's negotiation of past and future along the lines of Grosz's antimemorialization. Dolores LaChapelle, *D. H. Lawrence: Future Primitive* (Denton: University of North Texas Press, 1996).

20. See Preston, especially 172.

21. Gordon Craig, "Memories of Isadora Duncan," *Irma Duncan Papers*, archived at New York Public Library for Performing Arts.

22. Jacques Derrida, "The Animal That Therefore I Am (More to Follow)," in *The Animal That Therefore I Am*, ed. Marie-Louise Mallet, trans. David Wills (New York: Fordham University Press, 2008), 1. Hereafter cited in the text as *Animal That*.

23. Rebecca Tuvel, "'Veil of Shame;: Derrida, Sarah Bartmann and Animality," *Journal for Critical Animal Studies* 9, no. 1/2 (2011): 216.

24. Kimberly Engdahl Coates, "Performing Feminism, Transmitting Affect: Isadora Duncan, Virginia Woolf, and the Politics of Movement," *Interdisciplinary/Multidisciplinary Woolf: Selected Papers from the 22nd Annual International Conference on Virginia Woolf*, eds. Ann Martin and Kathryn Hill (South Carolina: Clemson University Press, 2013), 185.

25. Jack Anderson, "The Dance: Ann Carlson's 'Animals,'" *The New York Times*, February 7, 1988.

26. Tom Tyler, *Ciferae: A Bestiary in Five Fingers* (Minneapolis: Minnesota University Press, 2012), 229. Hereafter cited in the text as *Ciferae*.

27. Martin Heidegger, *The Fundamental Concepts of Metaphysics: World, Finitude, Solitude*, trans. William McNeill and Nicholas Walker (Bloomington: Indiana University Press, 1995), 185, 193, 196, 271.

28. Isadora Duncan, *My Life* (New York: Liveright, 1927), 166. Henceforth cited in the text as ML.

29. Edna St. Vincent Millay, "Sonnet XXI," *Harp-Weaver and Other Poems* (New York: Harper and Brothers, 1923), 73.

30. T. S. Eliot, "The Love Song of J. Alfred Prufrock," *Collected Poems 1909–1962* (New York: Harcourt Brace Jovanovich, 1963), 7.

31. Diana Fuss, *Human, All Too Human* (London: Routledge, 1996), 5. Henceforth cited in the text as *All Too*.

32. Ursula K. LeGuin, introduction to *Buffalo Gals and Other Animal Presences* (Santa Barbara, CA: Capra Press, 1987), 10. LeGuin goes on to write, "And for the people Civilization calls 'primitive,' 'savage,' or 'undeveloped,' including young children, the continuity, interdependence, and community of all life, all forms of being on earth, is a lived fact, made conscious in narrative (myth, ritual, fiction)" (11).

33. See Preston, especially her discussion of the female solo in Chapter One (*Mythic*).

34. See Rohman, *Stalking the Subject* and Nicole Shukin, *Animal Capital: Rendering Life in Biopolitical Times* (Minneapolis: Minnesota University Press, 2009).

35. Thus Duncan addresses the arabesque, a movement/position absolutely central to ballet history and aesthetics, as ultimately unnatural and to be avoided.

36. This title was used in the IDDC performance, February 27, 2014. Bresciani often uses the title "Ode to Dionysius" when restaging this excerpt. The Dionysian movement is also featured in the dance *Moment Musical* set to Chopin.

37. IDDC performance, Franklin and Marshall, February 27, 2014.

38. Georges Bataille, *Visions of Excess: Selected Writings, 1927–1939*, ed. Allan Stoekl, trans. Allan Stoekl with Carl R. Lovitt and Donald M. Leslie, Jr. (Minneapolis: University of Minnesota Press, 1985), 59. Henceforth cited in the text as *Visions*.

39. For a broad discussion of the centrality of animality to Nietzsche's oeuvre, see Vanessa Lemm, *Nietzsche's Animal Philosophy: Culture, Politics, and the Animality of the Human Being* (New York: Fordham University Press, 2009).

40. D. H. Lawrence, *Fantasia of the Unconscious*, in *Psychoanalysis and the Unconscious and Fantasia of the Unconscious* (Cambridge: Cambridge University Press, 2004), 79.

41. David Wills, *Dorsality: Thinking Back Through Technology and Politics* (Minneapolis: University of Minnesota Press, 2008), 213. Henceforth cited in the text as *Dorsality*.

42. IDDC performance, Franklin and Marshall, February 27, 2014.

Chapter 2

1. Fiona Becket, *D. H. Lawrence: The Thinker as Poet* (New York: St. Martin's Press, 1997), 29. Henceforth cited in the text as *Thinker*.

2. Peter Young, *Tortoise* (London: Reaktion Books, 2003), 7–8. Hereafter cited in the text as *Tortoise*.

3. D. H. Lawrence, "Tortoise Shout," in *The Cambridge Edition of The Poems*, ed. C. Pollnitz (Cambridge: Cambridge University Press, 2013), 316–318. Henceforth referred to with line numbers.

4. See also Derek Ryan, "Following Snakes and Moths: Modernist Ethics and Posthumanism," *Twentieth Century Literature* 61, no. 3 (September 2015): 287–304. His introductory essay discusses modernism's ethical encounters with animals, with a focus on Lawrence and Woolf, and outlines the entire special issue on "Modernist Ethics and Posthumanism."

5. Richard Ellmann, "Lawrence and his Demon," (originally published 1953) in *D. H. Lawrence's Poetry: Demon Liberated*, ed. A. Banerjee (London: Macmillan, 1990), 194. Henceforth cited in the text as "Demon."

6. I will discuss concepts of electricity and animal "magnetism" in relation to Lawrence later in this chapter.

7. For further discussion of the refrain, see especially chapters ten and eleven in *Plateaus*.

8. Kyoko Kondo, "Metaphor in *Women in Love*," in *D. H. Lawrence: New Worlds*, eds. Keith Cushman and Earl Ingersoll (Madison, NJ: Fairleigh Dickinson University Press, 2003), 168–182.

9. Lawrence's phrase "lapsing out" has been variously associated with his concept of "blood-consciousness" and a relaxing of mental cognition or mindlessness. It is usefully aligned with Deleuze's notion of becoming, given that both involve the dissolution of an Oedipal or centralized subjectivity. In *Women in Love*, Birkin claims, "You've got to lapse out before you can know what sensual reality is, lapse into unknowingness, and give up your volition. You've got to do it. You've got to learn not-to-be, before you can come into being" (WL 44). For further discussion of forms of knowledge in Lawrence, see Eric P. Levy, "Ontological Incoherence in *Women in Love*," *College Literature* 30, no. 4 (2003): 156–165.

10. William Connolly, *The Fragility of Things: Self-Organizing Processes, Neoliberal Fantasies, and Democratic Activism* (Durham, NC: Duke University Press, 2013), 156.

11. Gerald Doherty, *Theorizing Lawrence: Nine Meditations on Tropological Themes* (New York: Peter Lang, 1999).

12. Dalcroze was developed by the Swiss composer Émile Jacques-Dalcroze. A system of musical training that used movement, it was associated with "eurythmics" or self-expression.

13. Elgin W. Mellown, "Music and Dance in D. H. Lawrence," *Journal of Modern Literature* 21:1 (1997): 54. Henceforth cited in the text as "Music."

14. Mark Kinkead-Weekes, "Dance in Yeats, Lawrence, Eliot, and Williams," in *D. H. Lawrence: Literature, History, Culture*, eds. M. Bell, K. Cushman, T. Iida, and H. Tateishi (Tokyo: Kokusho-KankoKai Press, 2005), 246.

15. See Preston, *Modernism's Mythic Pose*.

16. Grosz's own view of race, which she elaborates in *Becoming Undone*, follows Darwin's view that "Racial differences . . . are those differences produced not by the direct effects of the environment (as sociobiology suggests), but through the operations of ideals of beauty and taste" (*Undone* 137).

17. See Chapter Four in Rohman, *Stalking*.

18. Many critics have corrected the view of Duncan as "purely" spontaneous by noting that her performances were highly crafted. She often choreographed into her works a "reaction" to musical cues that involved a few seconds' delay, creating a greater "illusion" of improvisation or spontaneity. Nonetheless, Duncan worked to develop movements that were less traditionally constrained and more connected to the body's own morphology, and to certain natural or material forces or rhythms. Thus, in my view, Duncan's association with the "unconscious" is not naïve or unjustified, if understood within a Deleuzian or even posthumanist theoretical register.

19. Andrew Harrison, "Electricity and the Place of Futurism in Women in Love," *D. H. Lawrence Review* 29 no. 2 (2000): 21. Henceforth cited in the text as "Electricity."

20. It is crucial to mention Nicole Shukin's incisive work on animal "magnetism" here. See Nicole Shukin, *Animal Capital: Rendering Life in Biopolitical Times* (Minneapolis: University of Minnesota Press, 2009). Shukin theorizes the "fantasy of 'painless transmission'" within electric transference that has been central to ideas about animal electricity since Galvani's work in the 1700s (Shukin 133). Shukin also insists upon a historical understanding of electricity that sees animal sacrifice at its core, reading the electrocution of Topsy the elephant in 1903 as a "founding symbolic and material gesture of early electrical and cinematic culture" (152). I do not have space to elaborate a number of Shukin's questions here, but it would be worth asking whether the disquiet of Gudrun (and Ursula's) experience constitutes a "painful transmission" that acknowledges, rather than elides, the Serrean "noise" of Gudrun's trans-species becoming.

21. See introduction, n. 25.

22. Deleuze, *Pure Immanence: Essays on a Life*, intro. John Rajchman, trans. Ann Boyman (New York: Zone Books, 2005), 28–29.

Chapter 3

1. This minor delay can by roughly approximated at several years if we consider the timeline between my book on animality in modernism, *Stalking the Subject* (2009)—which did not include Woolf among its considerations—and two recent books addressing Woolf and animality: Bonnie Kime Scott, *In the Hollow of the Wave: Virginia Woolf and Modernist Uses of Nature* (Charlottesville: University of Virginia, 2012); Derek Ryan, *Virginia Woolf and the Materiality of Theory: Sex, Animal, Life* (Edinburgh: Edinburgh University Press, 2013). The fall 2013 Virginia Woolf Miscellany on "Woolf and Animals" also signaled the rising interest in animals among Woolf scholars, as did the volume that I coedited: *Virginia Woolf and the Natural World: Selected Papers from the Twentieth International Conference on Virginia Woolf*, ed. Kristin Czarnecki and Carrie Rohman (Clemson, SC: Clemson Digital Press, 2011). That volume included, for instance, Jeanne Dubino's essay "Evolution, History, and Flush; or, The Origin of Spaniels." A few important essays had appeared earlier; see, for instance, Goldman, footnote 4. Other early essays included Craig Smith, "Across the Widest Gulf: Nonhuman Subjectivity in Virginia Woolf's *Flush*," *Twentieth Century Literature* 48, no. 3 (2002): 348–361 and Jutta Ittner, "Part Spaniel, Part Canine Puzzle: Anthropomorphism in Woolf's *Flush* and Auster's *Timbuktu*" *Mosaic* 39, no. 4 (2006): 181–196.

2. In this connection, Hermione Lee, an important biographer of Woolf, uses the phrase "her private interior zoo" (97) when describing Woolf's musings on interiority and the futility of biography. Lee's phrase comes after she quotes this extremely zoophilic portion of an entry in Woolf's diary: "As for the soul, why did I say I would leave it out? I forgot. And the truth is, one can't write directly about the soul. Looked at, it vanishes: but look at the ceiling, at Grizzle [the dog], at the cheaper beasts in the Zoo which are exposed to walkers in Regents Park, & the soul slips in. It slipped in this afternoon. I will write that I said, staring at the bison: answering L. absentmindedly but what was I going to write?" (qtd. in Lee 96–97). Hermione Lee, "Biomythographers: Rewriting the Lives of Virginia Woolf," *Essays in Criticism* 46, no. 2 (April 1996): 95–114.

3. See, for instance, Derek Ryan's fourth chapter, "The Question of the Animal in *Flush*," in *Virginia Woolf and the Materiality of Theory: Sex, Animal, Life*, henceforth cited in the text as *Materiality*. Recent essays on *Flush* include Jeanne Dubino, "Evolution, History, and *Flush*; or,

The Origin of Spaniels," in *Virginia Woolf and the Natural World: Selected Papers of the Twentieth Annual International Conference on Virginia Woolf*, ed. Kristin Czarnecki and Carrie Rohman (Clemson, SC: Clemson Digital Press, 2011); David Herman, "Modernist Life Writing and Nonhuman Lives: Ecologies of Experience in Virginia Woolf's Flush," *Modern Fiction Studies* 59, no. 3 (2013): 547–568, and Karalyn Kendall-Morwick, "Mongrel Fiction: Canine Bildung and the Feminist Critique of Anthropocentrism in Virginia Woolf's *Flush*," *Modern Fiction Studies* 60, no. 3 (2014): 506–526. Note again the earlier essays by Craig Smith and Jutta Ittner, cited above, which inform a number of these more recent investigations.

4. Bonnie Kime Scott, *In the Hollow of the Wave: Virginia Woolf and Modernist Uses of Nature* (Charlottesville: University of Virginia Press, 2012), 233, note 4. Henceforth cited in the text as *Hollow*.

5. Quentin Bell, *Virginia Woolf: A Biography* (New York: Harcourt, 1972). Henceforth cited in the text as *Biography*.

6. On the canine in Woolf, see Jane Goldman's influential essay, "'Ce chien est à moi': Virginia Woolf and the Signifying Dog," *Woolfian Boundaries: Selected Essays from the Sixteenth Annual International Conference on Virginia Woolf*, ed. Anna Burrells et al. (Clemson, SC: Clemson University Digital Press, 2007).

7. Kime Scott discusses Woolf's frequent visits to the Botanical Gardens at Kew alongside the Regent's Park Zoo in *Hollow*, 4.

8. Richard Epsley, "Woolf and the Others at the Zoo," *Woolfian Boundaries: Selected Essays from the Sixteenth Annual International Conference on Virginia Woolf*, ed. Anna Burrells et al. (Clemson, SC: Clemson University Digital Press): 86–99.

9. In the time since I began writing this book, Derek Ryan's *Virginia Woolf and the Materiality of Theory* (2013) has broken new ground in discussing Woolf's fiction and nonfiction in relation to Deleuzian concepts that include the concept of becoming. See especially his chapters four and five for readings that include questions of animality in Woolf.

10. The early, 1966 version henceforth cited in the text as *Thimble*.

11. See discussion of both the original and revised texts in Kristin Czarnecki, "Virginia Woolf, Authorship, and Legacy: Unravelling Nurse Lugton's Curtain," Bloomsbury Heritage Series (London: Cecil Woolf Publishers, 2013). Henceforth cited in the text as "Unravelling."

12. The later, 1991 version henceforth cited in the text as *Curtain*.

13. It is important to note that Hildick, when writing of his discovery in the *Times Literary Supplement* in 1965, seemed to have a more nuanced, or at least more speculative, set of notions about the relationship between the novel and the story. Wallace Hildick, "Virginia Woolf for Children?" *Times Literary Supplement* June 17, 1965. As Czarnecki mentions, he wondered whether the children's story gave Woolf a sort of relief from the violent themes in *Mrs. Dalloway*. See "Unravelling" 222.

14. Geneviéve Sanchis Morgan, "The Hostess and the Seamstress: Virginia Woolf's Creation of a Domestic Modernism," *Unmanning Modernism: Gendered Rereadings*, ed. Elizabeth Jane Harrison and Shirley Peterson (Knoxville: University of Tennessee Press, 1997), 95. Henceforth cited in the text as "Unmanning."

15. Sayaka Okumura, "Women Knitting: Domestic Activity, Writing, and Distance in Virginia Woolf's Fiction," *English Studies* 89, no. 2 (2008), 175. Henceforth cited in the text as "Women Knitting."

16. See, for instance, Hope Howell Hodgkins, "High Modernism for the Lowest: Children's Books by Woolf, Joyce, and Greene," *Children's Literature Association Quarterly* 32, no. 4 (2007): 354–367. Henceforth cited in the text as "Children's Books."

17. For an elaborated set of theories that locates aesthetics in *human* childrearing, see Ellen Dissanayake, *Art and Intimacy: How the Arts Began* (Seattle: University of Washington Press, 2000).

18. Gilles Deleuze and Félix Guattari, *Anti-Oedipus: Capitalism and Schizophrenia*, trans. Robert Hurley, Mark Seem, and Helen R. Lane (New York: Penguin Books, 2009), 26.

19. Michelle Levy, "Virginia Woolf's Shorter Fictional Explorations of the External World: 'closely united . . . immensely divided,'" in *Trespassing Boundaries: Virginia Woolf's Short Fiction*, ed. Kathryn N. Benzel and Ruth Hoberman (New York: Palgrave Macmillan, 2004), 148. Henceforth cited in the text as "Shorter."

20. Elizabeth Grosz, *The Nick of Time: Politics, Evolution, and the Untimely* (Durham, NC: Duke University Press, 2004), 19. Henceforth cited in the text as *Time*.

21. See my discussion of human "fur" in T. S. Eliot's "Sweeney" poems in *Stalking the Subject,* 35.

22. Czarnecki contacted Vivas to ask if she had seen the 1966 version that included Duncan Grant's paintings, and Vivas (who had read several of Woolf's novels) responded that she "had not seen or even known of the previous publication or Grant's pictures" ("Unravelling" 24).

23. As I will mention later in this chapter, the character Jinny in Woolf's novel *The Waves* discusses a monkey that "drops nuts from its naked paws" (*Waves* 176). Virginia Woolf, *The Waves* (New York: Harcourt, 1931). Henceforth cited in the text as *Waves*. Moreover, Louis in the same novel discusses his own social preening in similar terms: "it is for them that I do these antics, smoothing my hair, concealing my accent. I am the little ape who chatters over a nut" (*Waves* 128).

24. Bataille, like many twentieth-century thinkers and scientists, mistakenly understood tool use as an exclusively human capacity. See Chapter Two in *Theory of Religion.*

25. Gilles Deleuze, *Pure Immanence: Essays on A Life*, trans. Anne Boyman (New York: Zone Books, 2005), 28, 30. Henceforth cited in the text as *Immanence*.

26. Charles Darwin, *The Descent of Man, and Selection in Relation to Sex*, Volume 2, 1st edition (London: John Murray, 1871), 292.

27. Grosz reiterates that sexual selection is not best understood as exclusively adaptive or utilitarian: "Sexual selection is not the ability to choose the best genes for the following generation, but is rather the activity of spontaneous beings who operate according to their (sometimes) irrational desires and tastes to make bodily connections and encounters, sometimes but not always leading to orgasm or copulation, and even less frequently to reproduction" (*Undone* 131).

28. Gilles Deleuze, *Difference and Repetition*, trans. Paul Patton (New York: Columbia University Press, 1994), 28.

29. It is crucial to note here that Grosz's emphasis on sexual difference, following Irigaray, does not cancel out queer or transgendered identities and thus should not be glossed as such. When discussing Irigaray's claims about sexual difference, Grosz notes that Irigaray "questions, not homosexuality, nor ethnic identification, but only the disavowal of one's own morphological specificity. However queer, transgendered, and ethnically identified one might be, one comes from a man and a woman, and one remains a man and a woman, even in the case of gender-reassignment or the chemical and surgical transformation of one sex into the appearance of another" (*Undone* 109–110). As fluid and flexible, as historically contingent and malleable as sexuality may be, Grosz insists "there is no overcoming of sexual difference" (*Undone* 111).

30. See Carrie Rohman, "Disciplinary Becomings: Horizons of Knowledge in Animal Studies," *Hypatia: A Journal of Feminist Philosophy* 27, no. 3 (2012) and Rohman, "Animals," *Literature Now: Key Terms and Methods for Literary History*, ed. Sascha Bru, Ben de Bruyn, and Michel Delville (Edinburgh: Edinburgh University Press, 2016).

31. Jacques Derrida, *The Animal That Therefore I Am*, trans. David Wills (New York: Fordham University Press, 2008), 29.

32. Kari Weil, *Thinking Animals: Why Animal Studies Now?* (New York: Columbia University Press, 2012), xv. Henceforth cited in the text as *Thinking Animals*.

33. See Woolf's idea about a pattern hidden behind the "cotton wool of daily life" in her posthumously published memoir "Sketch of the Past," in Virginia Woolf, *Moments of Being: A Collection of Autobiographical Writing*, ed. Jeanne Schulkind (New York: Harcourt, 1985), 72. Ryan discusses this idea at the very outset of his introduction in *Materiality*, and his entire introduction is important in elaborating the relevance of new materialisms to Woolf's work.

34. Henri Bergson, *Creative Evolution*, trans. Arthur Mitchell (New York: Dover, 1998), 20, 23. Henceforth cited in the text as *Evolution*.

35. Gilles Deleuze, *Bergsonism*, trans. Hugh Tomlinson and Barbara Habberjam (New York: Zone Books, 1991), 99–100.

36. Gilles Deleuze, *The Fold: Leibniz and the Baroque*, trans. Tom Conley (Minneapolis: University of Minnesota Press, 1993), 7. Henceforth cited in the text as *Fold*.

37. Henri Bergson, *The Creative Mind*, trans. Arthur Mitchell (New York: Citadel, 1992), 95.

38. Cliff Stagoll, "Plane," *The Deleuze Dictionary*, ed. Adrian Parr (New York: Columbia University Press, 2005), 204. Henceforth cited in the text as "Plane."

39. See also Chapter Six in *The Fold: Leibniz and the Baroque*, in which Deleuze claims that events "are produced in a chaos, in a chaotic multiplicity, but only under the condition that a sort of screen intervenes" (*Fold* 76). Laci Mattison discusses the relationship between chaos and art (and the event) in this register, as well, in her essay "Woolf's Un/Folding(s): The Artist and the Event of the Neo-Baroque," *Contradictory Woolf: Selected Papers from the Twenty-First Annual International Conference on Virginia Woolf*, ed. Derek Ryan and Stella Bolaki (Clemson, SC: Clemson University Digital Press, 2012).

40. Rosi Braidotti, "The Politics of 'Life Itself,'" in *New Materialisms: Ontology, Agency, and Politics*, ed. Diana Coole and Samantha Frost (Durham, NC: Duke University Press, 2010), 212. Henceforth cited in the text as "Life Itself."

41. These critical observations are numerous in Woolf criticism. For instance, Poole and D'Amore link Rhoda's character to projections about Woolf's childhood sexual abuse; Roger Poole, *The Unknown Virginia Woolf* (Cambridge: Cambridge University Press, 1978; 4th ed.; Alice D'Amore, "Autobiographical Ruptures: Rhoda's Traumatic Displacement," *Woolf and the Art of Exploration: Selected Papers from the Fifteenth International Conference on Virginia Woolf* (Clemson, SC: Clemson University Digital Press, 2006): 44–49. Beer and Sypher discuss Bernard's role as primary narrator in the novel; Gillian Beer, *Virginia Woolf: The Common Ground* (Ann Arbor: University of Michigan Press, 1996); Eileen B. Sypher, "*The Waves*: A Utopia of Androgyny?" in *Virginia Woolf: Centennial Essays*, ed. Elaine Ginsberg and Laura Gottlieb (Troy, NY: Whitston, 1983): 187–213. Clifford Wulfman acknowledges and warns against the somewhat easy collapse of Bernard and Woolf's voices in his discussion of narrative failure in the text: Clifford E. Wulfman, "Woolf and the Discourse of Trauma," *Virginia Woolf and Trauma: Embodied Texts*, ed. Suzette Henke and David Eberly (New York: Pace University Press, 2007): 157–177.

42. *Merce Cunningham: Fifty Years*, Chronicle and Commentary by David Vaughan (New York: Aperture Foundation, 1997), 63. Henceforth cited in the text as MC.

43. See Derek Ryan, "Following Snakes and Moths: Modernist Ethics and Posthumanism," *Twentieth Century Literature* 61, no. 3 (September 2015): 287–304.

44. Virginia Woolf, *The Letters of Virginia Woolf*, 6 vols., ed. Nigel Nicolson and Joanne Trautmann (London: The Hogarth Press, 1975–1980): *Letters*, IV, 204.

45. It is important to note here the Deleuzian reading of *The Waves* that Beatrice Monaco presents in her book *Machinic Modernism: The Deleuzian Literary Machines of Woolf, Lawrence and Joyce* (New York: Palgrave, 2008). Monaco's reading has points of overlap with my own, and she compellingly discusses Woolf's novel as "a narrative 'organism' which pulses with cosmic, territorial and artistic life" (162). Monaco emphasizes the machinic elements of the novel, while I am more interested in the aestheticization of life.

46. Jane Goldman, ed., *Columbia Critical Guides: Virginia Woolf, To the Lighthouse, The Waves*, series ed., Richard Beynon (New York: Columbia University Press, 1998), 82. Henceforth cited in the text as CC.

47. Suzette Henke, "*The Waves* as Ontological Trauma Narrative," *Virginia Woolf and Trauma: Embodied Texts*, ed. Suzette Henke and David Eberly (New York: Pace University Press, 2007), 128. Henceforth cited in the text as "Ontological Trauma."

48. Patrick McGee, "The Politics of Modernist Form: Or, Who Rules *The Waves*?" *Modern Fiction Studies* 38, no. 3 (Autumn 1992): 386.

49. See the introduction in Rohman, *Stalking the Subject*.

50. Jane Marcus, "Britannia Rules *The Waves*," in *Decolonizing Tradition: New Views of Twentieth-Century 'British' Literary Canon*, ed. Karen Lawrence (Urbana: University of Illinois Press, 1992): 136–162.

51. In fact, Henke briefly mentions Jinny's dancerly tendencies and animal alliances, but Henke ultimately sees Jinny as exhibiting a childlike "hedonistic life-style," ending in a "swan song both for herself as a vulnerable subject and for Britannia's crumbling empire" ("Ontological Trauma" 136).

52. See also Derek Ryan's important engagement with similar questions about Jinny, where he deftly notes that Jinny is the only character in *The Waves* who refers to "a life" rather than

"my life," in his analysis of Baradian intra-actions and Deleuzian immanence in the novel (*Materiality* Chapter Five, especially 195).

53. For a discussion of this concept see Jakob von Uexküll, *A Foray into the Worlds of Animals and Humans*, trans. Joseph D. O'Neil (Minneapolis: University of Minnesota Press, 2010).

Chapter 4

1. Moira Roth, "Chronology," in *Rachel Rosenthal*, ed. Moira Roth (Baltimore and London: Johns Hopkins University Press, 1997), 205–206.
2. See USA Projects (2013), "Rachel Rosenthal Company," http://www.usaprojects.org/user/rachelrosenthalcompany, accessed July 1, 2013. Rosenthal died in 2015. At this time, her company continues to teach and perform.
3. Alexandra Grilikhes, "Taboo Subjects: An Interview with Rachel Rosenthal," in *Rachel Rosenthal*, ed. Moira Roth (Baltimore and London: Johns Hopkins University Press [1997; originally 1994–1995]), 60. Henceforth cited in the text as "Taboo."
4. See also Lourdes Orozco's discussion of *The Others*, in *Theatre and Animals*.
5. For a broad examination of the "ethic of care" tradition in feminist animal philosophy, see Josephine Donovan and Carol J. Adams, *The Feminist Care Tradition in Animal Ethics* (New York: Columbia University Press, 2007).
6. Myasthenia gravis is an autoimmune neuromuscular disease that is characterized by weakness, fatigue, and reduced functionality of the muscles.
7. Jacques Derrida, *The Animal That Therefore I Am* (New York: Fordham University Press, 2008), 28.
8. H. Peter Steeves, "Rachel Rosenthal Is an Animal," *Mosaic: A Journal for the Interdisciplinary Study of Literature* 39, no. 4 (2006). Henceforth cited in the text as RRA.
9. Phaedrus was an Athenian aristocrat depicted in Plato's texts as one of Socrates's primary interlocutors.
10. Considered by many to be Rauschenberg's most famous work, this piece was one of his "Combines" from the 1950s and early 1960s. "Combines" featured surprising combinations of found objects, clothing, debris, and traditional artistic materials such as paint, and taxidermied animals.
11. Compare also Steve Baker's discussion in *Artist/Animal* of Kim Jones's performance piece from 1976, in which he burned living rats on stage.
12. Rachel Rosenthal, *Rachel's Brain and Other Storms*, edited and with commentaries by Una Chaudhuri (London and New York: Continuum, 2001), 92. Henceforth cited in the text as *Traps*.
13. I want to thank Robert McKay for alerting me to Rosenthal's text several years ago in a discussion about animality and performance.
14. The written text deserves its own critical glossing, particularly given the pitched discussions of the affective in recent feminist animal studies work. For a discussion of the role of affect in feminist/animal studies, see *Hypatia: A Journal of Feminist Philosophy*, Special Issue: 'Animal Others,' vol. 27, no. 3 (July 2012).
15. Rachel Rosenthal, *Tatti Wattles: A Love Story* (Santa Monica, CA: Smart Art Press, 1996), 8. Henceforth cited in the text as *Tatti*.
16. Julia Kristeva, *The Kristeva Reader* (New York: Columbia University Press, 1986), 94.
17. See Derek Ryan's discussion of strains of skepticism toward Deleuze and Guattari's "becoming-animal" in animal studies, where he argues that rather than remaining primarily a too-sublime framework, Deleuzian becoming allows us to "enter into a zone or territory of proximity or indeterminacy, the shared event of becoming different, of becoming entangled with the other in a de- and then re-making of traditional ontological categories of human and animal" (539); Derek Ryan, "'The reality of becoming': Deleuze, Woolf and the Territory of Cows," *Deleuze Studies* 7, no. 4 (2013): 537–561. I clearly agree with the view of becoming as a productive concept for animal studies, though I want to remain alert to the tendency in Deleuze to associate animality proper with a form of packness, and thus to reinforce the notion that animals are not individuals or do not experience a form of self or subjectivity. As Rosenthal's text implies, animals ought to be considered in their singularities and their multiplicities.

18. Karlheinz Stockhausen, *Aus Den Sieben Tagen (From the Seven Days)*, trans. Rolf Gehlhaar, John McGuire, and Hugh Davies (Universal Edition UE 14790, 1968), 25.

19. Bonnie Marranca, "A Cosmography of Herself: The Autobiology of Rachel Rosenthal," in *Rachel Rosenthal*, ed. Moira Roth (Baltimore and London: Johns Hopkins University Press [1997; originally 1996]), 79.

20. Moira Roth, "Introduction," in *Rachel Rosenthal*, ed. Moira Roth (Baltimore and London: Johns Hopkins University Press, 1997), 15.

21. See Rachel Rosenthal, *Rachel's Brain and Other Storms*, edited and with commentaries by Una Chaudhuri (London and New York: Continuum, 2001).

22. Rachel Rosenthal, *Rachel's Brain and Other Storms*, edited and with commentaries by Una Chaudhuri (London and New York: Continuum, 2001). Henceforth cited in the text as RB.

23. See Kelly Anspaugh, "Powers of Ordure: James Joyce and the Excremental Vision(s)," *Mosaic: A Journal for the Interdisciplinary Study of Literature* 27, no. 1 (1994): 73–100.

24. David Wills, *Prosthesis* (Stanford, CA: Stanford University Press, 1995), 10. Henceforth cited in the text as *Prosthesis*.

25. See especially Chapter Seven in Wolfe, *What is Posthumanism?*

26. See Derrida's discussion of "carnophallogocentrism" in Jacques Derrida, "'Eating Well,' or The Calculation of the Subject: An Interview with Jacques Derrida," in *Who Comes After the Subject?* ed. Eduardo Cadava, Peter Connor, and Jean-Luc Nancy (New York: Routledge, 1991): 96–119.

27. For further discussion of the fur industry, see Chapter Four in Erin E. Williams and Margo DeMello, *Why Animals Matter* (New York: Prometheus Books, 2007).

28. See especially Part One of Bataille's *Theory of Religion*.

Chapter 5

1. Alastair Macaulay, "Merce Cunningham's Multifaceted Mirror, Held Up to Nature," *The New York Times*, January 6, 2017.

2. See Carrie Rohman, "No Higher Life: Bio-aesthetics in J. M. Coetzee's *Disgrace*," *Modern Fiction Studies* 60, no. 3 (September 2014): 562–578.

3. Alex Ross, "Searching for Silence: John Cage's art of noise," *The New Yorker*, October 4, 2010. Henceforth cited in the text as "Searching."

4. "Listen: John Cage-in love with another sound-01," interview excerpted from documentary film by Miroslav Sebestik, "John Cage: Compositeur," interview conducted February 4, 1991. Henceforth cited in the text as "another sound." Available at https://www.youtube.com/watch?v=2aYT1Pxp30M

5. *Cage/Cunningham*, a film by Elliot Caplan, 1991, 39:17.

6. *Merce Cunningham: Fifty Years*, Chronicle and Commentary by David Vaughan (New York: Aperture Foundation, 1997), preface 1. Henceforth cited in the text as MC.

7. Merce Cunningham, "A Collaborative Process Between Music and Dance," *TriQuarterly* 54 (spring 1982). Reprinted in *A John Cage Reader*, ed. Peter Gena and Jonathan Brent (New York: C. F. Peters, 1982), 176–177.

8. Carolyn Brown, untitled essay, *Dance Perspectives* 34 (issue titled *Time to Walk in Space*; Summer 1968): 29.

9. Carrie Noland, "The Human Situation on Stage: Merce Cunningham, Theodor Adorno, and the Category of Expression," *Dance Research Journal*, 42, no. 1 (Summer 2010): 47. Henceforth cited in the text as "Human Situation."

10. Noland notes developments in neuroscience that understand a form of motor, proprioceptive sense as largely preceding psychic interactions with the world. Neuroscientists use the term "protoself" to describe such interactions, and they understand this self as "evolutionarily prior" ("Human Situation" 55).

11. Merce Cunningham, *Other Animals: Drawings and Journals* (New York: Aperture Foundation, 2002), 14. Henceforth cited in the text as OA. I am grateful to Laura Kuhn, who is transcribing Mr. Cunningham's notebook entries, for confirmation of this segment, and for confirmation of the fact that Blotch was the last family cat Mr. Cunningham had. Blotch was a gift from the curator, Julie Lazar, from the Museum of Contemporary Art Los Angeles, in 1992, the day

after John Cage died. According to Ms. Kuhn, Julie thought Merce (and another cat named Losa) would be lonely after Mr. Cage's death.

12. Cunningham repeats similar sentiments on another page when he compares the skin of the iguana to "Byzantine jewels" (OA 44). Again, I am grateful to Laura Kuhn for helping me decipher Cunningham's handwriting.

13. See Chapter Five, "Revising the Human," in Rohman, *Stalking the Subject*.

14. See Dance Capsule for BIPED at mercecunningham.org.

15. Brian Massumi, "The Supernormal Animal," *The Nonhuman Turn*, ed. Richard Grusin (Minneapolis: University of Minnesota Press, 2015), 5. Henceforth cited in the text as "Supernormal."

16. See, for instance, Major Jackson's poetic exploration of this idea in "Metaphor," from *Hoops*. Major Jackson, *Hoops* (New York: W. W. Norton, 2007).

17. William E. Connolly, *The Fragility of Things* (Durham, NC: Duke University Press, 2013), 162–163. Henceforth cited in the text as *Fragility*.

18. See Terrence W. Deacon, *Incomplete Nature: How Mind Emerged from Matter* (New York: W. W. Norton, 2013).

19. See Carrie Noland's work, cited above.

Afterword

1. Elliot Caplan, *Cage/Cunningham*. DVD. West Long Branch: Kultur, 1991.

2. See also Steven Belletto, *No Accident, Comrade: Chance and Design in Cold War American Narratives* (New York: Oxford University Press, 2012), 13.

3. Brad Evans, "Humans in Dark Times," *The New York Times*, February 23, 2017.

4. Brad Evans and Bracha L. Ettinger, "Art in a Time of Atrocity," *The New York Times*, December 16, 2016.

BIBLIOGRAPHY

Accocella, Joan. "Mark Morris: The Body and What it Means." In *The Routledge Dance Studies Reader*, edited by Alexandra Carter, 269–277. New York: Routledge, 2010.

Aloi, Giovanni. "Animal Studies and Art: Elephants in the Room." Special Editorial. *Antennae*. February 2015.

———. *Art and Animals*. London: I. B. Tauris, 2012.

Anderson, Jack. "The Dance: Ann Carlson's 'Animals.'" *New York Times*. February 7, 1988.

Anidjar, Gil. "The Meaning of Life." *Critical Inquiry* 37, no. 4 (2011): 697–723.

Anspaugh, Kelly. "Powers of Ordure: James Joyce and the Excremental Vision(s)." *Mosaic: A Journal for the Interdisciplinary Study of Literature* 27, no. 1 (1994): 73–100.

Baker, Steve. *Artist / Animal*. Minneapolis: University of Minnesota Press, 2013.

———. *Picturing the Beast: Animals Identity, and Representation*. Urbana: University of Illinois Press, 1993.

———. *The Postmodern Animal*. London: Reaktion Books, 2000.

Bataille, Georges. *Theory of Religion*. Trans. Robert Hurly. New York: Zone Books, 1989.

———. *Visions of Excess: Selected Writings, 1927–1939*. Edited by Allan Stoekl. Translated by Allan Stoekl with Carl R. Lovitt and Donald M. Leslie, Jr. Minneapolis: University of Minnesota Press, 1985.

Becket, Fiona. *D. H. Lawrence: The Thinker as Poet*. New York: St. Martin's Press, 1997.

Beer, Gillian. *Virginia Woolf: The Common Ground*. Ann Arbor: University of Michigan Press, 1996.

Belilove, Lori. Master class. Isadora Duncan Dance Foundation of New York. Franklin and Marshall College. Lancaster, Pennsylvania. February 26, 2014.

———. Personal interview. February 27, 2014.

Bell, Quentin. *Virginia Woolf: A Biography*. New York: Harcourt, 1972.

Belletto, Steven. *No Accident, Comrade: Chance and Design in Cold War American Narratives*. New York: Oxford University Press, 2012.

Berger, John. *About Looking*. New York: Vintage, 1992.

Bergson, Henri. *Creative Evolution*. Translated by Arthur Mitchell. New York: Dover, 1998.

———. *The Creative Mind*. Translated by Arthur Mitchell. New York: Citadel, 1992.

Braidotti, Rosi. "Animals, Anomolies, and Inorganic Others." *PMLA* 124, no. 2 (2009): 526–532.

———. "The Politics of 'Life Itself.'" In *New Materialisms: Ontology, Agency, and Politics*, edited by Diana Coole and Samantha Frost, 201–218. Durham, NC: Duke University Press, 2010.

———. *Transpositions: On Nomadic Ethics*. London: Polity, 2006.

Bresciani, Jeanne. Telephone interview. January 26, 2014.

Bennett, Jane. *Vibrant Matter: A Political Ecology of Things*. Durham, NC: Duke University Press, 2010.

Broglio, Ron. *Surface Encounters: Thinking with Animals and Art*. Minneapolis: University of Minnesota Press, 2011.

Brown, Carolyn. Untitled essay. *Dance Perspectives* (issue titled *Time to Walk in Space*). 34 (Summer 1968).

Caplan, Elliot. *Cage/Cunningham*. DVD. West Long Branch: Kultur, 1991.

Carlson, Ann. "Visit Woman Move Story Cat Cat Cat." In *Animals*. Performance. Bessie Schonberg Theater. 1988.

Carter, Alexandra and Rachel Fensham. *Dancing Naturally: Nature, Neo-Classicism and Modernity in Early Twentieth-Century Dance*. New York: Palgrave Macmillan, 2011.

Chaudhuri, Una. "Animal Geographies: Zooësis and the Space of Modern Drama." *Modern Drama* XLVI, no. 4 (2003): 646–662.

———. "Queering the Green Man, Reframing the Garden: Marina Zurkow's Mesocosm (Northumberland UK) and the Theatre of Species." *Scapegoat: Architecture/Landscape/Political Economy*. Issue 2: Materialism (2011): 6–8.

Chaudhuri, Una and Holly Hughes, eds. *Animal Acts: Performing Species Today*. Ann Arbor: University of Michigan Press, 2014.

Cheney, Sheldon. "Introduction." In *The Art of the Dance*, edited by Sheldon Cheney, 1–11. New York: Theatre Arts, 1969.

Connolly, William E. *The Fragility of Things: Self-Organizing Processes, Neoliberal Fantasies, and Democratic Activism*. Durham, NC: Duke University Press, 2013.

Coole, Diana and Samantha Frost, eds. *New Materialisms: Ontology, Agency, and Politics*. Durham, NC: Duke University Press, 2010.

Craig, Gordon. "Memories of Isadora Duncan." *Irma Duncan Papers*. New York Public Library for Performing Arts.

Cunningham, Merce. "A Collaborative Process Between Music and Dance." *TriQuarterly* 54 (Spring 1982). Reprinted in *A John Cage Reader*, edited by Peter Gena and Jonathan Brent, 176–177. New York: C. F. Peters, 1982.

———. *Other Animals: Drawings and Journals*. New York: Aperture Foundation, 2002.

Czarnecki, Kristin. "Virginia Woolf, Authorship, and Legacy: Unravelling Nurse Lugton's Curtain." Bloomsbury Heritage Series. London: Cecil Woolf Publishers, 2013.

Czarnecki, Kristin and Carrie Rohman, eds. *Virginia Woolf and the Natural World: Selected Papers from the Twentieth International Conference on Virginia Woolf*. Clemson, SC: Clemson University Digital Press, 2011.

Czarnecki, Kristin and Vara Neverow, eds. *Virginia Woolf Miscellany* 84 (Fall 2013).

Daly, Ann. *Critical Gestures: Writings on Dance and Culture*. Middletown, CT: Wesleyan University Press, 2002.

D'Amore, Alice. "Autobiographical Ruptures: Rhoda's Traumatic Displacement," in *Woolf and the Art of Exploration: Selected Paper from the Fifteenth International Conference on Virginia Woolf*, 44–49. Clemson, SC: Clemson University Digital Press, 2006.

Darwin, Charles. *The Descent of Man, and Selection in Relation to Sex*. Volume 2, 1st ed. London: John Murray, 1871.

Davies, Stephen. *The Artful Species*. Oxford: Oxford University Press, 2012.

———. *The Philosophy of Art*. Malden, MA: Blackwell, 2006.

Deacon, Terrence W. *Incomplete Nature: How Mind Emerged from Matter*. New York: W. W. Norton, 2013.

Deleuze, Gilles. *Bergsonism*. Translated by Hugh Tomlinson and Barbara Habberjam. New York: Zone Books, 1991.

———. *Difference and Repetition*. Translated by Paul Patton. New York: Columbia University Press, 1994.

———. *Pure Immanence: Essays on A Life*. Translated by Anne Boyman. New York: Zone Books, 2005.

———. *The Fold: Leibniz and the Baroque*. Translated by Tom Conley. Minneapolis: University of Minnesota Press, 1993.

Deleuze, Gilles and Félix Guattari. *Anti-Oedipus: Capitalism and Schizophrenia*. Translated by Robert Hurley, Mark Seem, and Helen R. Lane. New York: Penguin Books, 2009.

——. *A Thousand Plateaus: Capitalism and Schizophrenia*. Translated by Brian Massumi. Minneapolis: University of Minnesota Press, 1987.

——. *What Is Philosophy?* Translated by Hugh Tomlinson and Graham Burchell. New York: Columbia University Press, 1994.

Dempster, Elizabeth. "Women Writing the Body: Let's Watch a Little How She Dances," in *Grafts: Feminist Cultural Criticism*, edited by Susan Sheridan, 35–54. London: Verso, 1988.

Derrida, Jacques. "'Eating Well,' or The Calculation of the Subject: An Interview with Jacques Derrida," in *Who Comes After the Subject?* edited by Eduardo Cadava, Peter Connor, and Jean-Luc Nancy, 96-119. New York: Routledge, 1991.

——. "The Animal That Therefore I Am (More to Follow)," in *The Animal That Therefore I Am*, edited by Marie-Louise Mallet; translated by David Wills, 1–51. New York: Fordham University Press, 2008.

Desmond, Jane. "Can Animals Make 'Art'?" Popular and Scientific Discourses About Expressivity and Cognition in Primates," in *Experiencing Animal Minds: An Anthology of Animal-Human Encounters*, edited by Julie A. Smith and Robert W. Mitchell, 95–108. New York: Columbia University Press, 2012.

Dissanayake, Ellen. *Art and Intimacy: How the Arts Began*. Seattle: University of Washington Press, 2000.

Doherty, Gerald. *Theorizing Lawrence: Nine Meditations on Tropological Themes*. New York: Peter Lang, 1999.

Donovan, Josephine and Carol J. Adams. *The Feminist Care Tradition in Animal Ethics*. New York: Columbia University Press, 2007.

Dubino, Jeanne. "Evolution, History, and *Flush*; or, The Origin of Spaniels," in *Virginia Woolf and the Natural World: Selected Papers of the Twentieth Annual International Conference on Virginia Woolf*, edited by Kristin Czarnecki and Carrie Rohman, 143–150. Clemson, SC: Clemson University Digital Press, 2011.

Duncan, Isadora. "Movement is Life" [ca. 1909], in *The Art of the Dance*, edited by Sheldon Cheney, 77–79. New York: Theatre Arts, 1969.

——. *My Life*. New York: Liveright, 1927.

——. "Notes for a Lecture." *Irma Duncan Papers*. New York Public Library for Performing Arts.

——. "Terpsichore," in *The Art of the Dance*, edited by Sheldon Cheney, 90–91. New York: Theatre Arts, 1969.

——. "The Dance of the Future" [1909], in *The Art of the Dance*, edited by Sheldon Cheney, 54–63. New York: Theatre Arts, 1969.

——. "The Dancer and Nature" [ca. 1905], in *The Art of the Dance*, edited by Sheldon Cheney, 66–70. New York: Theatre Arts, 1969.

——. "The Philosopher's Stone of Dancing" [1920], in *The Art of the Dance*, edited by Sheldon Cheney, 51–53. New York: Theatre Arts, 1969.

——. "What Dancing Should Be," in *The Art of the Dance*, edited by Sheldon Cheney, 71–73. New York: Theatre Arts, 1969.

——. "Youth and the Dance," in *The Art of the Dance*, edited by Sheldon Cheney, 97–98. New York: Theatre Arts, 1969.

Eastman, Max. Foreword. In Arnold Genthe, *Isadora Duncan: Twenty-Four Studies by Arnold Genthe*. New York: Mitchell Kennerley, 1929.

Eliot, T. S. "The Love Song of J. Alfred Prufrock." *Collected Poems 1909–1962*. New York: Harcourt Brace Jovanovich, 1963.

Ellmann, Richard. "Lawrence and His Demon" [1953], in *D. H. Lawrence's Poetry: Demon Liberated*, edited by A. Banerjee, 186-199. London: Macmillan, 1990.

Engdahl Coates, Kimberly. "Performing Feminism, Transmitting Affect: Isadora Duncan, Virginia Woolf, and the Politics of Movement," in *Interdisciplinary/Multidisciplinary Woolf: Selected*

Papers from the 22nd Annual International Conference on Virginia Woolf, edited by Ann Martin and Kathryn Hill, 183–189. Clemson, SC: Clemson University Press, 2013.

Epsely, Richard. "Woolf and the Others at the Zoo," in *Woolfian Boundaries: Selected Essays from the Sixteenth Annual International Conference on Virginia Woolf,* edited by Anna Burrells et al., 86–99. Clemson, SC: Clemson University Digital Press.

Evans, Brad. "Humans in Dark Times." *New York Times.* February 23, 2017.

Evans, Brad and Bracha L. Ettinger. "Art in a Time of Atrocity." *New York Times.* December 16, 2016.

Franko, Mark. *Dancing Modernism/Performing Politics.* Bloomington: Indiana University Press, 1995.

Freud, Sigmund. *Civilization and its Discontents.* Translated by Joan Riviere. London: Hogarth Press, 1930.

Fuss, Diana. *Human, All Too Human.* London: Routledge, 1996.

Giovannelli, Alessandro. *Aesthetics: The Key Thinkers.* New York: Bloomsbury, 2012.

Goldman, Jane, ed. "'Ce chien est à moi' ": Virginia Woolf and the Signifying Dog," in *Woolfian Boundaries: Selected Essays from the Sixteenth Annual International Conference on Virginia Woolf,* edited by Anna Burrells, Steve Ellis, Deborah Parsons, and Kathryn Simpson, 100–107. Clemson, SC: Clemson University Digital Press, 2007.

———. *Columbia Critical Guides: Virginia Woolf, To the Lighthouse, The Waves.* Series Ed., Richard Beynon. New York: Columbia University Press, 1998.

Goodall, Jane. "The Dance of Awe." Interview by Kimberley Patton and Paul Waldau. In *A Communion of Subjects: Animals in Religion, Science, and Ethics,* Edited by Paul Waldau and Kimberely Patton, 651–656. New York: Columbia University Press, 2009.

Gregg, Melissa and Gregory J. Seigworth, eds. *The Affect Theory Reader,* Durham, NC: Duke University Press, 2010.

Grilikhes, Alexandra. "Taboo Subjects: An Interview with Rachel Rosenthal" [1994–95], in *Rachel Rosenthal,* edited by Moira Roth, 60–76. Baltimore and London: Johns Hopkins University Press, 1997.

Grosz, Elizabeth. *Becoming Undone: Darwinian Reflections on Life, Politics, and Art.* Durham, NC: Duke University Press, 2011.

———. *Chaos, Territory, Art: Deleuze and the Framing of the Earth.* New York: Columbia University Press, 2008.

———. "The Creative Impulse." Interview by Julie Copeland. *Sunday Morning Radio National.* August 14, 2005. Accessed online January 11, 2009.

———. *The Nick of Time: Politics, Evolution, and the Untimely.* Durham, NC: Duke University Press, 2004.

Harrison, Andrew. "Electricity and the Place of Futurism in Women in Love." *D. H. Lawrence Review* 29, no. 2 (2000): 7–23.

Helmreich, Stefan. "What Was Life? Answers from Three Limit Biologies." *Critical Inquiry* 37, no. 4 (2011): 671–696.

Henke, Suzette. "*The Waves* as Ontological Trauma Narrative," in *Virginia Woolf and Trauma: Embodied Texts,* edited by Suzette Henke and David Eberly, 123–155. New York: Pace University Press, 2007.

Herman, David. *Creatural Fictions: Human-Animal Relationships in Twentieth- and Twenty-First-Century Literature.* New York: Palgrave Macmillan, 2016.

———. "Modernist Life Writing and Nonhuman Lives: Ecologies of Experience in Virginia Woolf's *Flush.*" *Modern Fiction Studies.* Special Issue: "Modernist Life Narratives: Bildungsroman, Biography, Autobiography." 59, no. 3 (2013): 547–568.

Hildick, Wallace. "Virginia Woolf for Children?" *Times Literary Supplement.* June 17, 1965.

Hodgkins, Hope Howell. "High Modernism for the Lowest: Children's Books by Woolf, Joyce, and Greene." *Children's Literature Association Quarterly* 32, no. 4 (2007): 353–367.

Ittner, Jutta. "Part Spaniel, Part Canine Puzzle: Anthropomorphism in Woolf's *Flush* and Auster's *Timbuktu.*" *Mosaic* 39, no. 4 (2006): 181–96.

Jackson, Major. *Hoops.* New York: W. W. Norton, 2007.

Kendall-Morwick, Karalyn. "Mongrel Fiction: Canine Bildung and the Feminist Critique of Anthropocentrism in Virginia Woolf's *Flush.*" *Modern Fiction Studies* 60, no. 3 (2014): 506–526.

Kinkead-Weekes, Mark. "Dance in Yeats, Lawrence, Eliot, and Williams," in *D. H. Lawrence: Literature, History, Culture,* edited by Michael Bell, Keith Cushman, Takeo Iida, and Hiro Tateishi, 236–258. Tokyo: Kokusho-KankoKai Press.

Kondo, Kyoko. "Metaphor in *Women in Love.*" In *D. H. Lawrence: New Worlds,* edited by Keith Cushman and Earl G. Ingersoll, 163–182. Madison, NJ: Fairleigh Dickinson University Press, 2003.

Kristeva, Julia. *The Kristeva Reader.* New York: Columbia University Press, 1986.

LaChapelle, Dolores. *D. H. Lawrence: Future Primitive.* Denton: University of North Texas Press, 1996.

Lawrence, D. H. *Birds, Beasts, and Flowers.* Santa Rosa, CA: Black Sparrow Press, 1995.

——. "Fantasia of the Unconscious," In *Psychoanalysis and the Unconscious and Fantasia of the Unconscious,* edited by Bruce Steele, 45–204. Cambridge: Cambridge University Press, 2004.

——. "Tortoise shout," In *The Cambridge Edition of The Poems,* edited by Christopher Pollnitz, 316-318. Cambridge: Cambridge University Press, 2013.

——. David Farmer, John Worthen and Lindeth Vasey, eds. *Women in Love.* Cambridge: Cambridge University Press, 1987.

Lee, Hermione. "Biomythographers: Rewriting the Lives of Virginia Woolf." *Essays in Criticism* 46, no. 2 (April 1996): 95–114.

LeGuin, Ursula K. Introduction. *Buffalo Gals And Other Animal Presences.* Santa Barbara, CA: Capra Press, 1987.

Lemm, Vanessa. *Nietzsche's Animal Philosophy: Culture, Politics, and the Animality of the Human Being.* New York: Fordham University Press, 2009.

Levy, Eric P. "Ontological incoherence in *Women in Love.*" *College Literature* 30, no. 4 (2003): 156–165.

Levy, Michelle. "Virginia Woolf's Shorter Fictional Explorations of the External World: 'closely united . . . immensely divided,'" in *Trespassing Boundaries: Virginia Woolf's Short Fiction,* edited by Kathryn N. Benzel and Ruth Hoberman, 139–155. New York: Palgrave Macmillan, 2004.

Lori Belilove and the Isadora Duncan Dance Company. Performance. Lori Belilove, director. The Ware Center, Lancaster, Pennsylvania. February 27, 2014.

Macaulay, Alastair. "Merce Cunningham's Mutlifaceted Mirror, Held Up to Nature." *New York Times.* January 6, 2017.

Manning, Susan. "The Female Dancer and the Male Gaze: Feminist Critiques of Early Modern Dance," in *Meaning in Motion: New Cultural Studies of Dance,* edited by Jane C. Desmond, 153–166. Durham, NC: Duke University Press, 1997.

Marcus, Jane. "Britannia Rules *The Waves,*" in *Decolonizing Tradition: New Views of Twentieth-Century 'British' Literary Canon,* edited by Karen Lawrence, 136–162. Urbana: University of Illinois Press, 1992.

Marranca, Bonnie. "A Cosmography of Herself: The Autobiology of Rachel Rosenthal" [1996], in *Rachel Rosenthal,* edited by Moira Roth, 79–89. Baltimore and London: Johns Hopkins University Press, 1997.

Massumi, Brian. "The Supernormal Animal," in *The Nonhuman Turn,* edited by Richard Grusin, 1–17. Minneapolis: University of Minnesota Press, 2015.

Mattison, Laci. "Woolf's Un/Folding(s): The Artist and the Event of the Neo-Baroque," in *Contradictory Woolf: Selected Papers from the Twenty-First Annual International Conference on Virginia Woolf,* edited by Derek Ryan and Stella Bolaki, 96–100. Clemson, SC: Clemson University Digital Press, 2012.

McCarren, Felicia. *Dancing Machines: Choreographies of the Age of Mechanical Reproduction.* Stanford, CA: Stanford University Press, 2003.

McCarthy, Jeffrey Mathes. *Green Modernism Nature and the English Novel, 1900 to 1930.* New York: Palgrave MacMillan, 2015.

McGee, Patrick. "The Politics of Modernist Form: Or, Who Rules *The Waves?*" *Modern Fiction Studies* 38, no. 3 (Autumn 1992): 631–650.

McHugh, Susan. *Animal Stories: Narrating Across Species Lines.* Minneapolis: University of Minnesota Press, 2011.

———. "Art and Animals." *Anthrozoos: A Multidisciplinary Journal of the Interactions of People and Animals* 26, no. 3 (2013): 474–477.

Mellown, Elgin W. "Music and Dance in D. H. Lawrence." *Journal of Modern Literature* 21, no. 1 (1997): 49–60.

Millay, Edna St. Vincent. "Sonnet XXI." *Harp-Weaver and Other Poems.* New York: Harper, 1923.

Monaco, Beatrice. *Machinic Modernism: The Deleuzian Literary Machines of Woolf, Lawrence and Joyce.* New York: Palgrave MacMillan, 2008.

Morgan, Geneviéve Sanchis. "The Hostess and the Seamstress: Virginia Woolf's Creation of a Domestic Modernism," in *Unmanning Modernism: Gendered Rereadings,* edited by Elizabeth Jane Harrison and Shirley Peterson, 90–104. Knoxville: University of Tennessee Press, 1997.

Morton, Timothy. "Guest Column: Queer Ecology." *PMLA* 125, no. 2 (2010): 273–282.

Noland, Carrie. "The Human Situation on Stage: Merce Cunningham, Theodor Adorno, and the Category of Expression." *Dance Research Journal* 42, no. 1 (summer 2010): 46–60.

Okumura, Sayaka. "Women Knitting: Domestic Activity, Writing, and Distance in Virginia Woolf's Fiction." *English Studies* 89, no. 2 (2008): 166–181.

Orozco, Lourdes and Jennifer Parker-Starbuck, eds. *Performing Animality: Animals in Performance Practices.* New York: Palgrave Macmillan, 2015.

Orozco, Lourdes. *Theatre and Animals.* Basingstoke: Palgrave Macmillan, 2013.

O'Sheel, Shaemas. "Isadora Duncan, Artist," in *Art of the Dance,* edited by Sheldon Cheney, 31–36. New York: Theatre Arts, 1969.

———. "Isadora Duncan, Priestess." *Poet Lore* 21 (1910): 480–482.

Poole, Roger. *The Unknown Virginia Woolf* (4th ed.). Cambridge: Cambridge University Press, 1978.

Preston, Carrie J. *Modernism's Mythic Pose: Gender Genre, Solo Performance.* New York: Oxford University Press, 2011.

Ridout, Nicholas. *Stage Fright, Animals, and Other Theatrical Problems.* Cambridge: Cambridge University Press, 2006.

Rohman, Carrie. "Animals," in *Literature Now: Key Terms and Methods for Literary History,* edited by Sascha Bru, Ben de Bruyn, and Michel Delville, 98-109. Edinburgh: Edinburgh University Press, 2016.

———. "Disciplinary Becomings: Horizons of Knowledge in Animal Studies." *Hypatia: A Journal of Feminist Philosophy.* Special Issue: "Animal Others." 27, no. 3 (2012): 510–515.

———. "No Higher Life: Bio-aesthetics in J. M. Coetzee's *Disgrace.*" *Modern Fiction Studies* 60, no. 3 (2014): 562–578.

———. *Stalking the Subject: Modernism and the Animal.* New York: Columbia University Press, 2009.

Rosenthal, Rachel. *Rachel's Brain and Other Storms,* edited and with commentaries by Una Chaudhuri. London and New York: Continuum, 2001.

———. *Tatti Wattles: A Love Story.* Santa Monica, CA: Smart Art Press, 1996.

Ross, Alex. "Searching for Silence: John Cage's art of noise." *The New Yorker.* October 4, 2010.

Roth, Moira. "Introduction," in *Rachel Rosenthal,* edited by Moira Roth. Baltimore and London: Johns Hopkins University Press, 1997.

Ryan, Derek, "Following Snakes and Moths: Modernist Ethics and Posthumanism." *Twentieth Century Literature* 61, no. 3 (September 2015): 287–304.

———. "'The reality of becoming': Deleuze, Woolf and the Territory of Cows." *Deleuze Studies* 7, no. 4 (2013): 537–561.

————. *Virginia Woolf and the Materiality of Theory: Sex, Animal, Life*. Edinburgh: Edinburgh University Press, 2013.

Scott, Bonnie Kime. *In the Hollow of the Wave: Virginia Woolf and Modernist Uses of Nature*. Charlottesville: University of Virginia, 2012.

Shukin, Nicole. *Animal Capital: Rendering Life in Biopolitical Times*. Minneapolis: Minnesota University Press, 2009.

Shusterman, Richard. *Pragmatist Aesthetics: Living Beauty, Rethinking Art*. New York: Rowman and Littlefield, 2000.

Smith, Craig. "Across the Widest Gulf: Nonhuman Subjectivity in Virginia Woolf's *Flush*." *Twentieth Century Literature* 48, no. 3 (2002): 348–361.

Stagoll, Cliff. "Plane," in *The Deleuze Dictionary*, edited by Adrian Parr, 204–206. New York: Columbia University Press, 2005.

Steeves, H. Peter. "Rachel Rosenthal Is an Animal." *Mosaic: A Journal for the Interdisciplinary Study of Literature* 39, no. 4 (2006): 1–26.

Stockhausen, Karlheinz. *Aus Den Sieben Tagen (From the Seven Days)*, 1968. Translated by Rolf Gehlhaar, John McGuire and Hugh Davies. Universal Edition UE 14790.

Sypher, Eileen B. "*The Waves*: A Utopia of Androgyny?" in *Virginia Woolf: Centennial Essays*, edited by Elaine Ginsberg and Laura Gottlieb, 187–213. Troy, NY: Whitston, 1983.

Tait, Peta. *Wild and Dangerous Performances: Animals, Emotion, Circus*. Basingstoke: Palgrave MacMillan, 2012.

Thacker, Eugene. *After Life*. Chicago: University of Chicago Press, 2010.

Tuvel, Rebecca. "Veil of Shame": Derrida, Sarah Bartmann and Animality." *Journal for Critical Animal Studies* 9, no. 1/2 (2011): 209–229.

Tyler, Tom. *Ciferae: A Bestiary in Five Fingers*. Minneapolis: Minnesota University Press, 2012.

USA Projects (2013) "Rachel Rosenthal Company," http://www.usaprojects.org/user/ rachelrosenthalcompany. Accessed July 1, 2013.

Von Frisch, Karl. *The Dance Language and Orientation of Bees*. Translated by Leigh Chadwick. Cambridge, MA: Harvard University Press, 1967.

von Uexküll, Jakob. *A Foray into the Worlds of Animals and Humans*. Translated by Joseph D. O'Neil. Minneapolis: University of Minnesota Press, 2010.

Weil, Kari. *Thinking Animals: Why Animal Studies Now?* New York: Columbia University Press, 2012.

Williams, Erin E. and Margo DeMello. *Why Animals Matter*. New York: Prometheus Books, 2007.

Wills, David. *Dorsality: Thinking Back Through Technology and Politics*. Minneapolis: University of Minnesota Press, 2008.

————. *Prosthesis*. Stanford, CA: Stanford University Press, 1995.

Wolfe, Cary. "Each Time Unique: The Poetics of Extinction," in *Animalities: Literary and Cultural Studies Beyond the Human*, edited by Michael Lundblad, 22–42. Edinburgh: Edinburgh University Press, 2017.

————. *What is Posthumanism?* Minneapolis: University of Minnesota Press, 2010.

Woolf, Virginia. *Moments of Being: A Collection of Autobiographical Writing*. Edited by Jeanne Schulkind. New York: Harcourt, 1985.

————. *Nurse Lugton's Golden Curtain*. Illustrated by Julie Vivas. New York: Harcourt, 1991.

————. *Nurse Lugton's Golden Thimble*, with pictures by Duncan Grant. London: Hogarth Press, 1966.

————. *The Letters of Virginia Woolf*, 6 vols. Edited by Nigel Nicolson and Joanne Trautmann. London: The Hogarth Press, 1975–1980.

————. *The Waves*. New York: Harcourt, 1931.

Wulfman, Clifford E. "Woolf and the Discourse of Trauma," in *Virginia Woolf and Trauma: Embodied Texts*, edited by Suzette Henke and David Eberly, 157–177. New York: Pace University Press, 2007.

Young, Peter. *Tortoise*. London: Reaktion Books, 2003.

INDEX

4'33" (Cage), 119

Adorno, Theodor, 125–26
Agamben, Giorgio, 119
Aloi, Giovanni, 3, 6–7
Althusser, Louis, 146
Anderson, Jack, 28
Anderson, Laurie, 1–2
animality
    Cage's works and, 13, 17, 119–21
    Cunningham's works and, 13, 17, 118–42
    Duncan's works and, 13, 15, 17, 19–22, 24–25,
        27–34, 40–41, 54, 119–20, 126, 140
    Lawrence's works and, 13, 15–16, 30, 38, 41–63
    modernism and, 13–14, 20, 22, 28, 32, 41, 51,
        57, 62, 75
    nudity and, 27–28, 77–78, 115
    prosthetics and, 113–14
    Rosenthal's works and, 13, 16–17, 99–117
    Woolf's works and, 13, 16–17, 41, 63–65,
        69–70, 72–79, 81, 84–86, 91–93, 95–96, 98,
        126–27, 133, 135–36, 142
"Animals" (Carlson), 28
"Animals, Anomalies, and Inorganic Others"
    (Braidotti), 4
animal studies
    animality in contemporary art and, 2–3
    anthropocentrism re-evaluated in, 4, 11–12
    dance studies and, 14, 19
    Deleuze's influence in, 7–8
    disability studies and, 114
    Freudian unconscious and, 32
    "inhuman humanities" and, 13, 30
    nudity and, 27
    performance and, 13–14
"The Animal That Therefore I Am" (Derrida), 27
anthropocentrism, 1, 4, 14, 75, 87, 110
Aquinas, Thomas, 121
Aristotle, 6

Art and Animals (Aloi), 6–7
The Artful Species (Davies), 5–6
Artist/Animal (Baker), 3
Art of the Dance (Duncan), 22
Atlas, Charles, 138, 141–42
Aus Den Sieben Tagen (*From the Seven Days;*
    Stockhausen), 105–6

Bacchanal (Duncan), 33
Bacchus, 32–34, 142
Bach, Johann Sebastian, 32
Baker, Steve, 2–3
Bataille, Georges, 33, 73, 117, 146
Beach Birds (Cunningham), 120, 137–41
Beach Birds for Camera (film), 138
Becket, Fiona, 42–43
Becoming Undone (Grosz). *See under* Grosz,
    Elizabeth
Beethoven, Ludwig van, 32
Bekoff, Marc, 11
Belilove, Lori, 23, 25, 29, 33, 41, 153–54n15
Bell, Catherine, 3
Bell, Clive, 63
Bell, Quentin, 63
Bennett, Jane, 24, 80–81, 146–47
Berger, John, 2
Berger, Stephanie, 130–32
Bergson, Henri, 71, 79–82
bioaesthetics
    Cunningham and, 118, 120, 122, 125–27,
        139, 145–46
    Deleuze and, 7–8, 32, 43
    Duncan and, 19–20, 22, 24–25, 27, 32,
        36, 41, 88
    Lawrence and, 43, 47–49, 87–88
    modernism and, 13, 17, 120
    Tatti Wattles and, 16–17, 110–12, 114–15
    trans-species nature of, 2, 5, 7–8, 15, 43,
        94, 147–48

171

Woolf, Leonard, 63–65, 78
Woolf, Virginia
  animality in the works of, 13, 16–17, 41, 63–65,
    69–70, 72–79, 81, 84–86, 91–93, 95–96, 98,
    126–27, 133, 135–36, 142
  animal nicknames among the family of, 63, 78
  bioaesthetics and, 64–65, 67, 78, 86–88, 90,
    94, 146
  "The Death of the Moth" and, 87
  Deleuze and, 51
  dogs and, 63–64
  Flush and, 63–64
  gardens and, 64
  Lee's biography of, 156n2

modernism and, 58
Mrs. Dalloway and, 64–65
new materialist readings of, 79
Nurse Lugton stories and, 16–17, 64–79, 81–86,
  120, 127, 133, 135, 142
posthumanist readings of, 64, 87–88, 93
The Waves and, 16, 64, 83, 86–98, 146

Young, Peter, 43–44, 49
"Youth and Dance" (Duncan), 32

zoē, 83–84
zooësis (Chaudhuri), 14
Zurkow, Marina, 14